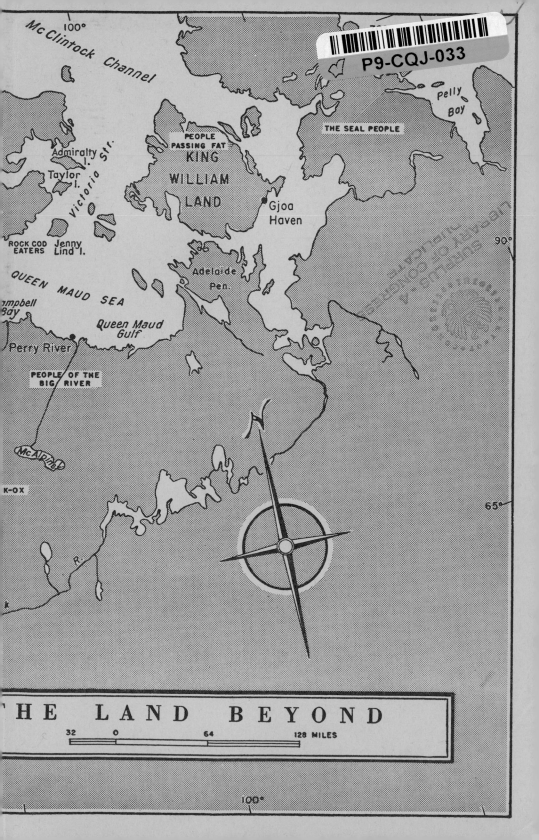

100°

Mc Clintock Channel

Pelly Bay

THE SEAL PEOPLE

PEOPLE PASSING FAT

Admiralty I.

Taylor I.

Victoria Str.

KING

WILLIAM

LAND

Gjoa Haven

90°

ROCK COD EATERS

Jenny Lind I.

Adelaide Pen.

QUEEN MAUD SEA

mpbell Bay

Queen Maud Gulf

Perry River

PEOPLE OF THE BIG RIVER

McAlpine

65°

K-OX

R.

k

THE LAND BEYOND

32   0   64   128 MILES

100°

AYORAMA

AYORAMA

BY

RAYMOND DE COCCOLA

AND

PAUL KING

ILLUSTRATED BY

JAMES HOUSTON

OXFORD UNIVERSITY PRESS
TORONTO
MCMLV

Oxford University Press, Amen House, Toronto
LONDON GLASGOW NEW YORK MELBOURNE WELLINGTON
BOMBAY CALCUTTA MADRAS KARACHI CAPE TOWN IBADAN
Geoffrey Cumberlege, Publisher to the University

Nihil Obstat

A. T. C. GRIFFITH, M.A.

CENSOR LIBRORUM

Imprimatur

✠ REVERENDISSIMUS GULIELMUS MARCUS DUKE, S.T.D.

ARCHIEPISCOPUS VANCUVERIENSIS

Die 16 Novembris 1954

Printed in Canada
by
MARACLE PRESS LIMITED

To

SUZANNE

CONTENTS

CONTENTS

PREFACE

They live in the Canadian Central Arctic and they call themselves the Krangmalit, or the People Beyond.

Their tribe embraces a number of groups with equally
fascinating names: the People on the Back of the Earth,
the People of the Bay, the Tom-Cod Eaters, the People of
the Caribou Antlers, the Far-Away People, the People of the
Falls, the People of the Rich Fishing Grounds, the Berry
Eaters, the People at the Bottom of the Inlet, and the People
of the Musk-Ox.

The last two groups are perhaps the least known of them
all, because few explorers have ever penetrated into their
traditional wintering grounds around the deep fjords of Bathurst Inlet.

The intimate day-to-day life of these primitive polar
people, as seen through the eyes of a missionary who spent
twelve years among them, is told in the following pages.

RAYMOND DE COCCOLA
PAUL KING

AUTHORS' NOTE

Every incident in this story is based upon actual experience or authenticated fact, though the real names of the characters have been changed and times and places have sometimes been altered to suit the narrative.

The Eskimo language in the dialogue has been translated literally where possible, but paraphrase has often been essential to make the meaning clear.

AYORAMA

1

NAOYAK THE SEAGULL

Angivrana was in labour. In the unsteady light of the stone lamp she seemed rough and nervous, with a prematurely old face that was at once large, broad, and strong. She sat squatting on the *iglek*, the built-up platform of snow covered with caribou skins, moaning and murmuring to herself as she rocked gently back and forth.

Angivrana was not alone. To her left, at the other end of the iglek, minding her own blubber lamp or *kudlek,* squatted a shrivelled-up nondescript shape, grandmother Manerathiak. On seeing me enter, she dropped the flat bone with which she had been scraping a caribou skin, stood up slowly, as if she would break in two if she hurried, and moved towards me with outstretched hand. A softening smile relieved her wizened, deeply lined face when our hands met.

'*Kranok ikpin?* How are you?' I inquired.

'*Namaktunga.* I am well,' replied the stooped old woman through teeth worn down to the gums.

'And how are you?' I turned to Angivrana, whose moaning had grown louder since my entry.

She placed her hand significantly on her abdomen.

'*Mane, iluane*. Here inside.' Several dirty satchels had been slung over her belt to protect her and the child against the evil spirits.

Suggesting that she try to keep quiet, I crawled out of the *iglu* to my dog-sled to get some bromide tablets. After the five-hour run that had brought me to Kagnekoguyak from my Mission in Burnside, my dogs were exhausted. They were resting in the snow, their collars attached by chains to the dog-line. It was still as grey and cold as when I left the Mission; the rawness penetrated through the double parka and into my bones. I hurried to the grub box on the sled and got the tablets from my medicine chest.

In a few minutes the drug had its quieting effect on Angivrana. Meantime the grandmother had brewed some tea in the kettle hanging from a driftwood rack, and was licking an enamel cup clean with her tongue before filling it with tea for me.

'*Nekretoren!* Have some food!' she said, motioning to the row of frozen caribou carcasses near the tiny door.

I had eaten some caribou fat and dry meat on the way to Kagnekoguyak in the morning, but the trip had sharpened my appetite and I took out my pocket knife and cut myself off a piece of the lean, tasteless meat. I had come to like it almost from the day I first set foot on the Barren Land off the schooner *Our Lady of Lourdes* the year before, and I never tired of it.

'Where is your husband?' I asked Angivrana, as I joined her on the iglek.

'He is hunting in the hills with our boy,' she said calmly. But the mention of her first-born brought on a fresh wave of self-pity.

I knew that while childbearing is normally a simple enough experience for the Eskimo woman, there are certain physical denials and discomforts she has to endure. For one thing, custom decrees that once the child is well on the way she must sleep by herself on the iglek, observing the ancient laws of the spirits. And she must abstain from eating such tender parts of animals as the liver, heart, and kidneys, and raw meat of all kinds. They, too, are part of the prenatal taboo.

When Angivrana's time arrived, the grandmother moved to her side as she knelt on the iglek, in obvious pain. With skilled assurance born of necessity, Manerathiak delivered the howling infant, deftly severing the umbilical cord by biting through it. She placed a piece of the cord in a satchel for Angivrana to hang around her neck later as a safeguard against sterility.

With the baby close to her breast beneath the parka, Angivrana lay back panting. Presently her breathing returned to normal, and she dozed off.

In my concern for the mother, I hardly had time to take a good look at the wailing babe. But I did notice the black hair, the partly closed dark eyes, and the tiny reddish body. She was a girl.

A girl! How would her father take the news? I should have known what to expect if it had been a boy. Nokadlak would have proudly invited the nearest friends to show off his latest man-child. 'Eh, eh,' they would have giggled approvingly, 'a little boy, a small man—*angutinuak, inugaluak!*' Before many winters had passed the boy would be hunting and fishing at his father's side; and one day, perhaps, he would be the family's sole provider in their declining years. But a girl— what good is a girl? A useless mouth to feed for months and years until she is taken away by another man, possibly never to be seen again.

I shuddered when I thought of what happens to so many

Eskimo baby girls. My recent conversation with Anarvik, an unusually fat woman I had seen occasionally at Burnside, burned in my heart. Matter-of-factly she had told me she did not raise a single girl in her family:

'I choked the baby girls because we could not have fed all my children.'

'That must have been because you did not love them, as you love Poktok and Ungerlak, your sons.'

She looked at me quietly and steadily before replying: '*Ayornorman*. There is nothing else we can do; it's our destiny.'

My anxious mind flashed back to Irkrarena. She was a tall well-built girl from Taseriuak Lake. In her last days of pregnancy she and her husband left the camp to visit some friends who were hunting on the Hanimor River. When Irkrarena returned to the camp a few days later, her figure was back to normal. She carefully avoided me, but I made a point of seeking her out.

'You look so thin and pale. Have you been starving on the trail?' I asked.

An odd expression came into her eyes, as a sad smile flickered on her full lips:

'The trail was rough and she was a girl. *Arnainaogame.* Alas, only a girl . . . .'

Outside, my dogs began to howl. Someone—probably Nokadlak—was approaching the camp.

I went out to see.

Nokadlak and his son Kudnanak were back from the hunt. As I walked towards their heavily laden sled, I found it difficult to tell Nokadlak's age. On his strong features, burned brown by the rigours of Arctic life, lay the impassive serenity of a man of the Barren Land. His chin was almost clean, although it had never felt a razor blade, and his upper lip carried a mere trace of whiskers. A few strands of his tough, thick black hair escaped the hood, partly covering his thin dark eyebrows beneath which two narrow slits betrayed jet-black eyes that glittered in the snowy whiteness.

I shook hands with him and his pleasant, alert twelve-year-old son. We exchanged greetings and I told Nokadlak I had been asked to come and see Angivrana because she was going to have a child. He did not seem surprised. I looked straight at him and said:

'The baby came this afternoon. It's a girl. Your wife is asleep with her.'

'A girl, eh?' He made no attempt to hide his disappointment.

'I'll help you unload,' I said, to divert his mind from the disclosure.

I noticed his good hunting luck and wanted to compliment him on his skill, but it would have been impolite. According to Eskimo etiquette, that should come later. Meantime, the tired dogs had to be put on their line, and the sled's contents transferred to the porch of the iglu. This done, we shook the snow off our parkas and boots and I followed Nokadlak into the iglu.

The old grandmother must have awakened Angivrana, because the latter was sitting up, saying to her husband: 'The baby is born. It is only a girl.'

'That's too bad,' Nokadlak said without expression. He took off his parka, shook it thoroughly to rid it of the last particles of snow and ice still clinging to it, and handed it to Manerathiak who hung it on the rack for drying.

'It's cold outside,' he murmured, plucking at the icicles in his nostrils and on the few hairs of his chin.

He sat down on the iglek, pulled off his boots, beat them with a stick, and gave them to the grandmother. Then he reached for a dry parka and short caribou boots stored at the back of the iglek, and put them on. Kudnanak did the same.

5

'*Teetoritse*. Let's have tea,' suggested Manerathiak. She filled a cup and slowly brought it to Nokadlak, muttering 'I am an old woman,' to excuse her slowness and any sloppiness that might accompany it.

She served me next, then Kudnanak, Angivrana, and herself in that order. Everyone also partook of the fish and caribou meat the old woman set before us in a dishpan.

Giving subtle airing to the thought that had been uppermost in her mind since her grand-daughter was born, Manerathiak finally said:

'My mother was called Naoyak. Only one of the dogs bears this name now. My mother could sew very well . . . .'

The hint fell on fertile ground. 'Naoyak—Naoyak. We'll call her Naoyak,' agreed Nokadlak.

That was over, at least. I sighed with relief as I considered the name. Naoyak meant seagull. It sounded fine to me—far better, in fact, than so many Eskimo names which find their origin in obscenity. And it seemed to apply well to the little girl, although, like any other Eskimo name, it could just as easily have been used for a boy.

'Great-grandmother Naoyak,' I thought, 'now the aimless wanderings of your forlorn and lamented soul are over! According to your tribe's beliefs, your refuge is in the newborn child. But for how long?' Nokadlak had given no indication yet.

Having politely waited till her husband had made himself quite comfortable, and noticing traces of blood between his fingers and on his forearms, Angivrana asked Nokadlak what luck he had had on his trip.

'It wasn't too bad. We travelled a lot, and brought back enough for a few days,' he replied modestly.

'Father shot a musk-ox and a wolverine!' Kudnanak put in excitedly.

His pride gradually getting the better of him, Nokadlak

began to relate the incidents in detail, choosing his words deliberately and speaking in a slow monotone that was punctuated from time to time by the baby's crying.

'We had no luck whatever on our first day out,' he said. 'But the following morning we saw tracks of Kalvik, the wolverine. I made a small tunnel of snow and placed a piece of caribou meat inside it. I tied one end of sinew around the meat and attached the other end to the trigger of an old rifle, which I also hid in the snow tunnel. Then we drove off to look for game.'

Eager to add his say, Kudnanak interjected: 'We had a good omen that day. Father shot a fox that had just killed a rabbit. So we got both for one bullet!'

'Yes, and Kudnanak helped me shoot many ptarmigans along the river banks,' the hunter conceded expansively. 'But the next day was stormy and we did not leave the iglu we had made on the river.'

'Father and I touched the weasels on our parkas that night, and the spirits of the land were good to us after that,' said Kudnanak solemnly.

'*Illa.* That's so,' rejoined Nokadlak. 'My old rifle killed the wolverine right between the eyes. It is a beautiful fur.'

'And on the way back we sighted three musk-oxen and Father shot one of them. It was *big!*' the boy added irrepressibly.

'The police might not like that,' I said, knowing full well —as did every Eskimo in the Bathurst Inlet territory—that killing musk-oxen was forbidden by the white man's law.

'Nobody saw me. Besides, we killed no caribou on this trip,' Nokadlak righteously justified his act.

Grandmother Manerathiak, who had not missed a word, now entered the conversation: 'I remember old Natkusiak saying that musk-oxen were plentiful inland during his younger days. He told me they had lots of meat and fuel and skins then. But one summer the ice did not melt on the sea. A blizzard struck. Cold rain was followed by sleet; then heavy frost mantled the land. Ice, thick and slippery, encrusted everything—rocks, moss, weeds. Musk-oxen drifted side by side with the caribou towards the sea. The terrible season pushed them clear off the land. They were not strong enough to break the ice and fill their bellies with grass. Hunger killed them right and left. Since then we have often starved.'

'Well, we are not going to starve today, grandmother!' said Nokadlak, and everyone laughed.

Angivrana listened interestedly as she fed the child and cleaned her little reddish body with the silky fur of an Arctic hare, and more particularly with her tongue. Once, when she lifted the baby towards her face, I saw a bluish spot, about the size of a twenty-five-cent piece, at the base of the child's spine. It was the Mongoloid mark, characteristic of all Eskimo children, which sometimes spreads across the buttocks but eventually fades and disappears in adolescence.

Angivrana wrapped her naked babe in the skin of a young caribou and placed her on the furs covering the iglek. She put on her parka, stood up slowly, and used the conventional excuse: 'I think I shall get some fresh air.' On the way out she picked up a stick to fend off the young dogs, and crawled out to the porch.

After she came back, Nokadlak reached the end of his proud narrative. He was getting tired and drowsy, but he was still in a good mood as he turned to his wife and said: 'You remember the good hunter Kakagun, who helped us in the past when we had no food? He has a boy who ought to be a good hunter, too, some day. Kakagun asked me once to keep a girl for his son. We'll keep Naoyak for him.'

I uttered a silent prayer of thanksgiving to God for preserving the little girl's life. I was glad to hear that Kakagun was to be the adopted father, because I knew him as one of the best hunters in the entire Central Arctic. Angivrana and the old grandmother seemed more relaxed now, but Kudnanak remained wholly unaffected by his father's decision to bring up his little sister.

That night, as I crawled into the sleeping bag, after Angivrana and Nokadlak had undressed and gone to sleep in their large family bag with the baby between them, I involuntarily thought of the morning a native named Hilro had come running into the Mission at Bathurst.

'*Fala, Fala!* Father, Father!' he cried.

'*Uvagor?* What is it?' I inquired.

'My child is without breath.'

'You mean your child is dead? What happened?'

'He died during the night. I and my wife killed the little man without knowing. We crushed his chest between us while we were sleeping. *Ayornorman tedja.* There is nothing to be done now. He is dead.'

Two years later Hilro and his wife accidentally killed another child in the same way. This time it was a girl. But, in true Eskimo style, rather than blame themselves, they attributed it to the inevitable destiny of the Barren Land. '*Ayornorman illa.* There is indeed nothing we can do about it,' they commented. In this succinct dismissal of the tragedy, I have often thought since, lies the Eskimo's entire philosophy of man's utter hopelessness in the Arctic.

Manerathiak was the last to get ready for bed, lingering by both stone lamps to lower their flames to a single wick. She reached into the excavation under the iglek and pulled out the *korvik* or tin can that served as a chamber pot and placed it within reach of Angivrana. Then she got another korvik and took it over to her own corner.

Mumbling and groaning to herself all the while, the tired old woman undressed as if her joints creaked and crept into her bedding, using her folded parka as a pillow. 'I feel worse every day,' she intoned to no-one in particular. 'I feel like a woman with child. Oh, a child! Of what use am I now?'

Although I had had a fairly strenuous and eventful day, my anxiety for little Naoyak would not let me fall asleep; nor did the various sounds in the dimly lit iglu help. Manerathiak's whisperings and incantations ebbed and flowed in the gloom, drowned out now and then by the baby's wails or by Nokadlak's heavy snoring, coughing, and spitting. I could see his head and Angivrana's close together resting on the edge of the iglek, steady streams of vapour rising from their mouths and nostrils in rhythm with their breathing. When the vapours hit the dome of the iglu, they turned into tiny crystals of snow that fell lightly on those sleeping below. But they were fully prepared for it. The edges of their *krepik* or sleeping bag were fringed with thick caribou fur that moved with their breathing and bodily movements, shaking off the crystals of snow and leaving their faces perfectly dry.

The diuretic action of the tea told on everybody, and the acrid smell from the array of makeshift chamber pots was in itself anything but soporific. Then there was the baby, waking periodically, crying hungrily. That, at least, was reassuring.

Thus, despite my weariness, I hardly slept at all. I just lay there—not thinking, not remembering any longer, as if I were one of these primitive, almost prehistoric people, temporarily cut off from the dangers of a heartless, barren, frozen land by a few blocks of snow and a caribou skin.

When morning finally came, I found I had worried needlessly about Naoyak's safety. Apart from waking to suckle, she had slept comfortably next to the warm bodies of her parents and was still very much alive.

The old grandmother, who had been tossing about fitfully during the predawn hours, was the first to rise, and busied herself at once with the stone lamp.

As the family was together once more, I was considering going back to the Bathurst Mission after breakfast when I noticed that Nokadlak and Angivrana had awakened and that the grandmother was welcoming them back to consciousness with cups of hot tea. Lying on his stomach, Nokadlak sipped the drink between bites on a big lump of frozen meat that Manerathiak had given him. He finished his breakfast in high spirits. Oh, but he had had a wonderful dream! They should all hear about it. Then, sucking his fingers and belching with complete satisfaction, he warmed to his story:

'As I said, it was a beautiful dream. I was a young man again, and I was hunting musk-ox. I spied one, a solitary bull, about the same time as he saw me. He came charging at me, with his eyes aflame and his little tail in the air—'

He did not finish. Suddenly, as if recalling reality at last, he asked the grandmother: '*Kranokikpa silla?* How is the weather?'

'*Nauna.* I don't know,' she said. 'I will have a look.'

She took the snow knife to cut her way through the outer entrance of the porch and crawled out.

'The wind is rising,' she reported on return. 'The sky is cloudy. It doesn't look good.'

If that's the case, I thought, I had better put off the trip until the weather clears. Meanwhile there was no time to waste if another sudden Arctic storm was in the offing.

Angivrana had nudged her son and told him to get up and help his father. When he saw his father almost dressed, the boy obeyed sleepily and presently joined Nokadlak and me outside.

Manerathiak was right. Everything pointed to an approaching blizzard.

2

THE PIRTOK

'The *pirtok* is coming. You'd better look at the dogs and then take care of the guns, the ice chisel, and the scoop; and don't forget the harnesses,' Nokadlak told his son.

I thought it best to take the same precautions with my dogs and equipment.

Silently Nokadlak studied the direction of the wind, which was already driving the fine snow in gusts along the Arctic floor. Then he started to cut blocks of snow with his knife. These he built onto the entrance of the porch at an angle to shield it from the icy blasts and the snow that were sure to follow as soon as the storm reached its height.

Kudnanak had removed the rifles from the sled and stacked them in the shelter of the porch. He knew enough not to carry them right into the iglu where condensation would form on them and they might rust or else freeze on being taken outside again. He then collected all the dog harnesses and arranged them on the sled beside a ten-foot chisel and an equally long-handled scoop made of the horn of a musk-ox. Eskimo hunters make a hole in the thick winter ice with

12

the chisel and then clear out the water and chips of ice with the scoop. Over this indispensable equipment Kudnanak placed a large cover made of skins and lashed the bundle securely to the sled with long narrow bands of caribou hide.

I was going through a similar routine with my sled when I noticed that the old grandmother had emerged from the snow-house and was taking the caribou skins off the sticks planted in the snow on which they had been put up for drying and airing. Normally Angivrana would be doing this chore, but Manerathiak was taking her place because of the baby. The old woman was not as useless as she would have herself believe!

She carried the skins into the iglu in bundles of four or five, making several return trips. No matter how long the storm might last, she, at least, would have plenty to do.

To make sure my sled would not be covered up with snow during the storm, I pushed it onto a little elevation. For the same reason Nokadlak helped his son glide their longer, heavier sled on top of the iglu.

As a precaution, Nokadlak cut several blocks of virgin snow, each about the size of a pillow. He gave one to Kudnanak to take in and leaned the rest against the lee side of the iglu. This was to be the family's water supply. Finally, he blocked the porch entrance to a height of a couple of feet to prevent snow from drifting in, and joined the rest of the family. I followed him in. Angivrana was nursing her baby. Kudnanak was already chewing on a chunk of dry meat.

'We have taken care of everything outside,' Nokadlak announced with a note of pride at his forethought and concern for the family.

'I didn't notice any chinks in the walls of the iglu, but if any snow sifts through, I can patch them from here.'

'I don't think anything will come through these walls,'

13

said the grandmother in a flattering tone. 'I remember how well you built this iglu. Angivrana and I helped fill the few holes. You laid the blocks very tightly together.'

Nokadlak took his cue. He smiled. 'My father was a good hunter and provider and taught me how to build the best snow-house in our land. Before he chose a site, he would say to me: "Now, look. To find the best spot you go around and feel out the snow with the rod as if it were a living creature." He would point out that the warmest place to build an iglu is over ice, above the sea, or lake, or even a river, because the water below is not as cold as the frozen ground. And if we were inland, and there was no ice around, my father would then look for a deep snowdrift which would keep the iglu off the ground.

'Even when I was a boy no older than Kudnanak I tried to build snow-houses like my father. And I remember one time another boy challenged me to see who could make a better snow-house. Not only did I build a better one, but I finished first and had a good laugh at his expense! Since then I have always been proud of my iglus.'

We all chuckled with Nokadlak, and I, for one, felt his infectious confidence allaying any misgiving I might have felt in the face of the blizzard.

As he boasted on, I recalled my first impression of an iglu's interior when I first arrived at Bathurst. I remembered being taken aback by the peculiar smell permeating it. I could not analyse it then, but later learned that it came from a mixture of furs, skins, rotten meat, dried fish, burnt seal oil or caribou fat, and plain humanity. Nokadlak's iglu was no exception.

But even a white man's nose eventually gets used to this effluvium and hardly minds it after a while. Instead, the sense of sight takes over, noticing the exact disposition of the blubber lamp and the drying-racks above them, masses of caribou skins and several sleeping bags spread out on the iglek, the pots and cups and other vessels lying here and there, the frozen caribou and seal carcasses heaped up on the floor near the tiny door, the bundles of frozen fish and dried meat, wasted bones, and sundry rags and feathers scattered about.

Snow serves as carpet, and a piece of ice at the top of the iglu as window. Blubber lamps supply most of what light there is, as well as heat for cooking. The inside temperature, of course, must be kept at about thirty-three degrees Fahrenheit; if there are signs of melting, the lamps are lowered and the caribou rag is taken out of the ventilation hole in the dome.

What always struck me even more than the physical appearance of an iglu was the friendly atmosphere of the whole household. The moment even an utter stranger entered the iglu, he became a welcomed friend who could share whatever his hosts had for as long as he wished. I don't know of any other place in the world where you can tumble into people's houses without ceremony or warning, and merely by saying that you have come a long way are at once made the centre of friendly greetings and open kindliness.

That was the way Nokadlak's family had accepted me from the start, and reciprocal feelings stirred within me. I wished I could somehow help them combat the storm. But the elemental fury was too powerful for mere man. There was nothing to do but sit it out in the iglu with my hosts.

As the day wore on, the temperature in the iglu dropped noticeably and we all put on our parkas.

Now and then Nokadlak looked through a peep-hole and listened to the wind and the snow pattering on the frozen floor.

'*Pirkrilertok*. It is really drifting hard,' was his invariable comment.

With snow sifting through minute chinks and weaknesses in the snow blocks, it seemed like a superfluous observation. But the family accepted it as we might receive a radio weather report, and Angivrana or the old grandmother would rejoin with: 'Yes, but I hope it won't last many days because our meat supply is not very high.' Though the danger of starvation during a prolonged storm is all too real to the Eskimo, no-one seemed to worry about it.

Nokadlak's wise, weatherbeaten face bespoke confidence and apparent unconcern towards the all-pervading terror of the frozen North—starvation in the Barren Land. And yet there was something in his eyes I could not quite grasp. Through the strength and the self-assurance I thought I detected a hint of brooding depression, of hopelessness beyond redemption. He said little all through the rising storm, as he quietly busied himself by mending dog harnesses with caribou sinew threaded through a triangular-shaped steel needle he had acquired at the trading post. Nokadlak was not one to prostrate himself on the iglek, plunged into sad torpor, as some Eskimos might do during a pirtok. His ingenious nature prompted him to find some useful occupation to combat his restlessness and boredom. All told, he was the picture of a strong and happy man who was proud of being a good provider for the family he headed.

Manerathiak was busy too. Squatting in her corner, with a caribou skin secured between her knees, she was scraping off the remaining bits of fat and meat with a spoon-like scraper made of musk-ox horn. As she worked rhythmically with her right arm, the old woman interspersed her mutterings about her lost children, her wonderful lovers of old, and her deceased friends, with monotonous songs. In the stillness of the iglu even her low humming was distinctly audible as she sang:

16

'*Kamaoktunga* . . . I am afraid and I tremble
When I remember my father and mother
Seeking the wandering game,
Struggling on the empty land
Weakened by hunger. *Eya-ya-ya* . . .

'*Kamaoktunga* . . . I am afraid and I tremble
When I recall their bones
Scattered on the low land,
Broken by prowling beasts,
Swept away by winds. *Eya-ya-ya* . . .'

I glanced at Angivrana. With her baby fed and asleep in
the back of her parka, she was now up and around, taking her
usual place in the household. Having scraped the stiff, bluish
spots caused by wetness off the heavy parka her husband had
worn on the hunting trip, she carefully checked every seam
and, finding a couple of small tears, mended them expertly
with a glove needle and sinew.

Her face revealed no emotion of any sort as she said somewhat wistfully to no-one in particular:

'It won't be too long before we give Naoyak away to
Kivgalo, the son of Kakagun. I wonder if the hunting is good
inland where they are.'

'If they are still at Taseriuak, they should do all right.
There is usually game there and Kakagun is a clever hunter,'
said Nokadlak.

'My father is a capable hunter too,' chimed in Kudnanak,
becoming suddenly animated as the conversation touched
upon his favourite topic. The boy had returned from the porch
where he had checked up on the pups, and was now quietly
sitting on the iglek. The pups were curled up like giant
doughnuts of fur, huddling close to each other in the increasing cold; they were safe enough for the time being.

17

'*Illa*. Yes,' agreed the grandmother, smiling. 'Your father is a great hunter. He has never let us starve.' She left unsaid what this actually meant to her. For had Nokadlak not been a good provider, she would have been discarded on the trail long ago as a useless chattel.

By association, my thoughts turned to Naoyak. The baby had awakened and was crying for her next meal. Angivrana swung the child off her back, under her left arm, and cradled her between her bulging breasts under the parka. Remembering Angivrana's passing remark, I wondered how soon Naoyak might be delivered to the hunter Kakagun.

Since the nomadic Eskimos never know when they may see their friends again, a promised girl is often adopted by her future in-laws almost from birth. They bring her up as their daughter until their son decides to set up housekeeping with her on his own.

My speculations did not bother Naoyak at all as she fed contentedly on her mother's warm, thick milk. But while the infant rested snugly next to her mother's bosom, oblivious to the seething world around her, her parents became more apprehensive. The pirtok seemed to be reaching its height. No-one spoke much any more. Nokadlak was paying less attention to mending the harnesses than he was to mending the cracks in the walls as winds of hurricane force pounded on the iglu, lowering the temperature and driving blinding drifts of snow before them.

We were all drinking tea more often than before to keep warm. But unlike the native broths of caribou or fish heads or animal bones with their abundant nourishment, the glowing effect of tea was passing at best, and merely increased the number of our trips to the porch. The pups did not stir or bother us, but watched our actions with understandable curiosity.

Out of courtesy to me as a guest, Angivrana and the grand-

mother from time to time filled an open sealskin bag with choice bits of fish, dry meat, and caribou fat, and put it back on the floor where we could all reach it. Between these semi-formal meal times, we all helped ourselves to slices of frozen caribou whenever we felt like it.

Towards evening, with the storm howling unabated, Kud-nanak anticipated the supper meal by announcing that he had some caribou legs stored in the porch. This revelation elicited a round of *'Illa, illa, namaktok!* Indeed, that's fine!' from his elders, as the youngster headed for the entrance. I followed him out to see what he meant to do with the caribou legs, and to stretch my own.

From a niche in the wall of the tunnel Kudnanak pulled out half a dozen front and hind caribou legs which he threw down on the hard snow underfoot. Then, taking one leg at a time, he crushed the bones with the dull edge of a short axe. The pups gathered round expectantly, hoping for chunks of meat to fly in their direction, not daring to bite into the whole animal legs for fear of getting kicked by the boy for their impertinence.

Outside, despite the terrific wind with its noise and swirling snow, the dogs began to howl, thinking someone was preparing their daily meal. But Kudnanak had the family supper in mind at the moment. He was crushing the bones for their frozen marrow—the Eskimo's butter.

Filled and warmed by his meal of meat, fat, and marrow, Nokadlak told his son that he was going out to feed the dogs. Kudnanak went with him to the porch where he held back the pups while Nokadlak cut high-smelling caribou into nine chunks of about two pounds each and dumped them into the sealskin bag Kudnanak had brought out of the iglu.

With the bag under one arm and his snow knife in the other hand Nokadlak ventured out into the blizzard. He moved slowly, bent almost to a crouch and carefully balanced against the wind, with his back to its icy blasts. Recognizing their master, the dogs stood up. Nokadlak went methodically up and down the dog-line, dropping a chunk of meat to each half-starved animal. Keeping their tails curled up between their legs for warmth, the huskies made short work of their rations and promptly rolled up for the oncoming night.

Nokadlak hurried back from the dog-line as fast as he could. Once in the shelter of the porch, he pulled off the parka over his head, revealing his bare, muscular torso, shook the snow off his garment, and replaced it before re-entering the iglu. Inside he knocked the snow off his leggings and gave them to his wife to place on the rack to dry. Like the rest of us, Nokadlak was ready to turn in for the night.

For five days the pirtok howled without let-up. Nokadlak had no conception of speed measurements, but I remembered being told at the Mission by another priest that its highest speeds ranged between eighty and ninety miles an hour. This is far less than the treacherous *uyaluk,* which strikes suddenly with hurricane force over an area of a few square miles, to vanish almost as soon as a passing tornado might in the middle States. But the oft-recurring pirtok, with its persistent, inexorable pounding by snow-laden winds, is just as fearsome to the people of the Central Arctic.

When the sporadic talk in the iglu turned to the pirtok, Nokadlak told me how one of his friends, who thought he could get back to his camp without making a shelter for himself when the pirtok began, was captured in a torrent of wind and snow.

'Iktutok had only one thought—to get out into a warm stillness, to escape forever from the roaring whirlwind of snow,' Nokadlak related unemotionally.

The freezing wind bit and clawed at Iktutok like a hungry bear, he said. Numb and stupefied, he began a monotonous refrain, moaning over and over again: '*Alapak, kaiornatok.*

I am cold, I am freezing.' He was past shivering now. He was slowly freezing under a burning bite. When Nokadlak discovered his friend as the pirtok subsided, his feet were partly frozen and all the toes had to be cut off.

'I don't know if Iktutok was lucky to live or not,' said Nokadlak. 'In his soul slumbers a restless dread of big winds. He is no good for travelling any more.'

Iktutok's fearful experience confirmed my decision to stay with Nokadlak until the storm had passed.

3

BURNSIDE MISSION

Even though I had left my sled on a slight elevation, I had to use a shovel to dig out the snow when I went out of the iglu on the morning of the sixth day after the pirtok first struck.

There was not a cloud to be seen in the sky, but it was still unusually cold, and the snow was running lightly on the frozen floor under a stiff breeze, like wisps of smoke out of a camp-fire. Snowdrifts had formed around the iglu and the dogs, making the surroundings even more desolate than before.

On top of the iglu, Nokadlak's *krammotik* seemed in far better shape than mine; only its runners were packed with driven snow. Kudnanak pushed the sled off the iglu, turned it over, and began helping his father to make it ready for the next hunting trip. This was urgent now, for the family's food stores had dwindled rapidly while we were prisoners of the pirtok.

With their snow knives, father and son meticulously scraped off the white ice coating that lay next to the protective two-inch layer of frozen peat on the steel runners. When he was satisfied that the coating had been completely removed, Nokadlak said laconically: 'Yuartok. It's ready.'

This was the signal for the boy to fetch the kettle in which his mother had melted granular snow, and a square piece of white bearskin from the iglu. Nokadlak took a mouthful of the lukewarm water out of the kettle and, finding its temperature about right, spat it out on the bearskin or *nanurak,* then quickly rubbed one of the upturned runners with the wetted rag. His successive applications of water, given with a rhythmic sweeping motion, made a smooth new ice surface for the runners. This done, Nokadlak scraped off the drops of water frozen to the sides of the runners, set the sled upright, and with Kudnanak's help dragged it back and forth to prevent snow from sticking to the new coating.

'*Namainartok.* That will be fine,' he said, panting. 'My rested dogs will fly over the snow with almost nothing to pull.'

I was using the same method to ice my runners and felt rather proud that it had taken me only one Arctic winter to learn a skill that the Eskimos pass on from generation to generation. Needless to say, Nokadlak and Kudnanak finished the job ahead of me, and were now straightening the dog harnesses.

Nokadlak had built his sled himself from trees he obtained after a long and arduous trip to the tree-line across an unknown land haunted by spirits and peopled by dangerous beings called Indians. He had secured the crossbars to the two heavy runners with strips of seal and caribou skin and had equipped the runners with steel for travel in the spring. Last fall he chopped some peat out of the marshy ground and thawed it out in a large cauldron above the blubber lamp. This, mixed with seal and caribou blood, he kneaded into a soft paste and plastered it lukewarm on the runners, high up on the sides and thicker in front to broaden the up-curving ends of the runners. When the peat coating was frozen solid,

23

Nokadlak went over all the rough spots with his snow knife. Then he dragged the sled across sandy ground to rub away any remaining imperfections.

In the extremely cold months from December to May his peat runners, properly ice-coated, would reduce friction to a minimum, whereas metal or wooden runners would drag in the snow and tire his dog-team to the point of exhaustion. Nokadlak knew that whale bones would make more durable runners for the winter snow, but whales are scarce in the frozen seas of the Central Arctic, and peat runners can take a lot of punishment on rapid trips, even with heavy loads. Nokadlak knew exactly how much abuse his sled could stand, and took all possible care to avoid running anything that might damage the peat runners or chip the ice coating. Wherever he went, his experienced eyes were searching the trail ahead for stones, sand, fresh dog's droppings, and glare ice. He iced his runners several times a day on his trips and always carried some peat for emergency repairs.

By the time I had finished rigging up my sled, Nokadlak was already loading his. He did it with method, both learned and inherited. First he laid some heavy caribou skins upon the cross-bars, folding them over to the exact width of the sled. Then he spread a large cover, made of caribou-cow hides, sewn together in such a way that it overlapped the sled on either side. On this he placed the heavy load in front so that the sled could be handled more easily on a rough trail. This consisted of his grub boxes and the dog-line. The rest of his equipment he piled evenly along the sled, with the sleeping bags in the centre, to make a comfortable seat for himself and Kudnanak.

With the load aboard, Nokadlak and the boy folded up the hems of the cover, wrapping up the contents and tying them like a huge mummy. Finally they inserted their rifles, ice-chisel, and snow-scoop between the ropes in easy reach.

Through all these preparatory steps Kudnanak had been helping his father without so much as a word of instruction, but now Nokadlak ordered him gently: 'Anchor the sled!'

This is the last detail that an Eskimo must remember before harnessing his dogs. Made of caribou antlers or old scraps of iron, or perhaps even a worn-out rifle barrel, the anchor or *kisak* is attached with a strong rope to the central pulling line.

With the dogs now excited and jumpy at the prospect of a warm run after their long rest in the chilly bed, Nokadlak wanted to make sure they would not pull the sled away before he was ready to leave.

Starting with the leader, the hunter and his son placed the light harness on each of the nine dogs. It was made of parallel straps with crossed leather bands attached to a backbar so that the dogs could pull with their shoulders and breasts with the least effort and greatest efficiency. They leashed the dogs in pairs with two lashes, one short—from the collar to the central trace—and the other five feet long tied to the backbar and the main trace, thus concentrating the dogs' combined pulling strength on the central trace. Only the lead dog was left by himself, free to move according to his master's commands.

I had stayed longer with Nokadlak's family than I had intended and was anxious to get back to my Mission at Burnside, but it was with a feeling of some regret that I said goodbye to the old grandmother Manerathiak and to Angivrana and her little dark-eyed girl in whom fate had arranged to interest me from the moment of her birth.

I thanked Nokadlak for his hospitality, wished him good hunting, and asked him not to wait for me to leave. Kudnanak seemed relieved to hear that nothing else would delay their departure. He picked up the anchor and jumped on the sled. '*Yo-ho, yo-ho!*' yelled Nokadlak in a voice filled with joy, and the dogs took off in a hubbub of yelping and scrambling. With the two women I watched them disappear from sight as they headed swiftly down a slope in a frenzy of reborn freedom.

Perhaps it was just as well that Nokadlak and Kudnanak did not stay to see me go. In the mad rush at the take-off, one of my dogs decided to relieve itself. Dragging its rump on the snow, it caused all the other dogs to get tangled up. It all happened so fast while I was trying to steer the sled clear of the droppings that I did not have time to break with the anchor. The sled careered ahead, jostling the dogs, and bringing on the inevitable fight.

I am sure a man like Nokadlak would have taken the incident in his stride. Lacking his experience, I was frankly disconcerted every time my team got fouled up. I summoned all my patience and tried to untangle the mess with good humour, but it was not easy. Several dogs seized upon the opportunity to settle their jealousies and differences in a roaring scramble, with the others joining in on the fringe. I had to whip the chief offenders with a thin chain to make them part. Eskimos believe that a good beating at the right time makes the dogs more faithful and obedient to their owner. They recommend the chain because it bites into the animal's skin without damaging its bones.

My finger-tips were almost numb by the time I was able to disentangle the ropes and the harnesses. It was with a relieved heart that I finally jumped on the load and shouted 'Takke, takke, Bobby! Get going, Bobby!' to my lead dog.

The dogs were pulling again as if nothing had happened and the krammotik, with its bow-shaped runners, glided easily along the hard snow. Here and there the snow was rough, but I reckoned that we were making five to seven miles an hour. At this rate I ought to be in Burnside, thirty-five miles to the south, before dusk.

Occasionally the trail led over hills that slowed the dogs to a walk, and then I gladly gave them a helping hand. The extra effort warmed me up, loosened my stiff muscles, and helped to relieve the monotony. Fortunately there were no greater obstacles to combat on this comparatively short run —no boulders of ice, no deep holes to tax the endurance and ingenuity of a man and his dogs. I did not face the back-breaking job of chopping my way out of rough ice with an axe, nor of filling up the dangerous holes with snow to get the team and sled across them. My dogs were spared the arduous, tortuous climbs over rocks and mountainous ice that can only result in ultimate exhaustion. These hazards I knew to be common in the Central Arctic, but we were not to encounter them on the way to the Mission.

We drove along the Burnside River, meandering in a desolate landscape, wildly beautiful with its crumbling serenity. In the overwhelming silence, broken only by the grating of the runners on the snow, my sympathy went out to Nokadlak and his people. How appallingly dreadful their way of living seemed to me! It is a monotonous enough life in the iglu; but to brave the elements day after day, year after year, in the continuous struggle for barest survival—how does the Eskimo do it? Aren't there moments when even the primitive man must be tempted to give up? These and like questions arose in my mind, but as yet I had no answers for them.

The light was failing when we climbed down through a creek to the sea floor and presently beheld the Mission buildings I had helped Father Delalande complete when I first arrived at Burnside in 1937. The main frame structure, thirty-one by eighteen feet, had been started by him the year before with materials brought from Edmonton by barge to Tuktuyaktuk via the Mackenzie River and thence by the schooner *Our Lady of Lourdes* across nine hundred miles of open sea and ice-fields to Bathurst Inlet on which Burnside stands. I had since added a smaller building for storing our supplies which also arrived once a year aboard the schooner.

It was nearly six hours since I had left Nokadlak's camp and I was glad to be back among more familiar surroundings. During my absence Father Adam had been holding down the station, and now he had a cheery fire going in the kitchen's coal stove. While I ate supper we exchanged our news of the past few days. He told me that if I was still keen to travel to Cambridge Bay for a local population survey I could have a travelling companion for the 200-mile trek north that very week.

'A young fellow named Otokreak, who arrived after you left for Kagnekoguyak, says he is planning to go back to his camp at Admiralty Island, and I am sure he won't mind if you go along. You can speak to him about it in the morning if you are interested.'

'I don't believe I know this young man, but since I have got to try to establish a station in Cambridge Bay sooner or later, perhaps I'd better travel with him at least part way. I'll see him tomorrow as you suggest.'

The hot meal of caribou-bone soup and steak, followed by steaming coffee, in a room comfortably heated with coal imported from Edmonton at $210 a ton, made me feel hot and drowsy. But I still had to feed my dogs and unpack the sled before going to bed. This I did in a half-daze.

Besides a good-sized living-room and the adjoining chapel, the Mission contained two small bedrooms, one of which belonged to me and the other to Father Adam. A moose skin, stretched to its full length and attached with rope to a bed of two-by-fours, served as both spring and mattress. On this taut hammock I placed my sleeping bag, and was soon fast asleep.

At dawn I woke up with a start from a vivid dream of

Nokadlak's family and the pirtok. Outside, in the half-light, the Mission's entire contingent of nearly thirty dogs and pups —including the nine dogs I had used on the previous day's trip—were echoing the melancholy howling of passing wolves.

Otokreak was asleep when I crawled into his little iglu on a bank of the Burnside Channel a couple of hundred yards from the Mission.

'*Teetoren!* Come and have tea!' I said loudly, knowing full well that if there is one thing that will wake an Eskimo it is an invitation to drink tea.

The young man—I judged him to be about seventeen— rolled over on his stomach, looked at me through half-closed eyes, and asked automatically: '*Kranok ikpa hilla?* How is the weather?'

'*Hillakrertok.* The weather's fine,' I assured him.

It was as impolite for either one of us to introduce himself as it was to ask the other's name. Those things had to await their turn. Talk of tea and the weather were properly more pressing.

The prospect of tea and the complete absence of heat in the iglu (he was probably saving his fuel) caused Otokreak to don his parka, breeches, and boots in record time, and follow me quickly to the kitchen. I had already cooked and eaten my breakfast of cornmeal and toast, and the room was now warm—too warm for my young friend. He sweated freely as he gladly accepted dry caribou meat and fat and several cups of unsweetened tea.

I learned that he had been gone from his camp on Kriki-takapfaluk or Admiralty Island for twelve nights, that he had visited some of his relatives at Gordon Bay, some thirty miles northeast of Burnside, and that he was returning shortly.

'Which way are you going back?' I asked.

'The same way I came here—through the Kulugayuk River.'

'Are you going to visit any friends at Cambridge Bay?'

'*Anertak*. Certainly. I must call there to pick up some things I have traded at the post.'

'Maybe Father Adam has told you that I too am a Father. I want to visit the people of Cambridge Bay, and I'd like to go with you.'

Although he was obviously flattered that a white man wanted to travel with him, Otokreak's native sense got the better of him. 'I haven't enough food for my dogs. My ammunition is low. And I have very little food for myself,' he complained. '*Mammianak illa*. Things are really bad.'

I did not let him down. 'All right,' I said, 'I'll feed your dogs and bring enough food for you and me on the trail. How's that?'

'That suits me fine,' he said, beaming, in an unabashed reversal of mood.

'If the weather is good, we can leave early tomorrow morning.' As the provider I now had to assume the initiative.

Otokreak rose to depart just as Father Adam returned with a load of ice for the Mission's water supply. I told him of our plans to leave the next day. He offered to help me prepare the necessary supplies for the long trip, and I gladly consented.

While I was cleaning my two primus stoves, the kind Father filled a large pot with chopped caribou meat and placed it on the kitchen stove. In another pot he put beans and rice, added water, and let them boil. As soon as they softened, he mixed the vegetables with meat and boiling caribou fat. Then he took the concoction out to the porch for freezing.

Otokreak returned unexpectedly with my harnesses and lines.

'Some of your ropes are worn out,' he said. 'I will change them. Also, three or four of the crossbars on your sled are loose and should be tightened for the long trip.'

His own few chores done, and his sled ready, except for icing the runners just before departure, Otokreak was obviously looking for something to do and I did not want to discourage him.

'There is caribou line in the store-room. If you need clips for the harnesses and dog collars, you will find them there too.'

Outside on the porch Father Adam was chopping the frozen minced meat he had prepared for me. 'There's enough to fill a gunny sack,' he said pleasantly. 'I guess that will do you for a couple of weeks at least, perhaps a little longer.'

'One sack should be plenty, thanks. But don't you think I ought to take a little extra coal oil?'

'Take eight gallons. Crossing new territory at this time of the year is a gamble. You can expect to be storm-bound for days.'

'How much dog food will you carry, Fala?'

'I will take what I need for my dogs for twelve days or more, and I will give you ten days' supply of dried meat.'

'*Namaktok*. That's fine.' The young hunter smiled. Then he added: 'Maybe we can visit the big camp at Taserkapfaluk. It is not far out of our way and I have friends there.'

The Eskimo has no regard for time since he has all his life to do whatever he pleases. 'Not far' may mean up to three days' travelling. Knowing this, I did not commit myself. The lake was not on the map, but I had heard of it from other Eskimos and its name fascinated me.

Ever-thoughtful, Father Adam reminded me to take my double sleeping bag and extra caribou hides to sleep on. 'It must be terribly cold inland,' he said. 'Last year, when I went up to the Hanimok River, the cold was so intense I could feel it burning through the soles of my boots.'

I was still comparatively new to the Arctic, and it to me. Thus, despite Father Adam's admonitions, I was looking forward to my trip in country unknown to the white man with considerable pleasure. Neither Father Adam nor anyone else could have persuaded me that during the next few weeks my cheerful mood would change into a nightmare of hopelessness.

4

BIG LAKE

With Otokreak's dog-team in the lead, we left the Mission soon after daybreak. Clouds covered the sky and it was bitterly cold, but otherwise the weather seemed passable. Almost at once we were picking our way between the clusters of tiny islands that dot the Burnside harbour. We skirted them and presently crossed Bathurst Inlet, which is only five miles wide at this point, then headed for Gordon Bay or Siorkretak, as Otokreak called it. That night we slept in an abandoned iglu in the foothills of the Umimaktok mountain range.

It took us nearly two full days of slow, tiring climbing to reach the plateau. But as we neared it I felt unusually elated, for so far as I knew I was the first white man to explore it.

Actually, there was nothing to chart until we reached the wind-swept Krimakton Lake, whose western bank we followed in preference to taking a chance over its treacherous glare ice. The oval lake lay precisely in the north-easterly direction we had decided to follow, and I was able to plot it fairly accurately with a compass. Perhaps I should have given it a white man's name, but at the time the thought did not even cross my mind.

We took advantage of the full moon, and despite the intense cold, pushed on to the two lesser frozen bodies of water known to the natives as the Kalgilik Lakes. We were now close to the highest point on the plateau and made camp on the more northern lake.

Over a cup of tea before going to sleep, I spoke to Otokreak about the trail: 'Is there much more climbing ahead of us now?'

'No, tomorrow morning we shall reach Taserkapfaluk if the wind is not blowing hard.'

Taserkapfaluk, Big Lake—the biggest one I was to discover on my travels—only hours away! I suppose I should have been excited at the thought, but I wasn't. Instead I asked: 'Whom do you expect to see at Big Lake?'

'I want to visit my friend Paoktok. He went up last fall to hunt caribou and trap foxes. The hunting is usually good there.'

'I suppose you are a fair hunter yourself?'

'*Ayuiktunga.* I'm pretty good because my father, who is the best hunter of all, taught me when I was young.'

'What is your father's name?'

'Kakagun.'

'Kakagun! What a surprise! I know your father. He is indeed a very great hunter and a very fine and kind man. But he never told me he had a son named Otokreak.'

'Perhaps it was because I was born not to his proper wife but to an exchange wife,' he said with a laugh. Then, in response to further questions, Otokreak explained what he meant.

It was a poor winter and Kakagun's wife was big with child when he decided to search for game in a distant part of the land. To help him tend the blubber lamp and mend his clothes, Kakagun took along Adjuk, the wife of his friend Karlik, leaving his own wife in the latter's care. Out of this

34

practical arrangement, common among friendly hunters, was born Otokreak. Kakagun adopted the boy and brought him up, but when Karlik drowned while hunting seals, he returned Otokreak, who had developed into a self-reliant youth of twelve, to Karlik's wife Adjuk for her support. Kakagun moved away from Admiralty Island to Taseriuak, and Adjuk was eventually taken as a wife by another hunter. Finally free to travel where he pleased, Otokreak set out to find himself a mate. Although he had been on the move all winter, he had not succeeded yet, for women were scarce. Now he was going back to Admiralty Island to look around among his former neighbours.

We had not gone far in the morning when our dogs sensed something ahead. Their heads up, they were looking round interestedly, and pulling harder to satisfy their curiosity. When they finally sighted an oncoming team, they began exchanging gleeful yapping with the other dogs.

We stopped at a convenient distance between the lead dogs, anchored our sleds to prevent dog fights, and walked ahead to shake hands silently with the unexpected stranger, whom Otokreak recognized immediately as Teretkrok.

After we had admired each other's dogs—the customary social icebreaker on the trail—we told him we were going to Big Lake. He in turn said that early that morning he had left the Kulugayuk River where his wife had just died, and that he was going to Kringaun or Burnside to trade his furs and see his friends. He did not have to add that he would be on the lookout for another wife, for no Eskimo widower remains in that state any longer than he can help.

I made a mental note of what Teretkrok said, so that I could notify the RCMP of his wife's death. It was a routine duty every Arctic missionary performed for the government. Several months later our paths were to cross again, but neither of us knew that. We parted without saying goodbye, for the word simply doesn't exist in the Eskimo language.

We reached the western bank of Taserkapfaluk at noon. Except for the bitter cold, abetted by a slight breeze, the weather was perfect, and the lake stretched eastward as far as the eye could see. No white man had ever beheld its expanse of glare ice, broken only by snow-drifts here and there. Otokreak had told me that his friend's camp was at the other end of the lake. It took us nearly five hours to traverse its twenty-five-mile length along the north shore.

We found four iglus there clustered within a radius of about fifty yards; two of them were joined together. Otokreak identified the owners of the twin iglus as his friends Miyuk and Amiraernek, both from Cambridge Bay. The third iglu of equal size, I found out later, belonged to Makara, while the fourth, much larger than the rest, housed Siksik with his two wives and their children.

As soon as they heard our dogs, the four men, the five women, and the ten youngsters streamed out to greet us. Miyuk's wife was carrying a baby girl on her back in her hood. As she approached Otokreak and me she smiled, shook hands without a word, then turned her head to the baby, pulled out its tiny hand, and said quietly: '*Attitoren*. Shake hands.'

The men had just returned from their trap-lines. Their sleds were still loaded, and heaps of rusty traps lay on them. They had placed their dogs on the dog-line and were refreshing themselves with tea when our arrival threw the camp into commotion. Dutifully the women went back to the iglus to keep the tea hot for their menfolk as the latter stayed outside to give us a silent hand with our dogs. The children clambered excitedly over our sleds, chattering all the while about our dogs and me.

'He is a Kablunak—a man with bushy eyebrows; not at

all like us,' some of them kept repeating in open wonder.

I had become accustomed to such scrutiny and did not let it bother me. I set up my dog-line and, with the help of Siksik and Makara, transferred my dogs to it, then took what I needed from the sled for an overnight stay in Siksik's iglu at his invitation. Aided by Miyuk and Amiraernek, Otokreak made short work of his unloading chores and headed for the twin iglus, talking and laughing with his friends.

The two iglus were connected by an archway, which simplified the heating problem for their inhabitants and enabled them to enjoy each other's conversation, songs, and jokes with a measure of comfort. As I entered his spacious iglu I could not help thinking that his two wives gave Siksik the sort of prestige a two-car garage brings a businessman. Bigamy for him represented virility and, in the eyes of his fellow hunters, added to his stature as a man. Personally, I considered Siksik's innate quality of kindliness his greatest asset, but his fine physique and strong features were undeniably attractive to every beholder.

Siksik's older son, a tall, red-faced, matured boy of fourteen winters, and the image of his father, followed us into the family iglu. The younger son chose to play round the sleds. Siksik's younger wife, whose name I learned later was Arluk, sat watching the kettle over the lamp, while his first wife, whom he called Kommek, was scraping a caribou skin on the commodious iglek. They were both shy; neither spoke, but they looked at me furtively when they thought I might not be watching.

To break the silence, I began describing our trip. Arluk poured tea and served everybody with meat, starting politely with me.

'Did you see any tracks of caribou, wolves, or foxes, or anything else?' Siksik inquired when I finished telling of the hard climb we had had and the lakes we had traversed.

'No, but this morning we met Teretkrok who was travelling from Kulugayuk River to Kringaun. He told us his
wife had died and he was going to trade at the post and visit
with his friends.'

At the mention of the chance meeting with Teretkrok the
women pricked up their ears, and I thought I detected a particular spark of interest on Kommek's face when I spoke of
his wife's death. Six months were to pass before I recalled and
wondered again about that momentary flash in her dark eyes.

Surfeited with play, Kommek's six-year-old boy and one of
his playmates joined us in the iglu, while over their noisy,
playful babbling, another young voice yelled outside:
'*Teetoritse!*' It was a reminder that tea also awaited me in the
twin iglus of Miyuk and Amiraernek.

I got some candies from my grub box, which I had left in
the porch, and gave a few to the two youngsters, taking the
rest with me for the other children in camp.

'*Goanna!* Thank you!' they chorused happily, popping the
candy into their mouths.

'I am going to feed my dogs and then go visiting,' I said,
after thanking my hosts.

'So am I,' said Siksik, and followed me out to the porch.

As I began to feed my dogs with dried fish, the other dogs
started howling, fearful of being neglected, and presently all
the men emerged with food for their teams.

I joined Otokreak and his friends and, accompanied by
Siksik, we entered the double iglu through the single tunnel
serving both.

To me there was always something fascinating about two
or more iglus joined together. Perhaps it was the rhythmic
arrangement of domes and archways whose effect increased
with the multiplicity of its component parts. Even three or
four iglus so linked gave me the impression of looking into

several mirrors at reflected images of shimmering white hemispheres with rounded arches between them.

'It is roomy and nice in here,' I said admiringly to Miyuk and Amiraernek. They beamed back proudly. Their wives were both in the first iglu, which belonged to Miyuk. Fussing with the preparation of tea and meat, they characteristically did not enter the conversation until later on. Miyuk's wife was still packing her baby girl in her hood, although the child was now asleep.

Otokreak had already told his friends about the various camps he had visited since he left home, and was now poking fun at my behaviour on the trail.

'Fala was half-asleep on the sled. He sometimes did not see the dogs' droppings and I had to help him unload and clean and re-ice the runners!' Everybody laughed good-naturedly.

Encouraged, my young guide continued: 'The day after we left Kringaun, we spotted a wolf in a valley. Fala said he'd go and shoot him. He took his rifle and went after the animal. I watched him get quite close to it. He kneeled down and fired. The wolf fell dead. Fala was very proud. He ran to the wolf as fast as he could. When he got to it, he saw the animal had a collar on him. It wasn't a wolf at all; it was a dog!'

This time even the women guffawed. 'Heh, heh, heh! He mistook a dog for a wolf! What a good joke, heh, heh, heh!' They chuckled so infectiously that they had me laughing too.

Miyuk and Amiraernek had two children each, and Amiraernek's wife, Arnaluak, was expecting a third. With the other children in the camp, Miyuk's boy and Amiraernek's two were playfully running in and out of the different iglus. No-one minded their antics. Here was freedom beyond that enjoyed by the children of our civilization, I thought. These happy youngsters could dash into anyone's iglu at any time and play in it or watch the family and nobody would say 'boo' to them. It was not only because with snow outside and a snow floor in the iglu they could not bring mud or dust into the dwellings; it was simply because Eskimo children are free to do whatever they like as soon as they can walk. They are never rebuked or beaten. The only parental restriction is that in stormy weather they are told to stay inside.

And yet, when one of Amiraernek's boys silently accepted candy from me, and I heard his mother say *'Goyalutin!* Give thanks!' he immediately obeyed.

Having partaken of tea, raw frozen caribou meat, and slices of blubber they had obtained from seals last fall in Bathurst Inlet, we adjourned from Miyuk's iglu into Amiraernek's part of the duplex.

Once again I could not offend the hostess by refusing tea. Impromptu entertainment was now provided by the three boys who took turns at swinging and stunting on a wooden trapeze bar suspended by two ropes from the centre of the dome. The ropes had been put right through the roof and were held securely by another piece of wood. The iglu's expertly shaped snow blocks had long since frozen into a single convexity whose structural strength could support far greater weights than boys or men on the trapeze.

Urged by one another to match or better the boys' acrobatic feats, Otokreak, Miyuk, and Amiraernek doffed their parkas and showed off. They mocked each other but always applauded well-executed stunts.

'Ilvitlu, Fala! And you, too, Father! *Takke, takke!* Come on, come on!' they chorused, expecting another good laugh at my expense.

Nature had not given me a large frame, but through school, college, and seminary I had been interested in gymnastics and felt at home on a trapeze. At the moment, however, I was full of liquid and food. Otokreak and my hosts took my hesitation to mean I did not know how to use a swinging bar. This gave them a sense of superiority over the little white man and made them all the more insistent.

'You are a Kablunak. Show us what you can do!' teased Otokreak.

'My stomach is filled with your good food, and I am tired from the trip, but I will show you one or two tricks,' I said at last. Bare to the waist, I repeated the hardest presses, swings, dips, and stands of the three well-muscled young men, dismounting with a fancy flip to the incredulous delight of all present.

They gathered round me. I stood panting heavily like a winded prizefighter, but I was inwardly pleased with my performance. They were all feeling my biceps with accompanying expressions of surprise and admiration that were summed up by the older Siksik, who had remained a spectator throughout: *'Angun ai-eh!* A man you are! You are small, but strong and capable!'

With all the acrobats sweating freely, the smell in the place was something to avoid.

'I am going to visit Makara,' I announced as soon as I replaced my parka. Leaving the women behind to clean up the makeshift gymnasium, the men trooped out with me.

My companions wasted no time in describing my prowess on the trapeze to the squat, moon-faced Makara, his impassive wife, and their two sons and daughter. I tried repeatedly to change the subject without success. Finally, over yet another cup of tea and slices of meat, Siksik did it for me:

'I will start with you tomorrow for Irkalututiak.'

The sudden decision of their unofficial leader to accompany me and Otokreak to Cambridge Bay received general approval. Otokreak's friends went back to their wives to warn them of the move. It was all arranged.

Everyone was still up in Siksik's iglu when he and I returned, for the entire Eskimo family habitually goes to bed at the same time. The night was cold but clear, with only a trace of wind raising powdery snow along the shore of Big Lake. There was nothing in the air to indicate a drastic change in the next twenty-four hours, and I was prepared to turn in with a loaded stomach and a light heart.

My composure was ruffled by Siksik, however, who casually asked me which of his wives I would like for the night. The tall, shapely, good-looking Arluk, and the somewhat older but also attractive Kommek both began to giggle at the proposal—not that it was out of the ordinary run of Krangmalit hospitality, but rather because they had never had the opportunity to sleep with a white man before.

I did not wish to offend Siksik or insult the ladies present —especially the red-cheeked Kommek, who was apparently under the impression that I was going to choose her.

Carefully picking my words, and using the politest tone I could muster, I replied: 'I am a Fala, and I am not supposed to accept such wonderful invitations, not even from such a good friend as you, Siksik.'

He had not expected my answer and seemed perplexed by it. The women were openly disappointed. Conversation lagged at this point, and I took the opportunty to undress and slip into my bag. The children stripped and lay down to sleep. Arluk crawled into Siksik's family-size sleeping bag, while Kommek took the younger child with her. I was left to my solitude and mixed emotions, accentuated by a gnawing in the stomach which, I suspected, resulted from overeating and overdoing the unaccustomed trapeze work.

5

ACROSS UNCHARTED LAND

The whole camp was bustling with preparations all next morning. The four families had come to Big Lake in the autumn of the previous year and, though they had built several snow-houses for themselves since then (two months being the maximum life even of a well-built iglu), it was their first move in six months.

My stomach-ache kept me awake for most of the night, and the morning found me making frequent sorties to a snow-drift. My new friends were quick to divine, with great amusement, that overnight I had developed piles.

By noon the sleds were made ready and loaded, the dogs harnessed, everyone seated, and the six teams took off, with Otokreak on his lightly-laden sled in the lead.

Travelling in the bitter cold and wind only made me worse. I was forced to stop from time to time, holding up the entire caravan, yet finding no real relief from the recurring pains.

To avoid the surrounding hills and more difficult terrain, we followed for about twenty miles the same shore route by which Otokreak and I had reached the camp the day before. Eventually the land flattened out on all sides and we veered sharply to the north in the direction of the Kulugayuk River. I glanced at my watch: it was four o'clock.

Dark, sinister clouds began to form in the west, shrouding the low sun and heading towards us. An hour later the wind struck with sudden fierceness and all at once a swirling blanket of snow enveloped our teams. Still we kept going, the tinkling bells of the leading dogs drawing us together. But soon we had to admit that we were lost.

The men decided to build two iglus. I wanted to help them but found that I had lost so much blood that it was all I could do to take care of my dogs. How my friends were able to construct their shelters of snow blocks in the face of onrushing waves of razor-sharp crystalline snowflakes, only an Eskimo could explain. While they struggled, some of the women and their crying children bunched closely together in the lee of their sleds, vainly trying to keep warm. The unencumbered women braved the merciless wind to unharness the dogs and tie the tired, shivering animals to the dog-lines. Then they shuffled over to the rising iglus and filled in the cracks between the blocks.

Siksik was putting the blocks together on one iglu and Otokreak on the other. The other men were cutting blocks out of the snow and passing them on to the two builders. Their faces almost hidden with frost and flying snow, they worked steadily, without rushing, yet quickly, methodically, and with consummate skill.

When Siksik's iglu was ready, his family and Makara's family got the blubber lamps going and took in the furs, sleeping bags, and meat. Miyuk, Amiraernek, their families and I followed suit as Otokreak's iglu was completed.

With ten of us in each iglu, crowding was the order of the night. Jammed side by side on the snow floor—there was no time to afford the luxury of an iglek—we kept reasonably warm, though not comfortable. Seeing my poor state, Otokreak offered to feed my dogs when his friends went out to look after their teams, and I accepted his kindness.

So weak and tired had I become, I did not know or care who lay next to me. No-one really slept that night. There wasn't room to turn. It was cold. The children cried often. As the wind increased with the passage of hours, Miyuk put everyone's misgivings into words when he said: 'We built the iglu in rather a hurry. I wonder if the blocks will hold as the wind gets stronger.'

The hunters' concern for the shelter never reached the point of worry or fear. It was just another bad storm and they would wait it out. Quietly they talked back and forth about the trip and how well the dogs had done so far, and even found humour in my misery when they saw me crawl out shakily through the small door hung with caribou skin. But their kindness overshadowed their playfulness, and frequent were their inquiries after my well-being and their offers of help.

Towards dawn the wind seemed to diminish its fury and I heard Otokreak suggest to Miyuk and Amiraernek that they might consider pushing on. His friends were not so sure it was a good idea, but agreed to consult Siksik and Makara as soon as they were up.

We were still about a hundred and fifty miles from Cambridge Bay—a matter of five or six days' travelling time with heavy sleds over uneven inland trails—providing we could find out our whereabouts in the first place. Otokreak's reason for resuming the trip despite the storm was that the longer we waited, the less food would remain for the dogs. Gradually the animals would get so feeble from hunger that they would be unable to pull the sleds and, lacking resistance, would freeze in their sleep.

Once they had looked over the situation outside, Miyuk and Amiraernek predicted that the storm would continue for several days. They were against moving on until it cleared. Makara sided with them. 'And what about the children?' he asked. 'Will they be able to stand the going? Will they not freeze on the sled if the wind grows stronger again?'

Siksik refrained from giving an opinion. Instead, his experienced eyes minutely surveyed the snow-bound surroundings, seeking possible landmarks. Suddenly he walked off in a northwesterly direction for a few hundred feet, then motioned the others to join him.

'Look,' he said, when the four men reached his side. 'I believe this creek is a tributary of the Kulugayuk River. If we follow it, we should reach the river in two days. Its high banks will give us more protection from the wind and we'll be able to travel faster along its shore-line.'

Only Makara, who was older than the others, was able to confirm Siksik's identification of the solidly frozen creek. Its meandering course was defined by a trough of packed snow, which showed no trace of the withered grass and rocks that normally constitute the floor of the Barren Land.

'Siksik is wise,' Makara said. 'We will follow him.'

Hearing no objections from his friends Miyuk and Amiraernek, Otokreak proclaimed: '*Aodlarta!* Let's go!'

Like grey ghosts in the flying snow and howling wind, the men went back to the iglus. Told of their decision, the women fed us all as much tea, dried fish, meat, and fat as we could take in anticipation of the long hours of sled-sitting ahead of us.

It was an effort to rouse the dogs into action. They lay curled up until the very moment they were harnessed, reluctant to believe that their masters were mad enough to travel in such abominable weather.

The younger children, in soft fawn-skin parkas, looked like

bear cubs who had been rolling in the snow. But they were not gambolling now. Their backs to the gusty wind, they sat quietly, almost motionless on the sleds between their parents, as the teams pulled away from the temporary camp.

Whipped by the wind, the snow clung to our eyelashes, sometimes so gluing the eyelids together that we could only open them again by rubbing them with our mitts. Some of the dogs were bleeding from the jaws—an unmistakable sign of extreme cold.

I had forced myself to eat with the rest for the sake of stamina and inner warmth. But my malady was further aggravated by exposure to the storm. If the others had let me, I think I would have gladly lain down in the snow and gone to sleep forever. Yet somehow I managed to survive the nightmarish ordeal.

In the afternoon we unexpectedly came across tracks of sleds and frozen dog droppings. The weight of the sleds had packed and frozen the snow where the runners had passed, and the tracks remained while the wind swept the softer snow alongside. Here and there the tracks were broken and no-one could really tell when they had been made. The mere sight of them, however, gave us the courage we needed, and even the sorely tired dogs pulled with renewed vigour.

Two hours later Siksik, who was in the lead, sighted black dots against the snowy backdrop. *'Inuit, inuit, inuraluit! Men, men, a lot of them!'* he yelled above the storm.

There were three families in as many iglus in the camp, and we spent that night with them. Our host was Avalekrat, who told us that they had moved up from the Queen Maud Gulf in early winter to retrieve caches of caribou they had killed in the fall, and were returning to Cambridge Bay when the storm overtook them.

Personally I could not have hoped for better news. At the

slow rate we were progressing, my diminishing supplies of dog food had me frankly worried. From my sickbed I asked Avalekrat if he could spare some carcasses of caribou, offering him a case of *krarkolak* or hardtack bread in trade, with further payment once we reached Cambridge Bay.

'For my children I can use the krarkolak,' he said. 'And I shall come to your iglu in Ikalututiak for some calico for my wife's dresses.'

The deal made, Avalekrat piled up six frozen caribou carcasses on my sled and helped himself to the pilot's bread.

Later that evening Otokreak, his face betraying an inward satisfaction, sat down beside me and said optimistically: 'Our dogs will be well fed from now on. Mine are getting so thin they look more like shadows.'

'Did you trade some meat?' I asked, wondering.

'Yes, indeed,' he grinned. 'Avalekrat gave me three caribou carcasses for nothing.'

I read between the lines. Everything pointed to my paying for nine instead of six carcasses.

The storm confined us to Avalekrat's iglu for two days and three nights. He built an addition to relieve the crowding and it was comfortable enough under the circumstances. The forced stop gave me a chance to rest my wasting body. To while away the hours, I talked at length with Avalekrat's mother, Itireitok. She was incredibly old for an Eskimo woman but bubbled with energy and good humour.

Perhaps because I paid more attention to her stories than her family did, the stooped old lady seemed interested in talking to me and helped me in every way she could.

'Do you know the big Bay of Kattimanek?' she asked me, by way of making an opening for one of her stories.

'*Illa*,' I nodded, recalling my previous visits to Arctic Sound.

'Well, a very long time ago a man lived there all by him-

48

self. He did not have a wife to look after him or a friend to visit him. But he was not lonely because he possessed a strange power not given to ordinary hunters.

'One day he went down to the seashore, saying to himself: "Let's see if there is anything moving in the water." He walked for a long time along the shore, peering into the clear water, but all he could see was smooth rock and pebbles.

'On the beach he found a piece of drift-willow and sat down to carve it with a knife. He cut out shavings of various shapes, leaving bark on some of them. He threw these into the water and called them salmon. To the smaller, barkless bits of wood he gave the different names of the white fish which we now find swimming in the lakes, rivers, and the sea.'

Itireitok's fanciful tale reminded me more of Greek mythology than of the bizarre Krangmalit stories that often start nowhere and end nowhere. Usually what little meaning such legends may have carried originally has been lost or hidden over the generations; but this one was refreshingly different.

The people of the Barren Land do not try to analyse the universe around them. They simply accept it. Life is too short and too much of a daily struggle against cold and famine as it is. Glances into the past by old people like Itireitok provided only fantastic notions about their world. From her, as from other Eskimos of the Central Arctic, I learned that their land is inhabited by supernatural beings, evil spirits and ghouls, who delight in surprising the unwary traveller and causing him trouble, disease, and pain.

'They are there all the time,' Itireitok assured me. 'They may be shy or fiendish. They are always breathing and whispering like the wind itself. Sometimes they look like men, sometimes like animals or mysterious hybrids raised out of nowhere, conceived like the hills and the mountains, the lakes and the sea.'

To Itireitok the earth and the heavens were animated beings that protected her against such superhuman forces. They were not spirits to her but visible helpers without a soul. She used the same word *anernek* to describe breath and the soul, since her own soul was a living, breathing thing, capable of survival after death.

'What happens to the soul when the body dies?' I asked her.

'It will go away for a while, keeping the same name as the body it leaves behind. Then one day the name will be transferred to a dog or a child.'

Try as I might, I could not get the old woman to tell me where she believed the soul went after death. She did explain that for a time the soul stays near the corpse on the bare ground, using some of the belongings left for its convenience. But she hadn't the faintest idea what happens to the soul after the name is passed on to someone else.

'Is the soul judged? Is it punished if found wanting, rewarded if deserving?' She had no coherent answers. She was definite only in her belief that the soul is linked to a name for as long as it is employed from generation to generation; and that other souls pivot around the same name, bestowing their qualities upon its bearer. Then she observed:

'Departed souls can be so troublesome! I am afraid of them. It is not good for them to be wandering about, forlorn and unattached. That is why we call a dog after the dead one if there is no new-born child in the family to receive the name.'

I had often come across such namings of dogs and noticed that the animals received no special treatment in the bargain. They were beaten with the rest of the team when the occasion warranted it, and they starved when their masters ran out of food. However, under no circumstances would they be killed by their owners. They had to die a natural death so that their names could be respectably transferred to other humans or canines.

That point was brought home to me during my first year in the Arctic. One morning, as the sun hung low over the mountains of Burnside, I saw a dog crouching in the snow on the slope to the channel. As I drew closer I realized that the animal was dying. His ribs were sticking out through his thin fur. There was no flesh on him, just bones. I tried to make him walk with me, but he would not even rise. I hated to see the poor old dog suffer the pains of slow death, so I put an end to his misery with a rifle shot.

It was deep twilight when a tall, powerfully built Eskimo entered my iglu. He came straight to the point: 'Why did you kill Manillak?'

'Manillak?' I echoed in surprise. 'Who is he? I've never killed anyone in my life!'

'Yes, Kablunak, you certainly did. Manillak is lying on the snow with a bullet through his head. He is dead. You shot him.'

The big man looked steadfastly at me, his face immobile. I did not know what to say. Finally he grunted: 'Manillak was my grandfather and my dog bore his name. Only my dog could not talk. He was very old and ready to die. Why did you have to kill him?'

After I got over my first fright I apologized to my visitor for my stupid mistake, offered him tea, and got him to talk about himself. That was how I first met Kakagun, the greatest hunter among the People Beyond. Our friendly paths were to cross many times after this initial misunderstanding.

Towards the third night the storm played itself out and everyone talked happily about resuming the interrupted trip on the morrow. I was feeling better and was able to feed my dogs myself.

It was exceedingly cold, but the clouds had vanished and the sky was aglow with *akraliak* or the northern lights. That night, after days of storm and stress, they seemed to me more beautiful than ever. From a dusky line of diaphanous haze a few degrees above the horizon, the multicoloured streaks ascended towards the heavenly zenith, assuming kaleidoscopic shapes and shades in their constantly quivering motion.

Siksik, Otokreak, and the other men hardly gave them a glance. I knew from previous experience with Eskimos that to comment on the beauty of the lights was a waste of time. They regarded the shimmering curtain in the sky with mixed feelings of fear and joy, and shunned any discussion of it. They were afraid of akraliak because they could not understand it, and also because it was often accompanied by falling temperatures; they were happy to see it only because it helped to brighten the long, gloomy winter night.

What had started out as a caravan of two sleds from Burnside now became almost an exodus as the families of Avalekrat, Igutak, and Avadluk joined us in the morning. To battle the cold, everyone wore double breeches and double parkas, which made us look like a procession of huge apes.

Well rested, the dogs pulled eagerly, and by noon we were able to reach the banks of the Kulugayuk River. We descended its steep embankment and found ourselves protected from the snarling westerly wind that was sweeping the barren floor above us.

But the ideal snow we had hoped for was not there. Sheltered from the wind, the snow lay soft in drifts. It was so sticky that the sled runners had little more chance of sliding along it than through sand or mud. Time and again grandmother Itireitok was told to walk ahead of Avalekrat's team. She was now excess baggage that could be discarded in case of necessity. Bent over her long walking stick, the poor old woman looked like a scarecrow in the incongruous Arctic setting. I wanted to help her but could not. Not only was my sled heavy with caribou, but it would have been improper to interfere. With an indomitable spirit, Itireitok plodded on. She never complained. She realized that she was altogether dispensable and acted accordingly.

We had to stop repeatedly for other reasons. Particles of the soft snow easily attached themselves to the hair between the dogs' paws, freezing into icy balls that irritated and cut them. Whenever he saw one of his dogs trying to bite its paws for that reason, Siksik, who was again in the lead, would stop his team and go to the dog. When he called it by name, it lay on its side and extended the paws to him. Down on his knees, Siksik raised the paws to his mouth and bit the icy pellets off as children bite at hard candy. The other drivers of the sleds, assisted by members of their families, emulated Siksik by examining all their dogs' paws and biting off accumulated ice.

Igutak's wife Oviluk seized such opportunities to take two newly-born pups to their mother for feeding. Picking them out of a caribou bag that was tied to the sled, she carried the yelping pups to the bitch, unharnessed her, and spread a caribou skin for her to lie on. The pups were the only survivors of a litter of eight; the rest had been killed because they were superfluous.

This time Oviluk noticed that the pups kept poking and pulling at their mother's teats without success. Suspecting the worst, she felt the breasts. They were frozen. In the turmoil of the morning's preparations for the trail she had forgotten to put the apron-like blanket of caribou skin over the dog's belly. Almost devoid of hair around the teats, the enlarged breasts froze solid.

Oviluk called over her husband Igutak.

'That's really too bad. What shall we do with the pups?' he wondered aloud.

'I have enough milk in my breasts for the pups and the

53

children,' she said without hesitation, and went back to the sled. Lifting her double parka she gave her breast first to one pup, then to the other, as naturally and unconcernedly as she did to her four-year-old daughter, the youngest of her three children.

Igutak re-harnessed the bitch, picked up the rug, and carried it back to the sled. To Avalekrat and Avadluk, who came to inquire what was up, he simply said: 'We forgot to cover the bitch this morning. Her breasts are frozen. Tomorrow before we pull away from camp we shall know just how badly she is frozen.' Word of this misfortune spread quickly to all the sleds, and the resigned comment was always the same: '*Mamianak*. It's too bad.'

The high embankments narrowed as we progressed, and huge granite rocks, partly covered by snow, lay in our path. The hunters stopped the teams when Siksik shouted to them: 'It is getting dangerous! The women and children should walk on the bank.' He was promptly obeyed. Ahead lay frozen rapids, boulders, and, here and there, seepage through the ice. Like a long, twisting snake, the dog teams followed one behind the other, the men skilfully manoeuvring the sleds to avoid damaging the runners.

Arnaluak, heavy with child, and Itireitok, depressed with the years, marched stoically along with the other women. They were all tired, but no-one grumbled. That was their lot and they took it in their stride, lightening their burden with gossip and laughter.

'Look at Makara,' one of them said. 'He must be getting old—he nearly upset the sled!' They all giggled, including his wife. Like children, they saw humour in everything.

As we passed the rapids we halted the teams to let the women catch up to us. The dogs were sniffing about busily, for they had discovered frozen droppings of wolves, wolverines, and foxes that had been attracted to the river by the carcasses of drowned caribou, now partly submerged by the river's frozen overflow.

'Why are there so many dead caribou here?' I asked Siksik, pointing to the bleached bones showing through the ice.

'Last spring the caribou tried to cross the river near the rapids to get better footing on the rocks, but the melting ice gave way and they were swept under by the current.'

It was the same all the way to the sea: glare ice, boulders, soft snow, and short-cuts through frozen rapids. Periodic stops to rest the dogs and ice the runners continued through the afternoon. While the women melted the snow and heated the water over the blubber lamps, the younger men—Oto-kreak, Miyuk, Amiraernek, Igutak, and Avadluk—scouted the sparsely willowed banks ahead for ptarmigan and *ukalek,* the hare. Although they had little time for hunting, they seldom came back empty-handed.

'*Akkimayunga!* I got more!' Miyuk exclaimed, waving a hare by its ears in front of Otokreak who had only managed to bag four ptarmigans, and both laughed.

Four good-sized iglus accommodated us that night.

In the morning Otokreak announced that he had slept like a *siksik.*

'Why like Siksik? Because he is a big man?' I asked him naively.

He nearly exploded with laughter. 'No, Fala, not like Siksik the hunter. Like a *siksik*—a squirrel.'

That morning we sighted the sea. It was still several miles off, but there was no mistaking its wide expanse of unbroken, level whiteness. The mere sight of it brought hopes of easier travelling to our weary band. Everyone's spirits rose, includ-ing those of old Itireitok who started to chant words that were picked up by the rest:

55

'*Namunme, sumunme* . . . Down to the sea I went
Where seals breathe through the ice.
Surprised, I heard:
Hai-ee-ya, hai-ee-ya, hai-ee-ya! Ee-ai, ee-ai, ee-ai!
The song of the sea
And the wail of the young ice:
Hai-ee-ya, hai-ee-ya, hai-ee-ya! Ee-ai, ee-ai, ee-ai!'

Their masters' heightened feelings infected the dogs. They pricked up their ears and pulled all the harder, sensing more open country. But as the land flattened out and we left the river, we again felt the bite of the westerly wind. Spurning the cold, we headed for Labyrinth Bay which was dotted with several small islands. My pains returned and I was forced to stop. Siksik, Otokreak, and Avalekrat gathered around me to shield me from the icy blasts. They did not joke any more about my condition.

That night we made camp near Melbourne Island. It was so cold that I could not light the primus stove I had brought along. The coal oil in it had turned into white jelly. From previous experience at Burnside, where we had a reliable thermometer, I knew that the freezing point of coal oil was about 55 degrees below zero.

Hoping to reach Cambridge Bay the following evening, we agreed to break camp before sunrise. It was grey and snowing when we left, but the wind's fury had decreased somewhat and we made fairly good time.

We were still about thirty miles from Cambridge Bay at two o'clock in the afternoon when we ran into a field of broken ice, formed in the fall by local winds and currents. Siksik signalled us to stop the sleds, and went ahead to reconnoitre. He reappeared from behind the jagged slabs and motioned us to follow his team. 'If he can get through, so can we,' I thought hopefully. But the difficulties we had surmounted along the Kulugayuk River paled in comparison with the hazards that now beset us.

Masses of ice rose at every step. The sleds bumped and slithered, often toppling over or falling into deep holes. To set them right again meant endless unloading and re-loading, then beating a passageway of snow. It was heartrending to see the dogs exert such desperate efforts to get out of the crevices. As for us, we lifted, pulled, and pushed the sleds till we were drenched in sweat, the chill wind notwithstanding.

Tossed and shaken in the struggle, Amiraernek's wife Arnaluak began to moan from the onset of labour pains. Amiraernek had no trouble persuading the other hunters to stop and make camp. We found four level spots and proceeded to build iglus on them. When the iglus were almost finished, I noticed that old Itireitok and Siksik's wife Kommek were supporting Arnaluak while she knelt on a caribou skin. The other women and the younger children gathered around them to shield Arnaluak from the wind. Bent forward as she knelt, Arnaluak was moaning so loudly that even the panting, played-out dogs began to howl as if in sympathy.

To everyone's relief the curtain was soon brought down on the pathetic scene as Kommek, her hands under Arnaluak's long parka, delivered the child. In her soft, worn voice Itireitok entreated the good spirits of the earth to protect the baby against Nananuak, the powerful evil spirit. A sinful murderess, Nananuak was feared by the Krangmalit because she had returned from the land of the dead in an attempt to indoctrinate them in the life hereafter.

'It's a boy, a strong little boy!' Kommek proclaimed with satisfaction, wrapping the tiny body in the fur of a caribou fawn and hurrying off into the first of the completed snow houses.

The scene took me back to Nokadlak's iglu and the birth

of Naoyak. I wondered what Amiraernek would have done if Arnaluak had presented him with a daughter. I wondered, too, how Nokadlak and his family had weathered the storms since I left them.

Supported by Itireitok, Arnaluak presently lay down on the iglek to rest, amid general rejoicing that another little man was added to the People Beyond.

'Kommek will clean your boy as soon as the water is warm,' the old woman told Arnaluak. 'Rest now, and I will get you hot water so that you can wash too.'

Kommek and Siksik's other wife, Arluk, remained with Arnaluak as Itireitok joined her son Avalekrat in another iglu, and the other women left to help their men unload and prepare for the night.

I took my sleeping bag to Igutak's iglu. Oviluk, his wife, was tending the blubber lamp. The two pups were whining for their next meal and, having scented their mother's presence in the iglu, were struggling to get out of the bag. Oviluk took one of the pups to the bitch, but the dog would not let her burning breasts be touched. Oviluk, whose own breasts were always full because her four-year-old daughter had not been weaned, let the pups have her milk.

By morning it was obvious that there was no hope for the dog. Her breasts were raw masses of red pulp, which she tried unavailingly to soothe by licking. Igutak did not harness her, letting her follow the sled when we moved off. The poor animal did not last long. The ice field taxed the strongest dogs. The sick had to be abandoned when they could not continue. The Barren Land took care of the luckless creature in its own impersonal way.

Night was falling when we finally surmounted the ten-mile-wide ice field and, after a seeming eternity, stood again on smooth snow. So weary was everyone that we barely had strength to build our iglus and crawl in to sleep.

Finally, at noon next day—ten days after Otokreak and I had left the Mission at Burnside—we reached the low coast of Victoria Land near Cape Colborn. The same evening we saw twinkling lights and white smoke rising against the overcast sky in a little cove of Cambridge Bay.

6

ENDS AND MEANS

The centre of life at Cambridge Bay was the Hudson's Bay Company trading post, operated by Scotty Moore, whose kitchen lights we saw as we approached. Storm lamp in hand, Scotty came forward to welcome me, a warm smile wreathed around the pipe in his mouth.

'Hullo, Father! How are you? I got a short-wave report that you had left Burnside over a week ago, and the Police boys and I were beginning to wonder what was holding you up. Come inside and tell me all about it!'

As we walked arm-in-arm towards the large, well-constructed building, Constables Tom Garland and Ray Stewart came out of the RCMP post to greet the new arrivals. I was glad to renew their acquaintance in Scotty's comfortable quarters. He had a nicely furnished living-room, but we preferred to sit in his warm, cosy kitchen.

Constable Garland looked at me for a moment and said: 'Father, you don't look as well as when I saw you here a year ago. Have you been ill?'

'I was fine when we left Burnside, but I got sick at Taserkapfaluk and grew worse along the Kulugayuk River. I think I'll live, though.'

They drank to my health and Scotty remarked: 'That's very strange, Father. Why didn't you come up through Melville Sound? It would have been much easier than going overland.'

I told him about Otokreak and the friends my guide wanted to call on at Big Lake.

'Well, you know,' Scotty mused, 'I never heard of any white men travelling across that country—not even the government surveyors. Have any of your fellows been in there?' he asked Tom Garland, who was Ray Stewart's senior by half a dozen years.

'Let me see your map.' Constable Garland was not one to give snap answers. Scotty brought in a topographical survey map from the living-room and spread it on the wooden kitchen table.

'This is the trail we took,' I said, tracing it with a pencil.

'You sure took a chance, didn't you, Father?' said Scotty, but before I could reply, Tom Garland exclaimed: 'I wish I had been along with you! So far as I know, none of the Police have ever set foot there!' Tom was an inveterate traveller and I knew he was genuinely sorry to have missed that trip.

Always a kindly host, Scotty asked if I would like to sleep in his quarters that night, but I thanked him and explained that I had planned to use my own outpost.

'Well, in that case I'll see you later. In the meantime, I guess I'd better stick around here, as your friends will be coming in soon for a cup of tea.'

'We'll give you a hand with your dogs, Father,' said Tom Garland when we stepped out into the freezing night air.

'Thanks a lot! I won't say no.' I climbed aboard the sled to cover the six hundred yards to my little post.

Siksik, as befitted his social standing of a great hunter, built his iglu in the place of honour near the RCMP buildings. The rest strung out their iglus between Siksik's large iglu and my house. This was a former trading post that I rented, simply furnished, from Scotty Moore for two foxes a year. It was a two-room frame building, with the living-room and kitchen forming one room and the bedroom separated from them by a wallboard partition. No-one had been in it since I vacated it the previous summer and its musty smell nearly overpowered me. I lit both the coal heater, which was placed in a cutaway in the partition to serve the living-room and the bedroom, and the coal stove in the kitchen.

When I went out, the two constables had already put my dogs on the line, and Tom asked me if I had enough meat for the huskies. We brought all my gear off the sled into the kitchen after feeding the dogs and left it on the floor to thaw out. The mildewy aroma was still thick, but the place was much warmer and more cheerful with the kettle singing on the range. To clear the air I opened the door and the Arctic night rushed in. I brewed coffee for my guests and closed the door, and we relaxed around the table.

'I don't think I've ever heard of your young friend Otokreak before,' Tom Garland said. 'Who is he?'

'He tells me he's from Admiralty Island and that his father is Kakagun, the great hunter.'

'Son of Kakagun, eh? If he's half the marksman his old man is, he should be a pretty good hunter.'

'So you know my friend Kakagun?'

'Know him! The year before you arrived at Burnside I was sent there to make a report on the Eskimos at Bathurst Inlet. Every native fancies himself as a pretty good hunter, so I was naturally surprised to find that wherever I went everyone admitted that Kakagun was the best hunter among the Krangmalit. I thought to myself: we'll see, the first chance that comes along.'

'Did you get the chance?'

'I'll say! The day Kakagun arrived in Burnside, your predecessor, Father Delalande, drew my attention to a lone wolf skirting the camp. I said: "I hear the great hunter Kakagun pulled in today. How would you like to call him so we can see how good he is with his rifle?" "I'll be glad to," says the Father, "Kakagun's a fine chap." And off he goes to fetch him.

'While he was gone, I studied the wolf through my field-glasses. He was a lean, long-legged fellow, a long way from where I stood. Father Delalande returned with Kakagun in quick time and I told him what was on my mind. The big hunter merely said that he'd try a shot.

'I kept my glasses on the moving wolf while Kakagun sat down on the snow, crossed his legs, rested his elbows on the raised knees, took aim, and fired. I didn't need the glasses to see that he'd scored a bull's eye. The wolf leaped into the air, came down, tottered, and lay still. Well, sir, that was proof enough for me! I've been an admirer of Kakagun's ever since.'

By contrast with the freezing temperatures in the iglus of the past ten nights, and the hard, often crowded iglek, my heated bedroom with its double bed and an old, well-used spring mattress felt like the height of luxury. I fell asleep as soon as I was in my bag.

The comfortable night's rest did wonders for me. I felt refreshed and strong once again. Resuming my priestly duties, I said Mass, breakfasted, and cleaned up the post. By noon I was ready to return the constables' visit.

Two dog-teams overtook me as I started for the RCMP buildings. They were driven by Otokreak and Amiraernek.

When they pulled up alongside, Amiraernek said: 'Arnaluak did not sleep very well last night. She had a backache. And the baby cried a lot.' He spoke flatly, without any display of feeling whatsoever.

'Are you also going to the Police Station?' I asked, taking the answer for granted. But Otokreak and his friend had other ideas. 'We are going to the sunken ship. We heard there is still lots of iron left on it.'

He was referring to the submerged hull of Amundsen's abandoned *Maud*, which lay in the ice in a cove between the RCMP buildings and the radar station. The Hudson's Bay Company had taken over the egg-shaped schooner, re-named her *Bay Maud*, stripped her of the vital parts and furniture, and left her there to die.

'I'll come and see it with you,' I said to Otokreak, and climbed aboard his sled.

Only the wheelhouse remained above the ice-bound *Bay Maud*. Her two masts had been cut and removed, with every-thing else of value to the white man. But Eskimo hunters had discovered that the innumerable spikes, set through the narrowly-spaced ribs and the heavy planking, made strong spear-heads and good hunting knives; while the strips of steel overlooked by the Kablunak could be fashioned into versatile *ulon* knives and, if they were long enough, into runners for sleds.

Otokreak and Amiraernek, however, were a little late. Search as they might, all they were able to salvage from the forgotten steamer were half a dozen long spikes. It took them the better part of the day to dislodge the bent metal from the oaken bed. I did not stay long with them but continued on to the RCMP buildings. Of these there were three: the bar-racks or station itself; a shack for the Eskimo couple who acted as interpreters, guides, and caretakers; and a warehouse. The latter contained a small jail that was built like a lion's cage with a steel floor and top. Its flat steel bars were covered with red anti-rust paint that gave them a gaudy circus effect.

Tom Garland and Ray Stewart were surrounded by all the normal comforts of home, except plumbing, in their five-room bungalow. Each had a nice bed-room; the spacious living-room had a three-piece chesterfield suite and cabinet radio; there was a compact office and a large rectangular kitchen with ample dining space. The house was very warm, as it should have been in return for the twenty-four tons of coal a year it took to heat it.

This was Ray's week to handle the cooking and serving chores, and the young man proved himself a credit to the Scarlet and Gold with the skillet. Later, when we adjourned into the living-room for a smoke and a chat, the Eskimo woman came in to do the dishes. She worked quietly and efficiently, using hot water from the kettle in a generous-sized dishpan.

'How are you coming along with that census of your district you started last year?' I asked Tom.

'It's all done except for some families between the Kulugayuk River and Sherman Inlet that we've heard about from other natives.'

'Could you let me have the names on your list so I can visit some of them before the breakup?'

'Sure thing, *mon vieux!*' Tom said, using one of several French phrases he had picked up from Father Delalande. The copy of the list he handed me was a revelation. Although he had carried out his investigation through his interpreter, the survey contained not only the names of the hunters, their wives, and their children, but also the background and police record of each family. I complimented him on the fine job and assured him I would treat the information as confidential.

'Just for that, Tom, I'll try to get you all the information I can on the people around Ellice and Perry Rivers.'

'Merci, *mon vieux*, that'll help a lot.'

The dishes done, the interpreter's wife asked Tom if there was any other cleaning he wanted done and, receiving a negative answer, smiled her way out.

'Did you hear what happened to her mother just a couple of weeks ago?' Ray asked when the woman left. I shook my head.

'Well, old Alunak was getting on in years, as you know, and everybody kidded her about her helplessness. That must have preyed on her mind till it got unbearable, because she went out into the storm that evening after visiting friends near the trading post and was never seen again.'

'That was the strangest thing, Father,' cut in Tom. 'About an hour after she left her friends her grandson arrived there with a sled to bring her home. They told him she should have reached the barracks long ago—it's only a mile along the bay. So the kid doubled back here to sound the alarm. Everyone in camp started looking for poor old Alunak, but it was useless.

'We found traces of her footsteps a couple of hundred yards away from the barracks. They led towards the river and suddenly vanished. The storm had reached its full strength, so we abandoned the search till morning. We never found any trace of her.'

'What do you think might have happened to her?' I said.

'I should imagine, Father, she fell from exhaustion and was covered up by the snow. We might find her remains in the spring.'

I had often seen young Krangmalit couples try their best to lighten the unenviable existence of their old parents in normal times. But when food got scarce and the family was on the verge of starvation, pity and kindness were repressed.

The old became a dead load on the sled, a dangerous hindrance on the trail. The lives of the young and the strong had to be preserved at all costs, and the weak and crippled had to be sacrificed. It was the unwritten law of the land.

But Alunak's case was different. Her people were better off than most Eskimos. There was no question of lack of food. Yet there may have been a feeling, heightened by her friends' taunts, that it was time she got out of the way. Or, again, she might have lost her way in the storm and frozen to death in a snow-drift as Tom supposed. 'At best, the Eskimo's mind is unpredictable,' I thought aloud.

'I'll tell you of another case, Father, to support that statement. This one's almost a crime classic!' Tom was warming up.

'A native woman—her name was Mapha—was brought into court at Coppermine for the murder of her husband, Ayalik, at Richardson Island where they had been wintering. She shot him but didn't quite kill him, so she grabbed fishing twine and strangled the poor fellow to death. It came out at the inquest that Mapha's lover, Aogak, was hunting near by when Ayalik was murdered, which provided the motive. A few days later Aogak killed his wife Kuptana and went to live with Mapha. Our headquarters at Coppermine got wind of the strange goings-on at Richardson, and Constable Campbell went over to investigate. He found Aogak stretched out in his sleeping bag, his brains blown out. The fellow had apparently seen the police team coming and shot himself through the ear by pressing the trigger with his toe.

'Campbell escorted Mapha back to Coppermine for the trial. The evidence being circumstantial, and the woman having three small children, she was acquitted.'

'Had she been found guilty she probably wouldn't have understood why she was punished anyway,' I said, recalling the circumstances that had put Orhena in jail.

Orhena was my former helper at Burnside Mission. As he told me his story he was chosen by the elders at Kraomavaktok to execute a couple of trouble-making hunters who had become a real menace to the camp.

'The medicine man and the elders fixed the day of the execution. They told me to get ready, for I was the best shot in camp. On the appointed evening the two bad men were invited into an iglu for a party. I hid behind the porch. One of the bad men did not stay very long inside. He came out and I shot him in the head. The other man, hearing the shot, ran out to see what had happened. He tripped over the body of his friend and I gave him a full charge in the neck.'

Orhena was given a two-year term for what the white man considered was double murder but what to him was a normal way of ridding the community of undesirable characters.

'You fellows must have quite a time now solving native murders,' I said to my hosts. 'The Krangmalit have learnt to fear the Police and tend to keep their secrets as far as possible from the post.'

'Yes,' agreed Tom, 'they are not making it any easier for us by doing their dirty work in the isolated hunting grounds. By the time word reaches us that a good hunter died on his way back from the tree line, or was killed among the caribou he was stalking, or disappeared in the sea on a bright, calm day, nothing is left of the body and the survivors have their stories pretty well rehearsed.'

Tom's ready admission reminded me of the circumstances surrounding old Tamarnek's death. Tamarnek wasn't a big man but he was proportioned like a professional wrestler. The one weakness in his otherwise powerful body was his eyesight. He was particularly susceptible to snow blindness, and went around all winter with bloodshot eyes. It was the fearful thought of being strong yet useless that prompted Tamarnek to ask his wife Anangayak to kill him. Dutifully she shot him while he was sleeping. Eventually Tamarnek's son Ikhik reported his father's death to me. 'His heart stopped beating,' he said in explanation.

Months later I called at Gordon Bay or Siorkretak on my mission rounds. There I ran into a young policeman on patrol from Cambridge Bay who had heard rumours of Tamarnek's death and was frankly curious about the case. We rounded up Ikhik to guide us to the spot where he had laid his father's body the previous fall. Among the scattered bits of bones we found a rusty gun, a tobacco tin containing needles, caribou sinew, some fine-cut tobacco, and matches— left there by his family for his soul's use in the happy hunting grounds.

The young constable was obviously disappointed. 'Let's go back, Father. I'll never get anything from this.'

'Wait a minute, Constable! There is one part of the human body that the animals cannot break or take away—the skull. Let's look for it.'

In a small creek near the open grave I found the skull, partly bleached by the wind and the sun. 'Look, here it is! Pretty badly cracked, too.'

'Oh, that's the work of a wolf, Father.'

'I'm not so sure. A wolf cannot break a human skull because it is too big for its jaw.'

His confidence slightly shaken, he examined it with me more carefully. A small hole showed in the back of the skull and three cracks, like shattered glass, extended to the forehead.

'Guess I'd better send it on to our experts in Ottawa,' he said.

The report came back next winter: a 25-20 slug had been found lodged in the decayed brain. Anangayak was tried and got a fifteen-month sentence. Yet, according to her son Ikhik she only did her husband's bidding. And while Eskimos generally disapprove of manslaughter, mercy killings are practised and condoned by the family concerned and the community at large. Here is yet another unbridgeable gap between the Krangmalit and the Kablunaks.

7

JIGGING THROUGH ICE

'How long do you plan to stay, Father?'

'You know me, Tom. I'd like to visit the different camps around here as soon as possible. But my dog food is running low, so I think I'll go up to the lake and try my luck at jigging.'

'Tell you what, *mon vieux*. I'll lend you enough rice to keep your dogs happy while you are fishing, and you can save everything you catch for travelling. I'll send my man Uttak over to you tomorrow. How's that?'

It was a thoughtful gesture, typical of the experienced Arctic traveller. 'Thanks, Tom, that's a deal. And by the way, is there anyone you'd like to recommend as a fishing partner?'

'Let's see—*mais oui, mon vieux*, I think your best bet would be Kunak if he's around. He belongs to the Ikralututiameun group and really knows the ropes.'

It was comforting to know that 'Ikralututiameun' is Eskimo for the People of the Rich Fishing Grounds and that my guide Kunak was an old acquaintance.

Next day Kunak and I went off to Ikralututiak Lake, eight

miles north of Cambridge Bay. 'First we have to find the right depth,' he said as soon as we arrived. Clearing the snow, he knelt down and peered through the thick clear ice, his hands shading his eyes, his nose against the frozen surface. He did this in several places until he found a spot with about six feet of water under the thick ice.

'*Namaktok!* This is fine! Let's bring the dogs closer.'

With the long-handled ice-chisel and scoop we took turns in digging a hole through the ten feet of ice. It was such warm work that we took off our outer parkas, although the temperature was easily thirty below. Half an hour after we started we finally struck water. It bubbled over the brim of the foot-wide opening with a gurgling sound like air being forced out of a kitchen tap.

Twenty feet away from the first hole we dug another so that we could both fish at the same time. Partly around each hole we put up a wall of snow blocks for protection against the freezing wind and spread a caribou skin over a block of snow to sit on.

Our fishing gear was of the kind used by the Krangmalit everywhere. The line was twine, wound around a curved piece of caribou antler; our home-made hooks were of copper, Kunak's riveted to a bear tooth and mine to a polished fragment of ivory. Like as not it came from one of the mammoths that once roamed the Far North and whose scattered bones are still found preserved in ice on river banks in the Western Arctic. For bait we cut strips of skin off a lake trout about the size of a little finger.

Slowly we lowered our lines into the watery holes until the hooks were in a couple of feet of water. Then we began jigging the line—up, down, up, down—with the precision of a pendulum. Sitting motionless all the while, lest we frighten the fish, we kept up this rhythmic toil for hours without a solitary bite.

I felt cold, restless, and miserable. Practically flat, mono-
tonously white, utterly void of any sign of life, and silent
except for the rustling wind, the cruel landscape filled me
with desolation. The only natural relief in the surrounding
flatness was a hill to the north called Mount Pelly or Uvayok
by the Eskimos because it looked like the belly of a pregnant
animal. Shaped like a loaf of bread, its top rose to the un-
glamorous height of 675 feet above sea level. And the only
man-made landmarks visible from where I sat were rocks arranged in narrow ovals between which the Eskimos lay their
dead to rest. Some earthly possessions of the departed were
still discernible through the light covering of snow—parts of
shattered sleds, rusty tea kettles, blubber lamps, and sundry
implements.

A primitive hunter born to the Barren Land, Kunak did
not show the slightest fatigue. He instinctively concentrated
all his attention on the water-filled hole before him. He
jigged the line with one hand and held a *kakivok* or trident
in the other like a winter-clad Neptune. His trident differed
from the sea god's in that it was made of two caribou antlers
with a steel spike between them set on the end of a long pole.

He seemed to be dreaming—and at times I'm sure he was
—yet no fish passed by or nestled in the weeds and gravel
below without his acknowledging its presence by jigging
harder and cheerfully mumbling to himself.

We fished right through till three o'clock, interrupting
our vigil only to stretch our stiffened muscles and warm ourselves with running and food. Perhaps the day was too bright
and visibility too good to trick the fish; whatever the reason,
we returned to Cambridge Bay empty-handed. So oppressed
was my body with the unremitting cold, and so depressed
my mind, I could not bear the thought of deliberately going
through that unrewarding experience next day. But when
Kunak stopped at his iglu and asked me if I wanted to fish

again, I automatically replied: 'Yes, I'd like to go back to-morrow morning.'

I was glad that Aniliak and Tuktugnak and their families chose that evening to drop in and renew our acquaintance of the previous year. They had heard that I had gone up to the lake with Kunak and were curious to know how I was getting along. Like Kunak, both Aniliak and Tuktugnak were native sons of Cambridge Bay. Aniliak was blind in the left eye and Tuktugnak had lost two fingers from his right hand. Both deformities, I learned, were caused by circumstances considered quite natural in the Barren Land.

As a boy, Aniliak had bitten into a chunk of caribou meat that he held with his left hand, and was about to slice it off at the mouth with a knife in his right hand when one of his younger brothers accidentally pushed his elbow. The blade pierced the youngster's eye and he was never to see with it again.

Tuktugnak was a fully grown hunter when ill luck crossed his path. He did not know that the seal he speared was an extremely large bearded seal. Stung to the quick, the big mammal used its powerful square flippers to drive itself down its breathing hole so fast that Tuktugnak did not have time to wind the harpoon cord of seal strips around his waist and brace himself against the pull. He had scarcely secured it around his hand when the heavy seal gave a mighty yank and the cord ripped through his fingers as the wounded creature escaped into the depths below the ice.

Over the loud crunching of hard-tack and the sucking in of tea, my guests and I exchanged information about the people we had met since our last meeting in the same post. When the subject and the laughs over my troubles were exhausted, we heard familiar noises on the porch. People were knocking the snow off their boots, blowing their noses, spitting; a woman was hushing her crying child; others were laughing. Suddenly, without as much as a knock on the door, they were in the kitchen. Miyuk, Amiraernek, their wives and children, and Otokreak came in noisily, smiling widely, muttering the customary words of admiration, and wiping their noses with the backs of their hand and arms at the sudden change in temperature.

'*Onartok illa*. It's really warm here. *Pignertok illa*. It's beautiful indeed,' I heard them saying.

They walked around, examining the pictures on the walls and laughingly questioning me about the various kitchen utensils and their uses. Their curiosity satisfied, they grouped themselves on the benches around the walls as I passed a tin of tobacco and cigarette papers. The women rolled their own as expertly as the men, and soon the place was so warm and thick with smoke I had to take their recurring hints of '*Onarpadlar!* It's too hot!' and open the door.

Everybody laughed when I told the new arrivals that I had returned from the lake empty-handed. And many were the helpful suggestions:

'Maybe you cut the hole too far from the shore, Fala.'

'Did you go early enough? The fish bite better then.'

'It was too bright today. The fish saw you were a Kablunak!'

At this point the suggestions began to grow obscene and the guffaws louder. There was nothing to do but join in the childish gaiety and then divert the conversation into another channel.

'Just as you came in,' I said, 'I was going to ask Aniliak and Tuktugnak about the *iluvek* on the lake shore. Who is buried there?'

Amiraernek took the bait. 'I well remember Pigadlak, an old woman who was left there. She belonged to the Korloktomeun group. She was with them when they went seal hunting on one of the small islands in Coronation Gulf. They

75

got a lot of seals and were enjoying themselves so much that they did not notice the ice break-up. When they discovered that the northwest winds and currents had broken the ice between their island and the mainland, it was too late.

'They did not bring their *kayaks* on their dog-sleds and had no way of crossing the water. They had spears, but they could not reach the seals without kayaks. They had no rifles, but even if they had had them, there was no game on the rocky island. All they had for themselves and their dogs was a large quantity of seals. When they ate all the seals, they started on the dogs. Some got sick and died. The others lived for a while on the bodies of the dead. Finally, only Pigadlak remained in the camp.'

'How did she manage to survive?'

'By feeding on the scraps of the corpses and the eggs of migratory birds and by jigging tom-cods off the rocks. Pigadlak was almost dying herself of starvation and disease when the sea froze again and a hunter took her to Nagiuktok Island.'

'What happened to Pigadlak there, Amiraernek?'

'She lived with some friends, got well, and found a husband. They had children and moved to Cambridge Bay, where she died of old age. When word got around about the many deaths on that island, the people called it Iluvek Island.'

'*Heh, heh, illa, illa, ayornorman.* Yes, indeed, it was hopeless,' concurred Amiraernek's wife Arnaluak, nursing her newborn son. 'Like my brother-in-law Mitkroernek. You remember?' she asked her husband rhetorically, and proceeded to tell us of his sad ending.

She said that when his family's food supply began to run low at Starvation Cove, Mitkroernek went hunting for ptarmigan up the Ekalluktor River. He had good success, and was about to return home when he was overtaken by a pirtok. He weathered the storm that night in an iglu, but—possibly driven by his impatience to bring food for his family—ventured out the next day. He had not gone more than half a mile when he was forced to make himself another iglu. It was a hurried job and could not have offered him much protection against the blizzard.

Leaving most of his equipment behind, Mitroernek, now lost and panic-stricken, pushed blindly on. He was found in a tiny shelter, his strength spent in fighting the icy blasts and swirling snow, his frigid body huddled in a last, vain effort of self-preservation. It was, as Arnaluak said, *'ayornor-man'*—there was nothing one could do about it.

As informally as they appeared, my visitors departed, and I wasted no time in going to bed.

For the next two weeks—except when it was stormy—Kunak and I fished in the same holes in the lake ice. After the first fruitless day, our luck wavered between good and indifferent. Our highest catch for one day was twenty trout for Kunak and sixteen for me, the fish ranging between three and twenty-five pounds.

Each time Kunak pulled out a fish, he promptly clubbed it over the head. I merely threw those I caught on the ice, where they froze in a couple of minutes. Whenever I fished from a boat or off a rock, I naturally clubbed the fish to make sure they would not jump out or slither off into the water; but I could not see why Kunak did it here.

'Kunak,' I said, 'why do you hit the fish over the head with your stick? Are you afraid they might fall back into the hole?'

'Because they die more quickly.'

It sounded like a logical reason, except for one thing: I knew that Eskimos have no feeling of pity for animals, birds, or fish. Kunak was holding the real reason back, and I resolved to find it out.

77

The next time Siksik dropped in with his two wives and two sons, I sounded him out.

'The fish want to speak evil words to the hunter, Fala. If he does not kill them at once, they will place a curse on him.'

I felt privileged to be told as much as that in such a straightforward fashion, for the Eskimo mistrusts the Kablunak. He can see or sense that the white man does not share his beliefs, and he guards them jealously for fear of ridicule.

Frequently I found that the Eskimo's reticence on matters supernatural merely reflects his inability to think in an abstract way. His customs stem from his own life and from the life around him. Through the generations his ancestors have stored up all the anxiety and terror of the Barren Land—the great burdens of the long winter nights, the dread of sudden storms, the hazards and disappointments of the hunt, the pains of slow starvation, the horrors of freezing to death. His attention is inevitably focused on things material. He shuns the uncertain, the spiritual, the unearthly.

Finally, the primitive man has been suddenly subjected to the white man's civilization by explorers, traders, missionaries, and police. By nature he worries neither over the past nor over the future. Such anxieties are at once the white man's greatest strength and greatest weakness in his eternal search for happiness. The Eskimo, on the other hand, simply accepts things as they are, and lets them go at that. If they do not work out for him, he will dismiss misfortune with one word: 'Ayorama'—'That's destiny, that's life, there isn't anything I can do about it.'

8

SPRING MADNESS

The mouth of the Ellice River lay a hundred miles to the southeast. I avoided the rough ice we had encountered on the way to Cambridge Bay by following the shoreline to Anderson Bay, then cutting across Queen Maud Gulf past the eastern tip of Melbourne Island. Here my compass went berserk, although the island was two hundred and fifty miles from the magnetic pole on Boothia Peninsula to the northeast. I resorted to nature's best guide used by the Eskimos—the sun—, and reached Campbell Bay on the third day.

Ten miles offshore I saw thousands of dark dots moving towards me. The dogs recognized them for what they were long before I did. They were migrating lemmings—Arctic mice—that had completed their life-cycle and were heading to the sea. Grey with white bellies, they averaged about four inches in length and were easily distinguished from the rat and mouse cousins by their short tails.

Although they broke ranks as we neared them, some of the lemmings did not move fast enough out of my dogs' paths and were promptly eaten by the hungry huskies. But if I had had a hundred teams of starving dogs, they would have hardly made an impression on their numbers. We saw them on all sides all the way to the mouth of the river.

It was evening, but the sun was still up in the early May sky as we travelled eight miles up the river to the falls where the Asiarmeum group—the People of the Berries—had their camp. I counted at least fifteen families there, some living in iglus with the roofs removed and replaced by caribou skins, and a few of the more optimistic housed in caribou tents. For the first time in months here was evidence of spring.

Reawakened hope and good cheer pervaded the little community as the reception committee—nearly everyone in camp—greeted me with 'Sillakrertok, nuna omalertok. The weather is beautiful, the land is stirring.'

It was easy to understand their enthusiasm. For the Krang-malit, as they greet each new spring, the sunlit hills and lowlands have never been so softly bathed with mauve; never has the sky been so blue, so clear, so filled with the cry of life. And after so many months of semi-darkness, of freezing on the trail, of near starvation—all of which combine to lull them into mental torpor—never has there been such joy of mere being.

The *sirenek* or sun transforms the dreary stretches of snow, ice, and rocks into a silvery landscape deserving a true artist's canvas. Even the cold becomes a sunny, exhilarating cold. Primitive instinct tells the People Beyond of the dearness and meaning of life. Every passing day becomes more precious to them now as light and warmth begin to permeate all nature. The mysterious powers of the universe give tangible evidence of their friendliness, gradually assuring them protection from the dangers of the polar night.

There was another reason for the general levity of spirit in the camp. The seal hunting had been good for the past few weeks in the Gulf, and now, as they awaited the coming of the caribou from the tree-line, the hunters and their families were going to have some fun with their friends, most of whom they had not seen all winter.

In anticipation of other arrivals from every direction the men had just finished building a *kalgik* or large community iglu, and everyone was going to the dance there that night.

In the tent of Kirluayok, one of the best hunters in the camp, the big drum or *kattuk* was being prepared by the host with the help of three musically inclined neighbours. While they held the frame, Kirluayok secured the stretched caribou skin around the wooden circle with caribou sinew. As I entered I joined Kirluayok's wife and several other onlookers who sat on a low matting of dwarf-willows covered with cari-bou furs, sipping tea and exchanging comments about the newcomers to camp.

Kirluayok's assistants tightened the drum and gave it to him to test with a stick the size and shape of the baton used by sprinters in relay races. Holding the flat drum by its handle in his left hand, he beat a brief tattoo.

'That's not right yet,' was the consensus, and Kirluayok handed the drum back. When it was re-tightened and wetted for extra tautness, he handed it over to me to the voluble de-light of all present. 'Fala, why don't you try the kattuk?'

The drum felt large, heavy, and awkward to hold, but I managed a fair imitation of a native drummer. 'That's better,' judged the experts, while the rest laughed and teased me.

The drum was ready; there was nothing more to hold up the dance. Gaily we all trooped over to the kalgik where we were soon joined by the occupants of the other tents and iglus. The dancing began at once. Nerlak, one of Kirluayok's tall young helpers, took the drum, wiggling and nodding solemnly to the assembly as if inviting appreciation for his performance. He began beating the drum slowly, his feet immobile but his body shaking up and down and sideways by fits and starts, like a dog just out of the water. Warmed up, Nerlak beat the drum louder and faster and moved around by jerks and leaps within the circle of standing spectators.

Encouraged on all sides, he added a song to his gyrations. As he sang he became more and more hysterical, increasing his frenzied tempo and emphasizing the rhythm of the song by hops and jumps, his face reflecting the mood of the moment.

Fascinated by the deep reverberations of the kattuk, the solemn-faced spectators wailed the endless refrain '*A-ee-ay, ee-ay-ay, a-ee-ay*' as the dancer kept quickening his pace until he was virtually in a trance. Lost in a magic dream, he was evoking his loves, his friendships, his hunting journeys, unashamedly unveiling the innermost secrets of his soul. Each time he beat the drum he spun around, finally bending forward as if to leap like a fox. Then, soaked in sweat and groaning with exhaustion, his voice hoarse and his mouth overflowing with saliva, Nerlak passed the kattuk to the nearest woman, muttering: '*Talva, numeren!* Take it and dance!'

All through the dance the children and adolescents kept coming and going, none of them content to stand passively in one spot. Outside they took every advantage of the complete freedom enjoyed by Eskimo children through their lives. Some of the boys invited the girls into the empty iglus and tents, others ran off with them into the snow in the dusk now settling over the camp. Having observed their parents through all stages of love-making, they let the excitement of the spring reunion run its natural course.

Normally the little girls are first shown by their parents how to submit to those little boys to whom they have been promised and to whom they will be married at puberty. If the

young hopefuls do not yield their bodies to the advances of their fiancés, or if they should prove unreceptive, the grown-ups will urge them on with words of encouragement and suggestive movements, or else will poke fun at them and tease them, all the while roaring with laughter.

Visiting neighbouring friends is another occasion for the children to fondle one another, to excite their animal senses, and to caricature the physical raptures of their parents.

Now here was an opportunity to explore newly found playmates, and the youngsters were not going to waste their time standing idly in a circle.

In the kalgik, by the flickering light of the blubber lamp, a woman named Tupertak was dancing and chanting:

'*Kranokme, kranokme* . . . how is it, how is it
That Kakit is so glad
And his voice so hoarse when singing? *A-ee-ay-ae-ay* . . .
I have never seen one like him anywhere.
His wife is an old woman
Whose breasts cannot drip milk any more. *A-ee* . . .
He came to me, Tupertak—
The name my mother gave me—
And he sat on the iglek. *A-ee* . . .
"I am a good hunter," he said,
"My wife no more creates in her body,
And I am still a young man." *A-ee* . . .
When I looked at Kakit
Staring into the gloom,
I saw a powerful man. *A-ee* . . .
I am not ashamed
That I submitted to him,
For a man must bring fruit. *A-ee-ay-ae-ee ay* . . . '

She danced like a man possessed, but her singing was high-pitched and more impetuous, more sensuous, more exciting.

No-one appeared to follow her voluptuous movements with more delight than chubby old Isaroitok who squatted on the snow floor beside his decrepit, wizened wife. A lascivious grin dented Isaroitok's jolly moon-shaped face, belying the startling fact that both his legs were cut off at the ankles. Neither this handicap nor his advanced age prevented him from travelling widely, and only slightly limited his reputation as a good hunter. I had met him originally on one of his trips to the trading post at Burnside, and he had told me then about the misfortune that overtook him at Gordon Bay.

A surprise storm isolated him and his wife from the Kiluitomeum group—the People of the Inlet's End. He was then young, strong, and restless. Impatiently he took to the trail. 'When we got back to our camp I could not feel my feet anymore, Fala. They were hard like soap stone. My wife started to cut off the toes. They fell off like chips of dry wood. I was crying and beat my wife. But my feet were so badly frozen I had to let her continue. She cut to the heels, where the blood began to trickle. She wrapped the stumps in small fur bags, binding them very tight. It was very painful, and for a long time I lay uselessly on the iglek—I, who had once been a great hunter!'

Isaroitok's sense of humour and his fondness for fun never deserted him. While he could not join in the dance, he always entered its spirit, his deep voice often rising above the rest at each refrain. His frail wife, nearly blind and partly deaf, huddled close to him, trying to sing in a thin, off-key wail. She rocked gently back and forth, her eyes closed, her mind recalling the gay dances of her spent youth.

From time to time others took over the kattuk as the previous dancers staggered out of the circle, drenched with perspiration, their tongues hanging out, their breathing fast and stertorous, like a tired dog's. Some, following Tupertak's example, revealed their loves; others sang of the scandalous incidents in their drab lives or of the personal faults of their rivals, male or female. Most of them resorted to songs passed on from generation to generation, recalling the golden age when game was plentiful and the land was inhabited by giants and kindly spirits. Hunting songs were popular, and so were such melancholy laments as the one sung by an old woman from Melville Sound:

> *'Kamaoktunga* . . . I am afraid when I see winter
> Swallowing the man-less land.
> I am afraid when my eyes follow the moon,
> The little moon, the big moon,
> On its old, old trail. *A-ee-ay, ee-aeeay* . . .

> *Kamaoktunga* . . . I am afraid when I hear
> The wail of the wind and the murmur of the snow
> Passing over the land;
> And when in the dark, distant sky
> The stars move on their nightly trail. *A-ee-ay, ee-aeeay* . . . '

Early in the morning, despite frequent excursions to their iglus for tea, the singers and dancers finally gave up. Some drifted back to their own iglus, others exchanged their mates, and the odd unmarried girl went off with two single men for the rest of the morning.

Winter held no more fears for anyone at Ellice River. Spring with its exploding passions and madness had taken over.

I slept late that morning, but as I emerged from my tent, my eyes blinking in the bright sun, only one man was on view. While the rest of the camp was still dozing, Isaroitok, the irrepressible amputee, was readying his sled for a trip.

'*Teetorlunuk*, Isaroitok! Come and have tea with me!' I did not have to repeat the invitation. With a smile splitting his face from ear to ear, he hobbled over on his knees.

'Are you going hunting today?' I asked.

'Yes, Fala, for small game. And maybe also to look from the hills for signs of the caribou.'

'I saw you last night at the dance. Did you and your wife have a good time?'

'*Anertak!* Most certainly! Only it is too bad my stumps and my wife's age did not let us dance. A long time ago I was one of the best dancers among my people, and my wife was pretty good too.'

'After the dance I noticed some of the men exchange wives. You know, Isaroitok, white men don't do that. Why do your people?'

'Because the hunter can dispose of his wife as he pleases.'

'What about the man?'

'He can lie with any woman as often as he gets a chance.'

'Even if he is fond of his wife?'

'Sometimes a man's wife is not responsive; then he gets another woman. Or a man gets tired of his own wife, so he changes wives with a friend for a while. It is a good feeling to have some change from the same thing day after day. It makes the men better friends, better partners in hunting.'

'Doesn't it make them jealous?'

'Why, Fala? The wives do not wear out. They come back to us happy and as good as ever.'

'Then why does a hunter go after the man who stays with his wife while he is away hunting?'

'That's different! If he does not ask the husband's permission, he is looking for trouble. And the wife will be beaten, too, for only her husband has the privilege of sharing her body with others.'

'Have your people similar customs for girls who are not married? Last night I did not see the boys ask anyone's permission to take them.'

86

'An unmarried girl can do what she wants. She has no hus-
hand to ask, Fala.'

'I realize she cannot ask her husband because she does not
have one, but what about her parents?'

'They don't care. Why should they? She has to learn, and
she has to find the right mate. If she and the boy enjoy each
other's company, they will live together. If my wife and I had
not liked sleeping together when we were married, we would
have parted company after a while. My people think that is
the right way.'

With the cock-like crowing of *'Teetoritse'*—the 'Come
and get it!'—the camp began to rouse itself to life in the
noon-day sun. When Isaroitok left, I circulated among the
iglus, curious to learn about 'the morning after'.

Answering the call for tea, a woman came out carrying her
baby in her hood. It took me a moment to recognize her as
one of the earliest dancers, the one who had sung about her
lover Kakit.

'You danced very well, Tupertak.'

'Illa, illa, heh, heh, heh!' she giggled with proper modesty,
patting her baby's bottom behind her back while her torso
shook in sympathetic rhythm.

'How is the infant? Is it a boy or a girl?'

'Indeed, it's a little man!' she sang out with pride, lowering
the hood a bit to show off the naked child. *'Attitoren!* Shake
hands!' she said to the baby.

'It's a nice looking boy you have, Tupertak.' As I held his
tiny hand I judged the little man to be about a year old. Set
in a round head, his slanted eyes matched his straight hair
for blackness. His brownish skin toned down his rosy lips.
His nose was running. He looked healthy and bright, but in
no way did his features resemble his mother's. It was only
too apparent that he didn't look like Tupertak's husband

87

either, the moment the latter approached us. To ask them if
he was the image of Kakit did not seem like the wisest thing
to do under the circumstances.

Of medium height and wiry build, Tupertak's mate wore
an ascetic look emphasized by his wide cheekbones below
which the face tapered sharply to a small chin. His parka
hood was down, revealing short-cut hair on top of his head
but a thick black mane falling down the back of his neck.

We shook hands. Then, after an appropriate silence, I said:
'I saw many men dancing last night but I do not remember
seeing you dance.'

'*Illa*. I did not dance, but I will tonight.'

'I forget your name.'

'I am Krilugok.'

Formal introduction over, I told him I was going visiting.

'So are we, Fala.' It was sufficient invitation to follow the
couple into the nearest tent.

The place was already crowded with visitors, some of whom
were sitting on the low iglek and others standing around
in groups. Everybody was either eating, drinking tea, or talking about the dance and gossiping about the newest arrivals.
I squeezed past and sat down on the fur-covered iglek beside Krilugok and Tupertak.

'Whose tent is this?' I asked them quietly.

'It belongs to the family of Pangun,' Krilugok said, in-
clining his head in the direction of the host.

'Which one is his wife?'

'There she is.' His eyes directed me to a big, broad-
shouldered woman with eyes so slanting they seemed closed.
She was pouring tea, a perpetual smile on her fat, red face.

'*Falamun*. For Father,' she told an old woman next to her,
handing her a cup. The old woman did not rise but passed
it along to an elderly hunter who in turn gave it to a young
couple, so that it eventually reached me.

'Krilugok, do you know everyone in this tent?'

'*Illa*, Fala.' He proceeded to tell me their names and I wrote them down in my diary. Some of the older people crowded around me, poking their faces into the little black book.

'Looks like lemmings' droppings,' someone observed, and everybody roared.

'There's a long string of them,' said another, amid renewed laughter.

'Maybe they have diarrhoea!' cracked a third. The joke had endless possibilities and they played with it till it died a natural death.

But when Krilugok included Unipksak in his list of names, the guffaws started afresh. 'Why is everybody laughing?' I asked, bewildered.

'Because that is a nickname. His real name is Nerlak, but we call him Unipksak the Storyteller—he likes to tell stories so much.' All eyes were now on Nerlak, the same who could not wait to open the dance the night before.

'How about telling a story for Fala?' Even the youngsters who had been running in and out of the tent paused in their tracks.

Pleased at all the attention, especially in front of a Kablunak, Nerlak strutted about noncommittally as if expecting further persuasion. When with the increased clamours came transparent suggestions that Nerlak was not up to telling stories after the dance, he readily took up the challenge and the invitation. In a voice still hoarse from the songs of the night before, he began:

'When I was a young man I had a friend whose name was Kahak. One winter when he was hunting near Cambridge Bay he met a hunter called Alikanek and his wife Ikralupyak. Kahak was not married, and when Alikanek went hunting he stayed with Ikralupyak. She liked my friend, so he ran off with her to Wilmot Island.

'Everything went well for Kahak until one day a red-headed policeman found him and took him back to Cambridge where he locked him up in jail. Kahak was about to go to sleep that night when the Amakro opened the door of the jail and said: "Here is a big kettle of hot tea for you. And here is an empty tobacco tin, your korvik for the night. Drink all the tea you want, but if you spill any of your urine on the floor, I will hang you in the morning!"

'It was cold in the little jail, so to keep warm Kahak drained the tea kettle. After a while he filled the korvik and fell asleep. He woke up during the night because his bladder was full again. He reached for the tin, but it was full. Although he was sleepy, he remembered what the policeman had said and was afraid. His belly became bloated like a bag full of blubber and he could not sleep any more.

'The Amakro returned in the morning. He looked in the kettle and found it empty. He looked into the tobacco tin and it was full to the brim. He looked at the floor and it was dry. He looked at Kahak and saw him squatting on the sleeping bag, his arms around his belly, a pained expression on his sleepy face. The Amakro began to laugh. When he had finished laughing, he said to Kahak: "You can go now, but don't steal your neighbour's wife again."

'Kahak left the jail like a pirtok, wetting his breeches as he flew out of the police station.'

Under the cover of the general laughter that followed Nerlak's story I made my escape from what I knew would develop into a dirty storytelling contest and went over to Isaroitok's iglu. He had already left, but his wife was alone. When my eyes became accustomed to the dim light I discerned two men squatting on the far end of the iglek. They had tied strips of caribou skin around their heads to cure their headaches and, as they wiped away their tears, they moaned in mournful unison: '*Ulureanartok—illa—ulureanartok*. It's painful—it hurts.'

'Why are they crying?' I asked the white-haired old woman.

'*Mamianak*. It's too bad. They are my sons and they have been snow-blinded.' She sat hunched over the blubber lamp and kept pushing bits of blubber closer to the flame, licking the fat off her fingers with a loud smacking of her shrivelled, colourless lips.

'How did it happen?'

'My boys came here yesterday with their families from far away. They had been travelling over hilly country for many days. It was hard going, they felt hot, and they took the wooden snow goggles from their eyes.

'They came in after the dance because it is not so bright here. But there is nothing I can do to help them,' she concluded.

'Here's some medicine that might relieve their pain.' I took a couple of tablets from my first-aid kit and, after dissolving them in cold water, squirted the solution into the men's inflamed eyes with an eyedropper. Then I applied ophthalmic ointment just inside the corners of their eyes. As I did so I noticed that the skin at the corners had recently been incised.

'Why did you cut your eyes at the corners?' I asked one of the men.

'There was too much blood in my eyes and it was burning them. I sliced the skin to let the blood out.' I had heard of this native remedy but had never before come across an actual case.

'Do your eyes feel better now?'

'They are getting better, thank you, Fala.'

'Where are your families—are they together?'

'Yes, in the big tent behind here on the deep snow of the river bank.'

'I am going to look them up.'

Several young children were sleighing on the slope of the river bank. They had harnessed pups to their little sleds and guided them after the manner of their fathers. 'Gee! ha!' they directed the pups, beating them with little whips when they did not obey.

A group of older boys and girls were playing *taptaoyak,* an advanced version of blind man's bluff. A blindfolded boy had just caught hold of a girl who was doing her best to stifle her giggles. Now he had to identify her by name. Ignoring the attempts of his playmates to distract his attention with queer noises and teasing of all sorts, the boy went methodically over the girl's face and body. She wriggled and squirmed, disguising her voice but making no attempt to escape his clutch.

It was an enjoyable game and the boy took his time. Finally he shouted out her name and, hearing his playmates applaud, untied the piece of calico from his eyes and fastened it round the girl's head. I did not stay to watch her catch and identify her victim, but went inside the large rectangular tent.

The two wives of the snow-blinded men were mending clothes and watching a younger woman being tattooed by a long-haired, bearded, and bewhiskered man. His beady eyes were intent on the sharp point of a long brass needle that he kept jabbing into her chin.

Her eyes closed, the girl recoiled almost imperceptibly at each stab of the needle as it drew drops of blood arranged in slightly curved vertical lines below her mouth. The girl's husband sat on the iglek near by with his boots off, showing no emotion. In fact he was too occupied with his own pedicure to be concerned about anyone else. Wielding a pocket-knife, he scraped the accumulations between his toes and, when the blade was full, wiped it off between his lips.

The line of bleeding dots on the girl's chin completed, the tattooer picked up a wooden needle and dipped it into a greyish-blue powder finely scraped from soapstone and the soot of blubber lamps. This he pushed into the perforations in her skin and another line was done.

Altogether five lines were customarily tattooed on the chin of a Krangmalek woman, three horizontal lines over each cheekbone, and three vertical lines in the centre of the forehead. It took hours of patient suffering to be marked for life with the brand of the People Beyond.

'I just saw your husbands and gave them medicine which made them feel better,' I told the older women.

They thanked me and offered me tea and lengths of boiled seal entrails resembling thick macaroni about the diameter of a little finger. Their rubbery texture was easy enough to chew and I found their sweet-and-sour taste to my liking.

Learning my hostesses' names, I asked them where they had come from.

'We spent the winter at the big lake inland.' I took this to mean McAlpine Lake, one hundred miles to the southeast.

'Are there any families living there now?'

'*Illa,* Fala, *taleman*. Five families.'

'Can you give me their names?'

Possibly because they were grateful for the little aid I had rendered their husbands, they told me not only the names of the hunters, their wives, and children, but also of their relatives and their last-known whereabouts.

Outside, the playful screams of children suddenly changed into a delighted chorus of '*Aodlan! Aodlaralluit!* Travellers! Many travellers!' Their cries rivalled the concerted howling of dogs and the general excitement of the adults rushing out to see the latest arrivals, among them Igutak, his pretty wife Oviluk, and their little girl who had followed me from Cambridge Bay.

93

More people in camp, more news to learn, more food to eat, more songs to hear, more dances to see, more women to choose from!

Life was wonderful!

Once again it was the effervescent Nerlak who opened the dance that night. His lithe long frame and the wild, faraway look in his dark eyes blended perfectly into the eerie setting, holding a particular fascination for the younger woman in the dance circle. Characteristically jealous of one another's looks, personality, and sewing skills, they mentally compared their husbands with the other men in camp and men like Nerlak.

'Who is Nerlak's wife?' I asked Isaroitok, the amputee, who sat with his spouse in their customary corner.

The old man laughed. 'Nerlak has no wife!'

'Why not? He is tall, and young, and gay.'

'No woman wants to depend on a simple-minded, irresponsible man. He may be a good dancer and storyteller, but he is a poor hunter, Fala.'

As I observed the gathering in the kalgik I received the impression that at least one of the women did not agree with Isaroitok. She was Oviluk. Her sparkling eyes, her radiant face, her general excitement all betrayed deep admiration for the dashing young man with the kattuk. And, poor hunter though he may have been, Nerlak was quick to notice the pretty newcomer who was so obviously interested in him. A natural show-off, he now danced faster, more sensually than ever before until he could dance no more. Wild-eyed, his long black hair ringing wet, he grinned triumphantly as he weaved over to Oviluk and silently, but meaningfully, handed her the drum.

When Igutak and Oviluk finally wended their weary way to their tent, as the dance began to break up at dawn, no-one was surprised that Nerlak tagged along and remained their guest for the next few days and nights; nor that Igutak, as host, gave his guest permission to sleep with Oviluk. Krangmalit hospitality was like that . . . .

By the end of the week, Igutak's usual smile and friendly manner had disappeared. Jealousy, hate, and helplessness had driven them away.

9

CARIBOU

By now several hunters had reported the arrival of scattered herds of caribou about a day's trip beyond the hills to the southeast.

This was the advance guard. It would be followed by the main migratory body numbering thousands. Instinct drove the *tuktuk* to the sea and its islands, where they could escape the brief but torrid heat of the inland summer and the clouds of large vicious mosquitoes accompanying the hot spell.

Usually there is no way of telling ahead exactly when or where the caribou will arrive. For years they may follow the same route, and then for no apparent reason shift their march by one or two hundred miles.

Sometimes a river's early overflow or premature breakup might cause detours and delay. Or a herd may be trapped by wolves in a narrow mountain pass; in the resulting stampede many caribou are crushed, while others scatter in all directions, galloping many miles off their natural routes.

Eagerly awaited by the hunters, the appearance of the

huge intact herd was another signal for jubilation and general excitement in the camp. When the peacefully grazing caribou drew nearer, only a few women with younger children remained in the camp. Everyone else, including youngsters from eight years up, set out joyfully for the hunt.

I had been following Krilugok's dog-team and pulled up when he stopped. 'The dogs are getting jumpy, Fala. Better to leave them here so that they cannot see, hear, or smell the tuktuk in the valley beyond.'

We took our rifles and climbed the hill. Below us spread a sight I shall never forget. Through a delicate haze that rose from the snow-covered land under the warm rays of the sun, caribou were visible everywhere. They were flowing from every gully, pass, and ravine, fanning out into the broad valley, pausing to graze, and then slowly pushing on towards the glittering island-studded sea.

Nimbly and silently we moved down the slope towards the endless herds. Some of the caribou nearest us scented an unfamiliar presence and raised their heads, pricking up their ears at the faint sounds from the sleeping land. Seemingly reassured, they went on grazing, scraping the hard surface-snow with their sharp hooves for the lichen below.

A series of sharp rifle reports shattered the silence of the land. The hunt was on! Krilugok and I took cover and began firing at the passing tuktuk. They were falling on all sides. Some of the surprised bulls and cows started to gallop aimlessly and then stopped to survey the ground. Bewildered, the great herds milled about in the valley while the hunters picked them off at will. Then, taking their cue from the leaders, the animals began to scatter, making their way out of the valley of death as best they could.

By now most of the hunters had all the meat they wanted —some thirty or forty carcasses for each family. This was what they had dreamed about all winter.

As the herds dispersed, Krilugok, his eyes sparkling with satisfaction, smiled and said; 'We have worked well. Let us go and get our dog sleds.'

On the way I tried to memorize each spot where the caribou I had shot now lay. Walking ahead of me, Krilugok too was surveying the carcasses on the side of the hill and the valley below when he stopped short by a boulder and yelled: 'Krayguit! Come quick!' I rushed forward.

Igutak lay face down in the bloodstained snow. There was a bullet-hole in his right temple. Oviluk had stayed in the camp with her daughter and there were no signs that anyone else had been near him. It might have been an accident, but Krilugok said reflectively: 'I wonder where Nerlak was hunting from.'

We did not have to sound any alarm. Some of the hunters instinctively felt that something was wrong and came over. Soon there was a crowd around us.

Everyone seemed mildy excited and there were general expressions of 'Mamianak. It is too bad. Igutak was a kind man and a good hunter.' No accusations were made, but the air was full of silent suspicion.

We carried Igutak's stocky body to his sled and I drove it to camp. Krilugok came along with his team, and a youngster volunteered to bring my dogs in. The rest went back to their work. The shooting was none of their business; it was a private matter.

Oviluk did not seem surprised at the sight of her husband's corpse, but for a few minutes she wept and moaned according to the Krangmalit custom. Then she brought a sleeping bag out of the tent and we placed the body in it. She pushed Igutak's knees up into the traditional sitting position and asked us to tie up the bag. Krilugok wrapped additional skins around it for protection against marauding foxes, and we secured the bag with caribou string. Neighbours gathered

round, howled formally, and moved the bundle behind the tent. There it would stay for the next two or three days so that the soul would still be with the family and not turn angrily against the survivors because they had isolated it. It could not have been left in the tent—that would have made the place taboo.

With the body out of the way, the hunters and their families resumed their occupations as if nothing had happened. Just as Krilugok and I were leaving camp, we saw Nerlak pull in with a load of caribou. No doubt some of them had been shot down by Igutak. He drove past his iglu and made for Oviluk's tent. He was now her provider and her husband.

Joining the hunters in the valley, we moved among the caribou we had shot, finishing off the wounded by driving our hunting knives into the base of each animal's skull right through to the brain. Hot and flushed, Krilugok pulled off his parka and his torso glistened with sweat in the bright sunshine. He grinned happily as he worked, and sang:

> '*Tuk, tuktuk,* come, come to me;
> I'll make boots with the skin of thy legs.
> Stay, stay with me, O creature of the land,
> Roamer of the mountains;
> Fear not, and let me catch thee.
> *Eyaya-eya-eya, eyaya-ya-ya . . .*'

He incised each leg from hoof to abdomen and then slit the carcass from head to tail along the belly. Thrusting his fist under the skin, he tugged at it with his hands and teeth until it came clean off. Deftly he cut the paunch and plunged his arms inside to the elbows. Blood trickled over his cupped hands as he brought them to his mouth and eagerly drank the thick red fluid.

'I have always been fond of it,' he said, noticing that I was watching him. 'It makes my own blood bubble with life. Try some, Fala! It is wholesome for man.'

Rather than hurt his feelings I scooped some blood with my hands and took a quick sip. It was warm and sticky. '*Mamartok*. It is good,' I said politely.

Fortunately I was prepared for his next move.

In the spring the caribou, like the musk-oxen, are infested with the larvae of the botfly, a wasp-like creature that follows the migrating caribou and lays its eggs on them. When the eggs hatch, the larvae bore through the thick hide, hollowing out sockets in the animal's flesh where they stay during the winter months. By May they look like hazel nuts covered with grey, fuzzy, raspberry-like skin containing sweetish yellow juice. At about that time they begin to emerge and fall on the ground, leaving scars on the caribou's hide.

Those larvae or *komak* are considered a great delicacy by the Krangmalit. Krilugok picked them off one by one, pressed them into his mouth, like a child sucking a grape, and said contentedly: 'Komak are the best! They make a man hungry for fresh meat. Eat your fill, Fala!'

My stomach turned over. As nonchalantly as I could I wiped my mouth with my hand in a gesture of '*Akreatorpadlarama*' (meaning 'I am now too full'), and moved on to the caribou I had shot.

Other hunters and their families were hustling about noisily, skinning the carcasses and loading them on the sleds. Children were cutting off pieces of cartilage and chewing on them. Then they pierced the animals' eyes with a bone and sucked them like candy to prevent the dead tuktuk from warning others against the hunters.

Hearts and livers being taboo for the Krangmalit, all the hunters tossed them to their dogs, leaving the rest of the entrails and the shedded skins on the frozen white floor. This was their offering to the helpful spirits of the land who had brought the caribou their way, as well as to the wandering souls of dead hunters.

Before loading the carcasses, Krilugok cut their legs at the knee joint and stacked them separately on the sled. He could not resist the temptation to pick out three or four shin bones and crack them by tapping along them with a rock. He pulled out the marrow with his fingers and devoured it as one might a thin, long sausage. The marrow had not yet had time to freeze and Krilugok promptly regretted his impatience. He vomited again and again.

'I could not wait,' he explained lamely.

'You have killed a lot of tuktuk. How many trips will you make to the camp to take all the carcasses?'

'It is not far, Fala. I can make three trips before dark.'

I had killed fifteen caribou, and even with only five dogs hitched to the sled I was able to take them in two trips. Seldom have I seen such industrious activity as greeted my eyes when I arrived with the first load. Everybody who could wield the fan-shaped ulon or any other suitable knife was busily carving the carcasses or skinning those tuktuk that had been brought in with their skins by hurried hunters.

Squatting with her baby on her back, Krilugok's wife Tupertak sliced the caribou flesh into strips of varying lengths and shapes, according to the part of the animal, and hung them over strong seal ropes suspended between the tall handles of the scoops, ice chisels, and tent poles. Chewing on parts of the ears and other gristle, she sang old hunting songs:

> '*Attorniartunga* . . . I will sing a song,
> A little song, about the white caribou.
> Perhaps it was a big bull, *eyaya-eya,*
> Running the plains of the earth,
> *Eyaya-eya-eya-ya-a* . . .'

When the sun sank towards the reddened horizon, and Kiilugok arrived with his final load, I asked him if he and Tupertak were planning to finish the cutting that evening.

'Certainly not, Fala! Everybody is full of fresh meat, everyone is happy. Now we will dance more than before! There will be plenty of time to hang up the tuktuk meat to dry tomorrow.'

Even as he spoke, the sounds of testing the kattuk in Kirluayok's tent reverberated through the camp. Somehow the great drum itself sounded louder than ever.

Igatuk was dead. That was too bad, but it could not be helped in any way now. This was life and one took it as it came. Nerlak and Oviluk danced, sang, and laughed far into the night. Spring madness continued its reign over the People Beyond.

10

ARCTIC SUMMER

For the rest of May and into early June the sun kept softening up the snow until the strong warm winds from the south arrived. In three days the snow was gone, exposing the Arctic tundra in all its nakedness. There was still little in that land, now criss-crossed with rivulets, to inspire anyone. Eroded by frost and winds from time immemorial, the barren floor looked as if it had been ploughed up by a careless giant and never harrowed. It lay in countless clods that the People Beyond realistically call the *angiptain* or the *niap-krotain,* meaning human skulls. Elsewhere, split limestone appeared at intervals like bristles in a giant brush.

There was not a single tree between the eye and the horizon—only scraggy bushes hiding in some of the depressions and creeks; dwarf-willows hugging the ground; and here and there clusters of moss, lichen, and grass. The rest was muskeg and gravel.

I had stayed at Ellice River longer than I had intended. Now I decided that I must get back to my Mission at Cambridge Bay.

As the river and sea were still frozen, I could travel by
sled all the way. I found my light fawn parka comfortably
warm on the trip, although the temperature dropped to the
freezing point morning and evening. But with the winter
winds a nightmare of the past, it was easy to agree with my
friends at Cambridge Bay that the summer was close at hand.

Puny though the Central Arctic plants and flowers are at
best, they brought me a feeling of reassurance and of a link
with the rest of the world. Primroses, buttercups, bluebells,
goldenrods, catspaw, dandelions, poppies, and other cosmo-
politan flora like ferns and heather gradually appeared, to
the delight of Kablunak and Krangmalek.

The native children spent hours roving over the sunny
slopes searching for the blueberries, cranberries, and other
Arctic berries. *Paunrain* was the name they gave to the most
common berry, with its various species, distinguishable by
the different colours resembling strawberry, raspberry, cur-
rant, and mulberry.

It was the season of bird migration, too, and succulent
duck and geese on the table. For nearly two weeks they
passed over us in a continuous northward stream. On the
way to their breeding grounds—the hundreds of islands in
the Arctic Ocean and on the inland lakes—where they can
raise their young out of reach of foxes and wolves, they
stopped to rest at the many lakes fringing the Bay.

Kunak showed me the best approaches to Ikalutuktiak
Lake, which always got a good share of the visitors. He knew
every rock and boulder that afforded the best screen from the
lake, and between these we crept towards the lakeshore.

Our arsenal contained 30-30 rifles, 25-20 carbines, and
shotguns, but we favoured our .22s because they made a minimum of noise and disturbance. The way the ducks and
geese reacted to our shooting reminded me of the big caribou
hunt. When one fell, the nearest birds would glance casually

at their luckless neighbour as if to say 'Poor chap! He must be dead tired,' and turn their attention back to whatever they were doing before.

After a couple of hours' rest, the leader would rise and the flock would follow him into the sky beyond. If no other birds seemed ready to descend on our small lake, we waded out in our waterproof seal breeches and collected the ducks and geese we had shot. Then we hid in ambush for the next flight.

Our silent vigil was broken one afternoon by a whirring noise in the sky so loud that I was sure there were planes above. When the flight came into view, Kunak did not have to tell me that the 'planes' were giant white swans. It happened that Kunak had packed his 30-30 rifle that day, and with it he took a quick pot-shot at the high-flying birds. He laughed when he missed, automatically reloaded his rifle and handed it to me.

'Here, Fala, you shoot the Kablunak's flying machines!'

There were possibly fifteen swans some six hundred feet above us, flying at a fast clip. The chances of my hitting one of them with a single shot were small indeed. But mathematics were never my strong point. I took a bead on the flock and fired. The impossible happened.

'*Makitor!* You hit him!' Kunak was just as flabbergasted as I.

Like an aircraft out of control, one of the swans began to fall crazily, favouring first one wing, then the other, finally crashing with a thud a hundred yards away.

The ducks and geese in the lake had taken off with the first rifle shot, so that we had nothing to lose by scrambling as fast as we could over the rocky ground. Although both its wings were broken and its breast badly bruised by the fall, it was easily the biggest, most beautiful bird I had ever bagged.

When I walked proudly over to the RCMP barracks that

evening with my prize, I intended to startle the constables, but I was not prepared for the jump Tom Garland gave or for the look of consternation on his face.

'Didn't you know, Father, that it's forbidden to kill swans?'

'You're not serious, Tom! I've seen many an Eskimo shooting at swans, and nobody ever said anything to me about a law against it.'

'Well, there is one. Ask Ray, if you don't believe me.'

Ray Stewart nodded solemnly. 'Unless there are extenuating circumstances, such as starvation, the penalty for killing a swan is jail.'

'There you have it, *mon vieux!* Will you come quietly or shall I slap on the handcuffs?' Tom chuckled. The upshot was that we took my unlawful kill to the Hudson's Bay post, where the four of us enjoyed a sumptuous feast—not omitting a toast proposed by Scotty to 'the man the Mounties didn't get'.

It was on such an occasion as this—in the security, warmth, and plenty of the Kablunak—that the continuous struggle of the Krangmalit for the barest existence in all the world stood out in sharpest relief.

The week I returned from Ellice River, all the natives (with the exception of the families attached to the HBC Trading Post and the RCMP Barracks, and my helper Kunak) left Cambridge Bay. They headed for various mainland points to await the caribou's southward trek in September, taking no chances of being caught by the sea's breakup in the latter part of July. In the spring the tuktuk's fur is nearly worthless; but his fall coat and the fat meat beneath it are the two most important items in the Eskimo's winter inventory.

Compared with the violent breakup of ice fields by storms in such open-sea places as Amundsen Gulf, Coronation Gulf, or Queen Maud Gulf, the ice breakup at Cambridge Bay on Victoria Land is a mild, unspectacular affair. Because of its sheltered nature and comparatively quiet waters, the ice there melts gradually, inconspicuously, yet just as surely as the tireless sun is up in the deep blue sky twenty-four hours a day.

As soon as open water appeared in the bay at the mouth of the creek draining the Ikalututiak Lake, the two constables, Kunak, and I set our gillnets for the salmon and lake trout rushing down to the feeding grounds in the sea. Their heads now disproportionately large against their long, starved bodies, the fish still made good eating for us and for the dogs.

We caught hundreds daily for about a week, split them, and put them to dry. The heads and guts we threw to the dogs or into empty oil drums from which we fed the huskies later. The sun beat on the steel barrels and a terrible smell exuded from them. Nevertheless the dogs seemed to regard the decomposing fish as a great delicacy.

Three weeks after it had blossomed forth, the summer began to fade.

11

THE LONE-WOLF HUNTER

In September Silla and Anoke, the chief spirits of the Barren Land, took over again. They made their presence known with a snowstorm that blew in all the way from the Greenland ice-cap across McClintock Channel and Victoria Strait. Silla is the dominant force of the land; Anoke is the wind. They are at once opponents and conspirators.

Resting on caribou skins on the floor of my living-room, where I invited him to spend the winter, Kunak spoke of the howling elements outside my little Mission:

'Listen to the spirits of the air, Fala! Silla is freezing the land until it becomes like stone. Then everything will be silent—so silent that the noise of the ice cracking under the cold sounds like thunder; so silent that the sound of steps on the snow frightens every living creature.

'But Anoke comes to battle Silla. Anoke brings movement and noise to the frozen land. He sweeps the snow, changes the land's face, screams across the barren floor, and gives life to the stony silence. But between them Silla and Anoke bring only destruction and death to the hunter and his family.'

Kunak was talking more to himself than to me now. 'The poor things. Listen to them! Hear the crying of dead children and of naked men and women rushing through space, pursued by the spirits of the air. How helpless they are against Silla and Anoke!

'My old mother was squatting on the snow one evening when she heard someone creeping stealthily across the land. She looked around, but there was no living creature, not even a lemming to be seen. Then she heard hissing voices, like the sibilant wafting of birds on the wing. She stood up and listened carefully. The hissing changed to fiendish laughter. Seized with terror, she ran back to the iglu. The voices did not follow her in; they rushed off to the hills and beyond. It is bad luck when the spirits of the air speak to one of us.'

For days on end—apart from venturing out to feed the dogs —we stuck close to our buildings. Whenever possible we exchanged visits, usually winding up at Scotty's or the RCMP barracks since my quarters were small and my furniture uncomfortable. Cards, conversation, and the radio provided welcome distractions during those storms, but I was particularly glad when Ray Stewart asked me to help him with the Eskimo language. Because of my Corsican birth I had grown up speaking both Italian and French. Perhaps it was this bilingualism that had made it easy for me to acquire a working knowledge of everyday Eskimo by the end of my first year in the Land Beyond. Ray's interests in the North were other than linguistic, and he had a hard time merely remembering the native words and their meaning, let alone twisting his tongue round them.

One evening our studies were interrupted by the arrival of an Eskimo family. Having built their iglu, they trooped into the barracks to greet us. The hunter, Nerreok, was tall and sombre-looking. His closely clipped hair gave his round head an appearance of being almost flat on top. His forehead was deeply furrowed. A flat, wide nose separated his narrow slitted eyes. He had a straight mouth, with a prominent lower lip and a thin upper lip above which a moustache spread in a wide crescent, curving down to a generous chin.

His face was expressionless, except for his dancing eyes. They seemed permanently amused at everything they saw. It was this peculiarity, rather than his general countenance or his name, that enabled me to recognize Nerreok as the lone-wolf hunter I had met two springs back at Burnside. He had just strung his six-foot bow and, noting my curiosity, handed it to me with the invitation to try it out. I huffed and puffed with all my strength but I could not draw it. His eyes laughed at me. 'Will you trade your bow?' I asked him in partial self-defence. '*Immana*. No. Not this one. It was made only for my strength.' I rather thought he was boasting, but during the next few days realized that no-one at the trading post could do any better than I.

His trading done, Nerreok departed as quietly as he had come and I did not see him again until now, but those eyes I never forgot. In the meantime I learned from others that, although he was one of the most powerful of Krangmalit hunters, Nerreok could not bear keen rivals and habitually hunted and lived with his family at Hope Bay in Melville Sound apart from other camps.

His wife was a small, thin woman who had borne him two boys and a girl. They were all shuffling about in the constables' kitchen, shy and uncomfortably warm after the cold trail.

Tom invited me to act as interpreter.

'Did you come from Aivartok?' Aivartok is the Krangmalit name for Hope Bay. It means 'he got a whale'.

'*Illa*, Fala.'

'What brings you here this winter, Nerreok? Isn't the hunting good at Aivartok?'

'There is plenty of game to trap, seal to hunt, and fish to jig, but we ran out of tea.'

'Have you been down to Kringaun recently?' I asked.

'I went down at the start of the trapping season to get more traps and ammunition.'

'Did you take the Kattimanek Portage?'

'*Illa,* Fala. I had a cache of seal at the Kattimanek Sound.'

'Did you meet Nokadlak on the Portage?'

'Yes, I saw him. He is getting a lot of foxes.'

'Is all his family well?'

'Angivrana and Kudnanak are fine, but the old grandmother is not very well.'

'What about Nokadlak's baby daughter Naoyak?' I asked as casually as I could, fearing the worst.

Nerreok shrugged his shoulders and the usual twinkle left his eyes. With obvious indifference, he replied: '*Ikkia, namaktokia.* Maybe she is all right.' She was a girl. However, I was relieved. If anything untoward had happened to her, Nerreok would have treated the subject differently.

Tired of the white man's small-talk, Nerreok turned to more significant news. His eyes shone as he said: 'Nokadlak told me he had heard from other travellers that Siksik had died at Taserkapfaluk.'

'You don't mean Siksik, the great hunter who had two wives?' I said incredulously.

Nerreok leered back: '*Illa, anertak.* Yes, certainly.' He had always been jealous of Siksik's fame as a great hunter and of his ability to keep two wives. Now his greatest rival was gone. There was unmistakable jubilation in his eyes.

'I'll be darned!' exclaimed Tom. 'It wasn't so long ago that we saw him here.'

'There wasn't anything wrong with Siksik. I travelled with

him all the way from Taserkapfaluk. He was in perfect shape. Better than all the rest of us.' I was completely baffled.

Seeing our agitation, and without waiting for any more questions, Nerreok went on: 'Siksik died and his younger wife Arluk and his older son died also. His older wife Kommek took the baby boy and went off with Teretkrok.' He paused to enjoy the effect on us.

'They sure disappear fast in this country!' commented Ray grimly.

I wasn't thinking so much of that, but rather of the look on Kommek's face when, some six months earlier, I had told Siksik and his household of meeting the widowed Teretkrok. Then in a mental haze I heard Tom say: 'Please ask him if he knows just what happened, Father.'

At first Nerreok hedged. *'Nauna. Naunartok.* I don't know. Nokadlak didn't say very much—Siksik, Arluk, and the boy all lost their breath.'

Finally he let it out: 'One morning—it was summer—Kommek made tea when they were in bed. Then she went out of the tent and brought back a big can of rotten fish. She gave them all some fish to eat. After a while they got sick—so sick they did not leave the iglek alive. Only the baby boy was well; Kommek did not feed him any fish. After they died she dragged their bodies to the lakeshore. Then with her little one she walked to Teretkrok's tent near the Kulugayuk River.'

'Who's this Teretkrok, Father?'

'He is the chap we met when we were getting close to Taserkapfaluk. He was heading for Burnside. He told us his wife had just died and that he was going to the trading post. I thought Kommek looked pleased when I relayed this news to Siksik. And I remembered Siksik quietly telling me: "Kommek is my first wife, but she is getting on in years and her blood is often cold. Now I have Arluk. She is tall and young and warm. I took Arluk from her husband Naogalluak who was sick. Later he cut his own throat with a knife." '

'Did Siksik tell you anything else?'

'He didn't have to, Tom. It was pretty obvious that Kommek resented Arluk, and it was just as clear that there was only one woman whom Siksik wanted. He slept with Arluk; Kommek slept alone.'

'I bet this would have been quite a case, *mon vieux,* but what's the use of speculating about it? Sure, Ray and I could go and bring this woman in and examine her former camp. And what would we find? Nothing would be left of the corpses by now, and, knowing the natives, we wouldn't get anything helpful out of them. They would all cling to the same story and laugh behind our backs.'

'I'm afraid you are right, Tom, when you say you won't get very far interrogating the natives. Even though they may be jealous of one another, they will not betray their fellow men to the Kablunaks. True, you might have found some additional evidence a few days after their death, but the fall and winter have swept over their bones since, and countless foxes, wolves, and wolverines . . . .'

The restless Nerreok only stayed a couple of days in Cambridge. Once he had all the tea he needed from Scotty, he could not wait to get back to Melville Sound, to his active life among his traps. But when I asked him on the eve of his departure why he was in such a rush to get away, he gave another reason. 'It's too cold, windy, and damp here, Fala. It is better in my camp. Nobody would ever come to Cambridge Bay if it did not have such good trapping grounds all around.'

He was right, of course, but he might have added that the other justification for Cambridge Bay was its harbour, the best on the south coast of Victoria Island.

12

THROUGH THE ISLANDS

Jenny Lind Island lies about eighty miles east of Cambridge Bay in windy Victoria Strait. There is little to distinguish it from dozens of similar small islands with their rolling hills and tundra vegetation except that it is completely surrounded by shallow, clear water, making it a favourite sealing ground in the summer.

When spring had erased the black memories of the Arctic night, I took it into my head to visit Jenny Lind Island and the few small camps on the way to it. At the end of the first day Kunak and I reached Sturt Point. We were greeted by all the occupants of the two iglus except one. This was Peruana, a woman of twenty-five who was dying of scurvy. While we put up our tent and took care of the dogs, her husband, Nuiterk, asked me if I would try to do something for her.

The poor woman lay moaning in her krepik. Her face, greyish blue and so horribly swollen that she could barely open her eyes, told me that she was beyond human help. Braving the stench, I drew closer and asked her how she felt. For what seemed like several minutes Peruana stared at me through the narrow slits in the monstrous ball of bluish flesh. Finally she whispered: '*Ayorama, taimanartok.* It can't be helped, I am nearing the end.'

Her mouth was a mess of sores. She was in nightmarish agony. Yet her mind was clear, for when I said 'Where does it hurt you most?' she forced herself to expose part of her chest, saying: 'Here.'

I saw that her body was disintegrating from decay. At best, her hours were numbered.

Outside, I asked Nuiterk what had brought on her disease.

'We were starving before spring came. I had no foxes to trade. She got sick.' As an afterthought, he added: 'I am going to call Anilianaher in again.'

I had not realized till then that the other hunter in camp was Anilianaher, the sorcerer. I had heard of him at Ellice River and I was curious to see him at work. He did not seem to mind my presence. He squatted on the snow floor and invoked his helping spirits over the moans of the sick woman.

Pitifully, like an ailing child, Peruana cried: '*Aniartunga, aniartunga.* I am sick. I am sick.'

As if in a trance the sorcerer chanted away without paying any attention to her: 'Who are you? Where are you? Do you hear me? Come here, come now!'

His pleas must have been heard by the good spirits, for presently he stood up and walked over to the dying woman. He tied a string to her ankle and began pulling on it, commanding the evil spirits to leave her.

But Anilianaher did not win the tug-of-war with his invisible foes. Hysterically the condemned young woman gasped: '*Ayolerama!* It can't be helped! Give me something to make me die!'

While Anilianaher chanted hoarsely on, the merciful spirits took compassion on Peruana. Although Nuiterk tried to forestall the end by pulling on her tongue 'to bring back her breath' (as he explained), she died late that night.

I helped Nuiterk prepare his wife for burial. Her legs were so puffed that we could not bend them according to custom. But we did manage to bend her body forward a little and place her hands on her abdomen. In this image of a child in the mother's womb she could be reborn to a new life. We carried her out through a special opening Nuiterk cut in the side of the iglu to conform with yet another Krangmalit tradition.

With the warm morning sun, the stench from the corpse exceeded human endurance. Nuiterk needed only a suggestion to move it away. 'Where are you going to take your wife?' I asked when we placed the heavy caribou-wrapped body on his sled. '*Kranilrome*. Just close by.'

Anilianaher and Nuiterk walked ahead of the dogs a short distance until they reached a little knoll overlooking the gulf. They lowered the body to the ground with the face turned towards the east. This would enable it to greet the rising sun —the source of all life and strength in the Land Beyond—as a kind protector. After wandering so much and so far during their lives, the Krangmalit invariably take their shortest journey after death. It is usually to a height of land commanding a pleasant view where the open grave can be easily noticed by passing wolves and foxes.

From a little bag Nuiterk took out Peruana's few personal belongings and arranged them near her remains. Before we left the iluvek or burial ground, he performed the final rite. Through the opening in front of Peruana's face (affording free passage for her soul), he touched her mouth, nose, and ears to secure her friendship and good fortune on the other side. Then, with real grief and loud cries, he looked for the last time upon his dead companion.

Back in camp the incident was promptly forgotten. There

was everyday work to be done, for the struggle for existence was never-ending. From my tent I could see Peruana's body on the little hill. In a few days it would be reduced to scattered bits of bones and a grim skull. The passing hunter would glance at them and say conversationally: *'Inugaluak talva.* This used to be one of us.'

From Sturt Point Kunak and I went straight on to Jenny Lind Island. Although it was late April and the sun was in the sky around the clock, it was still fifteen to twenty degrees below zero—too cold for the seals to crawl out through their breathing holes in the ice and sun themselves on it.

'Why not go to Taylor Island and hunt bear with Tulugak, Ablurek, and Nuvuligak, Fala?' Kunak suggested. These three hunters and their families had wintered on Lind, and were planning to go up to Taylor, fifty miles to the north, in a couple of days.

I fell in readily with Kunak's proposal, especially as I had heard that there were several families on that island whose particulars I could use in my survey.

We spent two days in preparation for the trip. While the women mended the caribou tents for the hunt, we men patched up our sleds with thawed peat and strengthened the cross-bars with additional lashes. Then we carefully checked our dog harnesses and tow-lines, our tools and our implements, our fishing and hunting gear, including the all-important firearms.

Ablurek, who spoke indistinctly (he had bitten his tongue in a wrestling match as a young man), was the most enthusiastic of all. He carried out his preparations with such infinite care that Tulugak nudged Nuvuligak and said, laughing: 'Ablurek is like a young lover grooming himself for a meeting with his woman!'

117

'I am sure the beautiful big bear is not bothering as much with his preparations!' exclaimed Nuvuligak.

'You can joke as much as you like,' Ablurek retorted in his thick, halting speech. 'I am tired of this place and of the same food. Seal, seal, nothing but seal all winter, except the odd hare. I want to travel and to find different meat.'

Three roofless iglus gaped at the blue morning sky as we left the camp and headed in the direction of Taylor Island. On the whole, the going was fairly good. Only occasionally did we encounter the heavy ridges of ice that the Eskimos aptly call the *koglunek* or fearsome thing. They are caused by cracks in the ice which, in expanding, build up huge mounds of sharp ice like the teeth of a saw. As the ice contracts, wide lanes of open water are left between the ridges.

Tulugak and Ablurek walked along such lanes ahead of the four teams, looking for narrow passages that could be crossed with safety. Now, having found a suitable crossing, they were waving and yelling to us to join them.

With a light, nimble jump, Ablurek leaped over the crack and was calling to his leading dog to follow him. Used to this sort of traffic, the rest of the team hopped unhesitatingly over the gap and the long sled spanned it easily, while the women and children aboard clung to the ropes around the heavy load.

The only casualty during such a crossing happened to be Sultan, one of my wheel dogs. He slipped and fell into the freezing water with his companion; and while they were scrambling up the other side of the crack, the sled ran over his left hind leg and broke it. I unharnessed the luckless husky and tried to make him walk, but he limped so badly that there was only one course. I took him on his leash behind an icy boulder. There he sank down to my side, looking up at me with his big, sad eyes. Unseen by the other dogs, I caressed Sultan for the last time.

'Here's something for you, old friend!' I put a piece of fish on the ground before him, and as he sniffed at it, I shot him through the head.

In the afternoon Taylor Island, which the natives call Aivak (Whale), rose in the haze ahead. It seemed to have no foundation, no anchor; it simply floated in a mirage.

'I have friends there, Fala. One of them is Kivgayuk.' Kunak intoned the name in such a way as to give the impression that there was something special about him. I tucked Kivgayuk's name away in my memory for future reference.

A moment later the dogs smelled some unusual presence and Ablurek, standing on his sled, pointed to a black spot on the ice about a mile away: *'Natsek talvane!* That's a seal there!'

The dogs broke into a run: they wanted to be in on the kill. When we were close to the lost, forlorn seal, the men told the women to hold back the dogs while they themselves walked up to the frightened animal. The poor creature must have crawled up on the ice through his *aglu* or breathing hole to sun himself in the spring sun, and fallen asleep. Meanwhile the drifting snow had probably covered up the watery opening and sealed it frozen. On awakening, the seal could not find his escape hatch, got helplessly lost, and became an easy prey for a polar bear, wolf, or passing hunter.

My male companions chuckled at this unexpected find. 'Killing this seal will be as simple as slipping on lake ice!' said Kunak. 'Watch Tulugak.'

The latter grabbed the seal by the flippers, turned the victim on his back, deliberately sat him up part way, and then with a quick forward jerk broke the poor fellow's neck. Although Tulugak did not hurry, the entire operation lasted less than ten seconds and—more important still—required no ammunition. Pulling him by a flipper to his sled, Tulugak hoisted the hundred-pound seal on his sled like a sack of coal and said, grinning: 'We'll all eat him tonight.'

The camp on Taylor Island was located on a promontory jutting into Victoria Strait, some five miles up the eastern coast of the mushroom-shaped island. Far to the north the snowy banks of Driftwood Point glittered in the evening sun, beckoning us to Admiralty Island. Several Eskimos came forward to greet us. Their children were highly excited at the sight of such an expeditionary force. Poorly dressed, their noses running freely, they gathered noisily around my team, making me the uncomfortable centre of attention.

'*Kinalikia tamna, kablunaoyok, eh!* Who can this one be? A white man, eh!' a couple of the older boys shouted.

I humoured them. '*Kablunaoyunga illa.* I am indeed a white man,' I said, pulling the silliest grimace I could muster on such short notice. This frank admission and histrionic display seemed at once to satisfy and amuse them. Laughing and chattering, they ran back to their elders to describe the strange little man with white skin and dark eyebrows who could speak their language and make funny faces.

When I had a chance, I asked Kunak which of the hunters was Kivgayuk. He nodded his head in the direction of a medium-sized young man whose long black hair, carelessly parted down the middle, made him almost indistinguishable from a woman. His features were regular enough, except for a prominent hooked nose and a lower lip so full it drooped under its own weight.

'Kivgayuk is a Natchilik of Orshoktok,' he volunteered, meaning that he belonged to the Seal People from the Blubber Grounds of King William Island. It seemed unusual for a Natchilik to be living with members of the Kivalereit Group, and I asked Kunak for an explanation.

'He ran away from the Natchilit because he killed a man.'
'Where?'

'At Orshoktok. He was crossing a big bay with his friends Pangun and Ugiuk. They were hunting together. A storm came. They built an iglu in the lee of a boulder of ice. The wind grew worse and worse. On the third day it ripped off a block of snow from the top of the iglu. Pangun, Ugiuk, and Kivgayuk were eating at the time. Pangun said: "We must patch the roof." Ugiuk said: "I will do it."

'He was a little man, but very fat and strong. He put on his parka, took his snow knife, and went out. Pangun and Kivgayuk ate their frozen meat and listened to Ugiuk scrape and cut snow above them. Then Pangun bent back his head and through the hole in the roof saw his friend's naked belly protruding under his parka.

' "Pangun," whispered Kivgayuk, "look up! Ugiuk's belly is as big as a pregnant woman's." "Yes," said Pangun, "his belly is white like a seal's." Kivgayuk picked up his snow-knife, stood up on the iglek, and plunged the blade into Ugiuk's belly.'

'Why did Kivgayuk kill his friend?'

'*Nauna*. I don't know. It was not a nice thing to do, but it was such a big belly, Fala.'

After a day of visiting back and forth with the four families on the promontory—which they picturesquely called *tikerk* or forefinger—we headed east towards the middle of Victoria Strait for the realm of Nanuk the Polar Bear, the king of the Land Beyond.

13

NANUK THE BEAR

Our destination lay only twenty miles away to the east, but rough ice and frequent lanes of open water stretched it into a tiring all-day trip. The water made the going hazardous, but it was reassuring at the same time. Polar bears feed almost entirely on seals, and they naturally find it easier to catch them by diving after them into the water than by stalking their breathing holes in the ice.

That night, as we rested in our tent, Kunak reminisced:

'When I was a boy my father took me hunting on the sea-ice with other men. They said Nanuk prowled near the lanes of open water and blowholes, patiently waiting for the seals to come up, just like the Krangmalit hunters. The men used their dogs to attack Nanuk. It was always a great fight to watch in those days.

'The dogs circled Nanuk and jumped on his back, trying to tear him apart. Then the men rushed in with their long spears and plunged them into Nanuk's ribs. Many dogs were usually wounded or killed during the battle, and it was a tricky job for the men, too. But the old way was much more exciting, although even now nobody can foretell what a wounded bear might do.'

I had never been on an organized polar-bear hunt, but I had naturally heard other hunters' stories about the unpredictable white giant of the Arctic wastes. Kakagun, for instance, always claimed that Nanuk was a playful character. 'If Nanuk can find a barrel near a trading post or mission, he will take it up a hill and roll it down like a little boy. Then, when he gets tired of the game, he flattens it with a blow of his paw. Nanuk likes to play with the trap-line, too. He has real fun dragging the snares across the ice. But if a fox who follows him gets caught in a trap, Nanuk will tear it to pieces.'

When Tulugak and Ablurek dropped in for tea, Nanuk was on their minds, too.

'*Ilaranaitok*. He is good-tempered when he is full of seal blubber, but I don't trust him,' said the former.

'That's right,' agreed Ablurek. 'When Nanuk is hungry he will eat the whole seal and anything else he can kill. I have known a starving Nanuk to attack my dogs on the dogline and even go after a team on the trail.'

'Did a bear ever attack you, Ablurek, when you were travelling?'

'*Illa*, Fala. One evening my friend Okpinuak and I were returning to camp after hunting foxes. We were smoking and talking quietly about our young days. Our dogs sensed something. First my leader, then the other dogs, glanced back and broke into a gallop. I looked back. So did Okpinuak. It was easy to see a *nanuk* was chasing us. Then I remembered that when we packed up after the hunt we had wrapped everything, including our rifles, in caribou skins. You should have seen us trying to get the rifles out while the dogs tore as fast as they could for camp. Okpinuak's team was faster than mine. And Nanuk was faster, too. He was getting closer and closer, and still I could not get my 30-30 rifle unpacked. At last I got it. But I could not shoot from the bouncing sled, so I jumped off. Nanuk was very close now. I knelt down and fired. That was my only round. The rest of the ammunition was still packed away in the sled. Nanuk bounded a few more leaps towards me and fell. I was lucky. We had a good time in camp that night. Everybody said I was a good hunter.'

With these hunting stories still ringing in my ears, we left the women and children in camp next morning and set out in search of bear tracks. They crisscrossed here and there, and the trick was to pick out and follow the most recent ones. From the tops of intervening ice ridges the four native hunters and I surveyed the surrounding ice fields for a sign of Nanuk. At best he was difficult to spot against the white background. For, although the polar bear's fur has a yellowish tinge to it, it is white enough to blend perfectly into the Arctic landscape. But the men I was with were not to be deceived indefinitely.

'*Talva!* There!' Kunak whispered excitedly. I trained my telescope on his discovery. At first I could not make it out at all. Then the rare sight took shape. Yes—it was a bear, reared on his hind legs, motionless, like a grotesque snowman.

'Why is he standing like that, Kunak?'

'Watch. He is waiting over a seal hole. If the seal comes up for air in this hole, Nanuk will get him.'

'But each seal has several breathing holes. He may not use this one at all.'

'Nanuk is clever. He is almost a man. He finds the other holes and covers them up with snow. The snow freezes. The seal has no choice. He has to use the only one that is left. Keep watching. Maybe you will be lucky.'

Ablurek, Nuvuligak, and Tulugak sat glued to their telescopes. They were all of one mind—to let the bear have his fun and then to take him. Minutes ticked by. The bear was poised like a marble statue. My eyes began to blink from steady staring. Then it happened. In a flash the statue crumpled, its powerful paws crushing the seal's head and scooping it up on the ice almost in one movement.

We watched silently as the bear had his meal of fresh seal blubber. The hunters knew that the more Nanuk ate the less dangerous he would be, and were content to wait until he had had his fill. When the time came, each of us unharnessed a dog or two and led them to the bear's tracks. Then we let them go, and with loud, excited yelps they hurled themselves across the snow. We followed with our sleds until we were about a hundred yards from where the huskies held their quarry at bay. Nanuk knew how to handle them. Sometimes standing up, sometimes almost sitting down, he swatted at them as if they were hornets. So quick were his movements and so well did his heavy, coarse mantle shield him, that no dog really got its teeth into him.

We anchored our sleds, and Kunak and I watched them while Ablurek, Tulugak, and Nuvuligak walked towards Nanuk with their rifles. When they were about halfway between us and the bear they sat down a few yards apart, crossing their legs in the usual shooting position. Their actions were unhurried, deliberate, and methodical.

Instinctively the bear knew who were his real enemies. He kept beating off the snarling dogs, but his attention was fixed on the strange two-legged beings who did not seem to be afraid of him.

The three hunters raised their rifles, elbows steady on their knees. Nuvuligak, who was in the middle, glanced at his companions and said in a quiet, level voice: 'Let me try it.' His request was respected in silence. Deliberately he waited till he could zero in Nanuk's shoulder. When his mark was exposed, with no leaping dog in between, Nuvuligak pressed the trigger.

With a roar of pain the bear bit the wound and sprawled on his belly. The dogs pounced on him with glee, but their joy was short-lived. In a moment the bewildered bear was fighting back, now mad with rage. One of the daring dogs got in the way of one of his wild swings and fell dying in agony. The rest attacked with fury heightened by the sight and smell of Nanuk's blood, but they were no match for him. He ploughed on, despite them, towards the hunters.

Two more shots, fired almost simultaneously by Ablurek and Tulugak, stopped his further progress. Then all three hunters fired once more to make sure. The bear was in his final convulsions as they closed in on him. Now he was still and, as if by command, the dogs stopped yapping and began licking the bear's blood and their own wounds. Nuviligak kicked the nine-foot carcass a couple of times and then poked it with the butt of his rifle. There was no response. Nanuk, the king, was truly dead.

With his long-bladed hunting knife Nuvuligak ripped out the liver, walked off to a crack in the ice and dumped it.

'Why did Nuvuligak throw the liver away, Kunak?'

'So that the dogs could not get it, Fala. If a dog eats Nanuk's liver, it will get sick and lose its coat.'

'Is it all right for a man to eat it?'

'*Immana.* Certainly not.'

'Why not?'

'He'll vomit. And he will have sores on his skin.'

It took all five of us to roll the thousand-pound carcass onto Nuvuligak's sled, but the task of taking it off again was lightened by many willing and excited hands in camp. With the prospect of feasting on Nanuk for the next two or three days, the women fell eagerly to the task of stripping off the hide and dividing the carcass among the families. They laughed gaily as they toiled.

Each family packed off its share of the bear, filled the big

cauldron with its meat, fat, and bones, and waited impatiently for the blubber lamp beneath to do its duty.

Ablurek's wife was the first to call out: *'Nanutoritse! Nanutoritse!* Come and have bear meat!'

Although Ablurek's tent was crowded when I got there, he
made room for me on the iglek and his wife brought me a
slice weighing about a pound. It was half-boiled and bleeding.
I found it tough to eat. But the others swallowed large chunks
of it, barely chewing the pinkish flesh. My dogs could have
learned no table manners in this company. And yet it was
a happy, almost dignified assembly.

I was wrestling with a bone when Ablurek smiled and said
for all to hear: 'Why don't you eat the marrow, Fala? It is
even better than the caribou's!' All eyes were on me, and they
were all grinning.

'Give Fala an axe!'

Afraid to shatter the bone with the axe's sharp edges, I
hit it with the flat side. The bone held together. Everyone
giggled. Again and again I hit the obstinate object, but
succeeded only in raising waves of laughter all around. At last
Ablurek admitted the truth: 'There is no marrow in Nanuk's
bone, Fala. It is made strong like a stone!'

The feasters moved on from Ablurek's tent to Nuvuligak's,
thence to Tulugak's, winding up the night with an outdoor
dance in a weirdly beautiful Arctic setting. The sun, looming
large and crimson near the horizon, had turned the snow
into shimmering pink, and so grotesquely lengthened all
shadows as to make the whole scene unreal.

Everyone relaxed next day. Even those who had not over-
estimated their capacity and paid with sickness for their folly
loafed in the spring sun. But early on the following day—
with the bear meat almost gone and the hunters restless once
more—we went after more bear tracks. We were lucky. In a

broad lane of open water a female bear was giving swimming lessons to her cubs. Two balls of fluff, with black eyes and noses, they crouched hesitantly at the water's edge. Their mother called to them to come in. They refused, almost crying. She climbed on the ice, went behind them, and gently pushed them with her snout into the cold, dark blue water. The cubs dog-paddled, keeping their sharp-nosed heads above the surface. The mother bear dived in and gave them a pick-a-back ride to the ice.

While the swimming instruction continued, the hunters crept up as close as they dared, taking cover behind the ridges of ice. Once again the she-bear was in the water, inviting the cubs to join her. Again they refused, and she was about to return to push them in when four shots rang out in rapid succession. The frightened cubs leapt into the water, seeking her protection. Valiantly the wounded bear struggled to swim to them, but before she reached them a second round finished off all three.

'We were lucky to find Nanuk in the water,' remarked Kunak. 'On land she would fight worse than the cubs' father. And if one of the cubs was killed or wounded first, nothing would stop her from attacking the hunter.'

Tulugak voiced the practical viewpoint:

'Our women can make some warm *karlik* [breeches] and heavy *puelluk* [mittens] from the young bearskins for next winter. And, if there's anything left over, we'll have soft sled runners for hunting seals.'

When the wind did not bring the floating bears to the icy shore fast enough to suit him, Tulugak tossed his harpoon and we all helped to pull the victims in.

Our hunting trips were frequently interrupted by high winds, by snow storms, and occasionally by *taktuk*, the fog, which came after unusually warm days and forced the hunters to stay in camp.

When we had been at Taylor Island for two weeks, a terrific storm blew in from the southeast, marooning us for three days.

'That rumbling does not sound exactly like thunder, Kunak. What is it?' I asked at the height of the storm.

'That's ice breaking in the sea. The smaller floes are driven by the currents against the larger ice fields, and when they crash and the ice piles up in ridges you hear this loud noise.'

'I'd like to see how much ice has been broken.'

'We can do that when the storm blows over, Fala.'

The entire camp must have been stung with the same curiosity when the bitter cold gave way to warmer temperatures as the wind subsided. For, as soon as their sleds and supplies were ready, the hunters took their wives and children for the day's hunt.

'Fala, you heard the big noise during the storm?' Ablurek asked me.

'Yes. Kunak said it was ice breaking up.'

'That's right. Now there will be more open water and we might need a kayak. My krammotik is loaded with the family. Can you take my kayak for me?'

I was glad to oblige Ablurek. The precautionary measure seemed well advised, and I could easily handle another eighty or ninety pounds on the sled. We all travelled together for nearly ten miles. Then the dog teams began to fan out as the hunters followed the various bear tracks. Only Tulugak's sled continued straight on. Kunak and I inclined a little to the left when he picked out a fairly fresh set of tracks. From the top of a hummock we checked the surroundings for Nanuk and the progress of the other hunters. There was no visible sign of Nanuk himself. Nor did any of the hunters wave his arm to signal the rest that he had spotted one and needed help.

I noticed that Tulugak had stopped his sled by a long lane

of open water and was sizing up its extent before venturing across. Apparently satisfied that the crack was not endless but that the ice ahead was connected to the main ice, he took his team over the narrowest part and proceeded to the outer fringe a couple of miles beyond.

When I surveyed the scene again a little later, Tulugak had anchored his team and was now sitting on the water's edge, his rifle ready for action against any seal that might bob up for air. Beside him sat his wife Aligunek and their young daughter. They made an appealing picture of family life. Involuntarily my mind flew back to the verdant, semi-tropical valleys of Corsica, and hunting and fishing trips with my own father.

Without warning a thunderous crackling noise filled the air and I was facing stark reality again. Tulugak had been tricked by one of the evil spirits. His ice field had broken away from the main frozen mass.

I saw him pick up his little girl and dash for the sled, the portly Aligunek hurrying behind. With every passing moment the chasm of deep open water widened slowly, inexorably. By the time they reached the near edge of the immense floe they stood no chance of bridging the gap.

The other hunters sped towards their friends. Seeing Ablurek among them I remembered his kayak on my sled. I ran to my team, picked up the anchor, and headed for the meeting point.

Nuvuligak, the first to reach the edge of the main ice, wasted no time in trying to establish a line of contact with the marooned family. He kept flinging his spear, to which was attached a cord of caribou strips, but his best efforts fell short.

'My *niksik* will be better!' shouted Ablurek, unpacking a four-pronged hook resembling a miniature anchor weighted with scrap metal. A long twine, gathered around a stick, was tied to the niksik. Ablurek wound up like a softball pitcher

and let the niksik fly with an underhand throw. It was a long, straight pitch, the one the hunters use in bringing in shot seal. But it was not quite far enough either.

'There's only the kayak to save them, Fala,' he said. 'Let's get it into the water!'

We placed the long, slender craft in the water alongside the ice. While Nuvuligak, Kunak, and I held the kayak steady, Ablurek stepped into it carefully and sat down, stretching his legs in front of him. I handed him his double-bladed paddle. He found his balance with it and pushed off. It looked deceptively easy.

'Get your krammotik ready for crossing!' Nuvuligak yelled across the widening water. Despite the cross-wind, or perhaps having himself guessed Ablurek's plan, Tulugak began taking his rifles, ammunition, and knives off the sled. Meanwhile Aligunek anxiously watched the approaching kayak, her little girl clinging close to her.

'I'll take the girl inside the kayak, Tulugak. Aligunek can stretch out on top. You push the dogs in. I'll come back for you next trip.'

The little girl wormed her way into the belly of the boat and lay snugly on the bearskin covering the bottom amidships. Ablurek took up his place in the oval hole, which resembled in miniature a conning tower I once saw on a submarine in the Mediterranean. He spread his legs so that the girl's head rested between his knees, steadied the kayak, and asked Aligunek to get aboard behind him.

Although it was long—perhaps twenty feet—and extremely buoyant, the kayak dipped appreciably when Aligunek climbed cautiously on it. It took all Ablurek's skill to prevent it from rolling and tipping while she first squatted, then followed his curt orders. Without once turning around to look at her, he was balancing the kayak with the paddle like a tight-rope walker using a long pole and saying:

'Hold on to my parka. Now get down on your knees. Easy. Stretch your legs back slowly. Right out. Stay flat and be sure to hang on. *Iyuarpin?* Are you set?'

'*Iyuartunga, illa.* Yes, I'm ready,' she giggled back, as if all danger had long since passed away.

'*Utirluta!* Let's go back!' The kayak moved off.

Tulugak had brought his lead-dog to the edge of the floe. Now he pushed it into the water while all the dogs yapped in protest. Ablurek called to him, and the leader began to swim for the kayak. One after another the dogs, and finally the sled, were pushed off the ice by Tulugak, who remained cheerfully behind, confident of rescue.

The strange convoy ploughed on tediously through the rippling waters, its speed controlled by the slowest dog. My sympathy went out to Aligunek, straining to stay motionless in the cold breeze.

Ablurek successfully brought the kayak to our waiting hands. Aligunek alighted stiffly, but her round face was beaming. 'How's my daughter?' she asked.

'She's fine,' replied Ablurek, vacating his seat to let the child out.

Presently the dogs were scrambling on the ice. Freed of their harnesses, they were booted or whipped into motion to keep them from cringing and freezing. They ran off, stopping only to shake themselves, and then rolled in the snow to dry themselves.

Ablurek did not wait while we pulled up the sled. He was off to get his friend whose silhouette was receding into the sun. The immense floe was picking up speed in the strong currents.

No trace of apprehension remained in the group. Gathered around the rotund Aligunek and her little girl, they laughed gaily at the near-disaster. When Ablurek and Tulugak landed safely, Tulugak and his wife thanked Ablurek.

'*Goiyalutin.* Say thanks,' Aligunek told her child. This brief formality, which Ablurek did not acknowledge verbally (the Eskimo language has no formula for this), was the only break in their chain of gaiety.

To me it was almost incomprehensible that any normal person could remain unperturbed and smiling no matter what misfortune befell him. Yet this resigned acceptance of whatever happens to him as an inevitable act of nature is the Eskimo's finest defensive weapon. His relatives might perish in a storm; his family may be starving or freezing; death in many guises may brush past him—but he will give the evil spirits no satisfaction. He will conceal his emotions. He will grin and say: '*Ayornorman illa!* Indeed, there is nothing one can do about it. That's life!' Any deviation from this behaviour would be construed as weakness. And weakness has no place in the Land Beyond.

Much more demonstrative than their masters were the hunters' dogs. Still licking the salty water off their shaggy hair, they were obviously unnerved by the unexpected swim and even more so by the distant rumbling of breaking ice.

'The dogs are listening and they are afraid,' said Kunak. 'Let's help Tulugak harness them and get back to camp.'

14

NATSEK THE SEAL

After our dinner of seal meat that evening the conversation inevitably ran on the dangers of breaking ice. It was agreed that the day's experience was a warning to move closer to land, and the hunters decided to set out next day to look for their friends on Admiralty Island.

There a surprise awaited us. Driftwood Point, the site of the main camp, was deserted. We found caches of winter implements wrapped in bearskins and stored on steep boulders out of reach of animals. They were the only signs of orderliness. The rest of the campsite was littered with messy bits of caribou and sealskins, ptarmigan feathers, lumps of frozen peat, and dog droppings.

Dirty patches of snow marked the several spots where the tents had been pitched. Table-high blocks of snow indicated where the hunters had hoisted their sleds to work on them. Ablurek and Tulugak searched the ground for the freshest sled tracks and decided rapidly exactly which way their friends had gone.

'What sealing grounds lie in that direction, Ablurek?'

'Uyaraguit Bay, Fala. Good hunting there in the spring.'

The sun was bright in a clear sky next morning when we started along the southern coast of Admiralty Island. There were hardly any pressure ridges here, and we were able to cover the thirty-two miles to Prince Edward Bay in seven hours. Kunak and I were well ahead of the other teams (not only were my dogs of superior breed but they were regularly fed) when we spotted some dark objects in the distance.

'Those things are tents, Fala. We'll see new people and have a good time!' my companion exclaimed.

We were welcomed with the usual hospitality by the entire population of the five-tent community. Then we watched the other teams pull in. Decked out in their best parkas (they had changed a few miles out of camp for the occasion), the three hunters and their wives were yelling at the top of their voices at their dogs to show off their animals, not to mention themselves. The huskies were tired and paid little attention to their masters' exhortations to run faster and pull harder. But our friends' efforts were not entirely wasted. They succeeded magnificently in displaying their importance before the gathered multitude of admiring men, women, and children, and howling dogs.

Their vanity satisfied, they climbed off the sleds and went about shaking hands with the camp's twenty inhabitants. Among the latter I was glad to see my young friend Otokreak. We exchanged greetings, and he said: 'You seem to be travelling a lot, Fala.'

'Yes, I like to visit as many people as I can. What about you? Have you found yourself a wife yet?'

'I found one and I am trying her out now. She is a little old, but she sews well.'

'Last winter I saw Nerreor in Cambridge Bay and he told me that he'd heard about your father. He said Kakagun was inland at Taseriuak where he was getting a lot of foxes.

Nerreor also told me that Kakagun has adopted a little girl, Naoyak, promised to your half-brother Kivgalo. Did you know that?'

'Nobody told me about it, Fala. Who is this girl Naoyak?'

'She is the daughter of Nokadlak. She was born two years ago when I was visiting his camp at Kagnekoguyak.'

Otokreak showed no further interest either in his young half-brother or in the latter's wife-to-be. He was more curious to know when I might be returning to Bathurst.

'I expect to go back to Kringaun next winter or next spring. Then I think I will give travelling a rest and stay one or two seasons with the people there. Why did you ask?'

'I may go with you. The land is too cold here and hunting is often poor during the winter. We nearly starved last winter. Some friends came from the far end of Uyaraguit Bay to stay with us. For a long time they had nothing to eat except tom-cods and sealskins. Things got so bad they lost most of their dogs. We gave them some blubber for their lamps, but we were short ourselves and we had to spend many days on the sea-ice hunting seals to provide for everybody. Even then we got only just enough to avoid starvation.'

'Have you got many seals lately?'

'No, Fala. We arrived only two days ago. But tomorrow we are all going after Natsek. The sun is warm now and they are beginning to come out of their aglus on the ice.'

Leaving Otokreak, I wandered from tent to tent, chatting with the Eskimos and taking down their names and other particulars. One name—Akraliak—I had heard before. Eskimos at Cambridge Bay had told me of his strange build—legs so short that they seemed to have been amputated, and long, apelike arms. His wide face was a labyrinth of concentric wrinkles arranged around a large flat nose, and his shifty eyes were almost crescent-shaped. I had heard his story, too. His wife had been taken away by his elder brother, and Akraliak had let his anger stew until it boiled over. He drove to his brother's camp and stealthily entered his iglu while the couple were asleep. Akraliak crept up close and blew his brother's head to pieces with his rifle. He dragged the naked body out of the sleeping bag and into the cold Arctic night. Then he crawled in with the woman and told her he would adopt his brother's frightened son.

My census notes showed that Akraliak had kept his promise; also that his wife had since borne him a boy and a girl. Mittek, the adopted boy, was now old enough to hunt with the men. This must have made Akraliak somewhat uneasy because of the Krangmalit tradition of ultimate revenge.

A hunter can kill his neighbour without fear of being punished by his elders, who consider it his own business so long as it does not injure the community as a whole. But with relatives of the victim it is another matter altogether. Custom imposes upon one of them the duty of destroying the murderer. This is a purist's vendetta, executed without anger, without passion—just like killing caribou or any other game. And the patient stalking and waiting for the opportune moment is an essential part of the manhunt.

Even if the murderer knows that an avenger is chosen and that he is a doomed man, he does nothing about it. In fact he will even raise the children of the man he has killed, realizing all the while that one of them will ultimately slay him. Meantime the executioner—and everyone else—treats the murderer as if nothing had happened. But everyone knows that sooner or later, even if it takes years, the avenger will strike him down.

In the morning all the men fanned out across the sea 'floor' while the women stayed in camp to carry on their favourite occupation—gossiping with the newcomers. Kunak wasn't enthusiastic about the trip. He would have much preferred to stay in camp with the women, he told me. But when I insisted that I needed him, he consoled himself. 'I'll have time to enjoy myself at the dance tonight. Now I'll show you how good a seal hunter I am!'

To make doubly sure of seeing experts in action, I decided to stay close to Otokreak and Tulugak. As we were leaving, Akraliak and Mittek pulled alongside my sled, and the former asked Kunak:

'Are you and Fala going by yourselves?'

'No, Fala is joining Otokreak and Tulugak.'

A shadow passed over Akraliak's face, but he answered cheerfully enough. 'We'll meet you later at the dance!' he said. 'Don't eat too much fresh seal liver today!'

We travelled north. I turned to Kunak, who was unusually silent, and asked: 'Did you ever meet Mittek before?'

He answered slowly and thoughtfully. 'Yes, I knew him when we were boys. He was younger than I, but we used to trap weasels together near the camp. Then his father was killed and he went away with Akraliak.'

'Is this the first time you've seen him since?'

'No, Fala. I have seen him several times, mostly at the trading post in Ikalutuktiak.'

'Is he a good hunter?'

'He is quite a good shot, Fala.' This was said in a condescending tone.

Behind us Otokreak was having trouble with his team. I knew his dogs had diarrhoea, but this fact alone could not account for his falling so far back. I asked Kunak what was the matter.

'It's his sled. It's too heavy for the dogs. Otokreak traded his good sled for a new rifle when he got himself a woman, so he built a sled with runners of willows wrapped in caribou skin and sealed in ice. Now his team crawls like a worm on a piece of dry meat, and Tulugak has to stop and wait for him to catch up.'

'Don't you think we should be seeing seals soon, Kunak?'

'Let's turn up to this ridge and look around.'

From the mound of pressure ice we scanned the frozen sea. Drifts of snow lay like downy pillows on the lee sides of the ridges of rough ice. But where the ice was smooth the snow covering was thinly spread.

Kunak pointed to some distant flecks on this silvery expanse.

'Those little lemmings are seals, Fala. Watch and you will see them shifting, swaying, and turning in the sun.'

'I can see some of them moving. But many seem to be quite still. Are they asleep?'

'Not for very long. They put their heads down to doze, then raise them to look around. Keep looking at only one *natsek* and see what he does.'

I picked one out and watched through my tinted glasses. Kunak was right. In a few seconds the seal stirred, looked warily about, and resumed his catnap. I timed his waking intervals. They occurred about forty seconds apart. He was nearly as accurate as my watch.

'What is he so afraid of, Kunak? I can't see anything else around except seals.'

'Natsek knows he is not the only living thing on the ice. His main enemy, Nanuk the Bear, may be prowling about; and there might be other strange, dangerous shapes that he should shun.'

'Tell me, just how does the big fat seal climb on the ice?'

Kunak laughed. 'First of all Natsek sticks his head out of his aglu. If he sees nothing to fear, he places both fore flippers on the edge of the aglu and with a push of his rear flippers flops out on the ice. He stays there—always close to the edge of the aglu so that he can plunge back into it at the first sign of danger.'

'Does every seal use his own aglu?'

'The mature natsek always does. But two or three young

ones might share the same aglu. Sometimes they get playful and overconfident. They crawl away and if it is a little foggy they lose their way. Then they might crawl towards the shore. It looks to them like a stretch of open water.'

Otokreak and Tulugak came up with us now. 'Fala is watching the seals over there,' Kunak told them. They studied the sealing ground as a field commander might the disposition of enemy troops.

Tulugak said: 'There's a wary one. He's all alone and unhappy in his sleep like an old woman with bad dreams.'

'A hunter must be tricky to get a restless natsek like that,' said Otokreak.

Kunak agreed. 'Natsek is aware of his usual enemies and of his friends basking in the sun. But he is not so sure of other moving objects. A hunter must try to look like a seal and act like one; or else he must not be seen by Natsek at all. The only way to do that is to advance when his head drops for a few moments of sleep. That's what I think we should do now.'

Otokreak and Tulugak went down to their sleds and made off. In high spirits they kept running back and forth alongside their sleds, pausing now and again to glance at the occasional openings in the network of ridges. Recalling what Otokreak had told me of the hardships of the previous winter, I thought: 'They must be feeling the very joy of life. After months of struggle for the barest existence, the Barren Land now promises them warmth and food.'

To give Otokreak and Tulugak—and ourselves—plenty of elbow room, Kunak and I proceeded in the opposite direction. We stopped a few hundred yards from a couple of seals and hid my team out of sight behind a mass of rough ice. The dogs sprawled on the snowy bed, glad of the chance to cool off.

'Now, Fala,' said Kunak confidently, 'I'll show you that Inuk is more capable than a Kablunak.'

From the sled he picked up a parka and a pair of over-pants, both made of sealskin. He spoke as he changed his parka: 'We picked the right couple. They are mating. Look at them! They are too busy to notice us.'

Exuberantly he stepped into the karlik, pulling its top to his waist so that the bottoms reached down just below his knees.

'I'll stay close to the dogs,' I said, 'to keep them quiet and see they don't run off somewhere. I'll be able to watch you at the same time.'

He disappeared between the ridges. Now I could see him at the edge of the rough ice. Two hundred yards separated him from the loving couple, alternately nuzzling each other and catching a few winks of sleep. Kunak moved with cat-like furtiveness. When the seals lowered their heads, he stepped out of his hiding-place and ran for a few seconds towards them, falling prone to anticipate their re-awakening. Even then, his presence did not entirely escape the seals' notice. They raised their heads and stared at him. But the intruder was acting very normally. He lifted his head, shifted, and wriggled his sealy body as if he was trying to make himself more comfortable by his aglu.

In starts and stops, regulated by the seals themselves, Kunak kept gaining yards. 'But why doesn't he shoot?' I wondered. 'He can't be more than fifty yards away from them now.' Yet he kept on inching towards his quarry.

Suddenly he leapt up like an Arctic hare and was on top of the seals in a flash. He clubbed them right and left with the butt of his rifle as if possessed. But he wasn't quite fast enough to handle them both. Stunned though it must have been by the blows, one of the seals managed to scramble to the aglu and dive out of sight.

My dogs sensed the mortal battle. Yapping away, they would have galloped off had I not been able to grab the sled in time and quieten them down with the whip.

141

Kunak was waiting for me, leaning on his rifle and beaming all over. '*Ayuitunga, eh,* Fala? I'm pretty good, eh, Father?'

'You definitely are. Any woman would be proud to have you as a husband.'

'I have been thinking about that. But where shall I find a wife?'

He cut open the seal's belly and pulled out the steaming, bloody liver. To drain off the excess blood, he dropped it in the snow and waited for a few moments. Then he sliced off several lumps and threw one away to the spirit of the sea as a token of his goodwill. Finally, motioning me to help myself, he plunged in with gusto.

'Eat, Fala. This is good even for a Kablunak!'

He had flung the glove of challenge. I had to show Kunak that a white man could do as well as an Eskimo, at least when it came to *eating* game. However, it was so obvious that my gorge rose that my friend said mockingly: '*Ayorpialertok, Kablunak.* The white man is really hopeless.'

We loaded the seal aboard the sled and looked around for Otokreak and Tulugak. We could just discern them heading north towards a lead of open water. 'Seals must be crowding along the crack like mosquitoes on a child. Let's go there too,' Kunak said impulsively.

'What's wrong with this one on our left? He should not be too hard to get. There are plenty of spots where you can take cover and shoot at close range.'

'*Taralik, illa.* Yes, there are shadows. Wait for me. I am going to get him too.'

In much the same fashion as before, Kunak proceeded towards his goal; but he seemed puzzled, even as I was, for the seal did not move. 'Must have made a pig of himself at supper and now he's sleeping it off,' I surmised.

Within easy range, Kunak fired. Still the seal did not move. He shot again and then raced towards the motionless prey.

My dogs, excited by the rifle shots, ran to Kunak's side hoping to be present at the kill.

Even before I reached him I realized that it was my turn to chuckle at his expense. For a moment he was speechless with embarrassment. Then sullenly, lamely, he said: 'One of the hunters had to get rid of his sick dog. I thought it was a seal, but I was not really sure . . . .'

'I'll have a good story to tell in camp tonight! The women are bound to enjoy it.'

'No doubt they will, Fala,' he said, recovering his confident manner. 'But they will like me all the more.'

I was still trying to fathom his logic when we joined Otokreak and Tulugak who had halted in the lee of a hummock near the open crack in the ice floor.

'Where did you shoot Natsek?' Tulugak asked, looking at my sled.

'Kunak didn't shoot it; he clubbed it,' I answered for him.

'But we heard rifle shots.'

'Oh! That was when Kunak mistook a dead dog for a seal!'

Tulugak and Otokreak roared with laughter at my cocky friend.

'I am going to make tea,' said Kunak tersely.

'Let me know when it's ready.' Otokreak was still laughing, but his mind was once more on live seals. 'I'm going to have a try at those natsit by the open water.' He strolled off, his rifle dangling in his right hand.

'The best Otokreak can do is kill one natsek,' said Kunak. 'They are excited at meeting so many friends, but there are always some of them on the lookout. If he shoots at one, the rest will plunge to safety.'

None of us spoke while we watched Otokreak crawl or take cover behind the snow-drifts. He had one decided advantage: he was advancing into the wind. In the silence of the land the same wind brought us the characteristic noises of seals at play—something between the snorting of an impatient horse and the friendly grunts of a well-fed hog.

Otokreak had apparently gone as far as he could go without scaring off the entire school. He raised himself slightly off the snow, aimed, and fired. The frightened seals, their flippers pounding on the ice, slithered off into their watery refuge.

'He killed one,' said Tulugak. 'He is a good hunter.'

Otokreak was at the smitten seal's side in a matter of seconds. He bent over to rip open its belly, pulled something out, and began to pace round it.

'What's he doing, Tulugak?' I asked, mystified.

'He is marking the snow with Natsek's guts.'

'Why?'

'To show other hunters it belongs to him.'

'Has he a special mark?'

'No, Fala.'

'Then how will they know it was Otokreak's seal and not Kunak's, for instance?'

'They won't.'

'I don't understand.'

'If Otokreak leaves the seal where it is and others find it, they will know that someone shot it and they will not take it. It is Otokreak's.'

'You mean that if a seal is wounded and crawls away to die and no-one leaves any markings around him, whoever finds him can keep him for his own?'

'That's it, Fala.'

On top of the ridge Kunak was waving his arms, motioning Otokreak to join us at tea. It was steaming and we sipped it in a cheery mood. Otokreak brought his contribution to the table—the seal's warm liver.

'*Akreatorama*. My belly's full,' Tulugak said for the rest

of us when the liver was gone. I passed around a tin of tobacco and we relaxed on the sleds.

A muffled shot rang out.

'That might be Akraliak,' suggested Kunak. 'I think he is
the only one who was going to hunt in this direction.' True
to his restless, boastful self, he looked out at the lane of open
water and teased me: 'Fala, you are a Kablunak. Where
should we go now?'

'Perhaps it might be better if I followed you, Inuk. You
were born on the ice. You have spent your life on the ice. You
must surely know where to go and what to do.'

He accepted the implied sarcasm as a compliment, saying:
'Let's go to the water.'

Our little tea party over, I set our course for the open lane.
Once again Otokreak and Tulugak drove off in the opposite
direction. The crack was about twenty-five yards wide for
the most part, narrowing to ten or fifteen feet in places and
stretching as far as Kunak and I could see.

'I am going to get off here, Fala, and wait for a while,' he
said. 'Maybe Natsek will pop up.'

I continued alone. It was an extremely bright day, warm
and languorous. The dogs did not want to pull at all, and I
could not blame them. The sled was scarcely moving. I
watched the water for something to do. By contrast with the
glittering white surroundings it looked almost black. Unexpectedly, out of this dull blackness rose the shiny black head
of a seal. I don't know which one of us was more surprised at
seeing the other. I only know that while Natsek stared at me
with his big glassy eyes, my hand automatically reached for
the rifle and I shot at him.

There was a loud splash as he disappeared. Blood marked
the spot, but the seal was nowhere to be seen. I waited for a
while but without success. With nothing to keep me there I
urged the dogs to move along.

About an hour later, when I had turned around to rejoin Kunak, my lead dog noticed something unusual lying on the ice ahead. The whole team joined Bobby in a race for what soon took on the outline of a seal. I stopped the dogs just before Bobby reached it. It was the natsek I had previously shot.

Expecting little resistance, I grabbed the seal by the back flippers to pull him away from the water. But I had under-estimated the big fellow. I found myself being drawn to the edge of the ice against which he anchored his fore flippers. My adversary's breathing was wheezy, he was almost gasping for breath. At first I thought it was caused by fear or the strain of our tug-of-war. Then I saw a trickle of blood on his short, thick neck and realized I had shot him through the gullet.

Under the seal's supreme efforts to free himself the ice suddenly cracked and I lay prostrate with my legs still on the ice floor and my torso on the broken chunk of ice nearly two feet lower. The seal had accomplished his purpose. I let him go and hung on for dear life like a bridge between the main ice and the little floe. If I slipped any more it meant a watery grave. I could not turn or move without this risk. I yelled for all I was worth, hoping that Kunak would hear me: 'Imalertunga! Ikayorlanga! I am drowning! Help me!'

Two minutes passed—the longest two minutes I think I've ever counted—before Kunak came to my rescue. He was about a quarter of a mile away when he heard my call and he arrived panting from the run. Without wasting words he grabbed my feet and pulled me back on the ice floor.

'Goannarivaktor. Thanks a lot. You came just in time, Kunak. That water is too cold for bathing, and the ice bank would have been too high for me to scramble up.'

He hardly listened. He was shaking his head and laughing.

146

'Kablunak may be capable of doing many things. But in the Land Beyond he is always like a useless old woman.'

I was in no position to take offence. It was the way of the land to laugh at danger anyway.

The wounded seal apparently found it even harder to breathe in the water than on the ice. He had crossed the narrow lane of open water and had climbed up on the ice, snorting in pain. I put him out of his misery with a shot through the head. Kunak fetched his niksik off the sled, threw the four-pronged hook past the dead natsek, and brought him in as the hook caught the seal's side.

We hoisted it aboard the sled and sat down to wait for Otokreak and Tulugak. With our rifles ready we kept the water under observation. Within the hour four seals were unlucky enough to raise their heads. They didn't stare at us for long. We shot all four, fished them out of the water with the niksik, and piled them on the sled. Other seals within earshot dived down. It was late afternoon now and they had had enough warm sun for one day.

Otokreak and Tulugak sat proudly on their seals' bellies as they drove up. 'We had good hunting today, but it should be better still in the next few days when more seals will be coming from the north along the leads of water,' the former said brightly.

'You should have come with us for a good laugh,' smiled Kunak. 'Fala was going to have a swim with Natsek and then changed his mind.' They both relished Kunak's embroidered description of the incident, and it was a happy group of hunters that headed for camp in the red sunset.

On the trail our dogs did not share our lightheartedness. Several of them were limping, and spots of their blood were beginning to show up on the snow.

'We should put their boots on next trip, Fala. The snow has been thawing and freezing. It makes icy needles. Some of the dogs are not tough enough.' Kunak was wise after the damage had been done. I had left the dog's boots behind, not expecting to need them on a single day's trip.

'Something is wrong,' he told me as we pulled into camp. 'Those three teams are leaving.' He hailed the nearest driver: 'Where are you going?'

'Mittek came back with the news that his father Akraliak had fallen into open water and disappeared. Mittek is going to show us where it happened.'

As the sleds glided by I saw young Mittek sitting on one of them. I turned to Kunak: 'Why are they going after Akraliak? If he is drowned, as Mittek says, nobody can help him.'

'It is not good to leave a body alone. It will cause the wrath of the evil spirits to descend upon the whole camp. They are going to fish Akraliak's body out of the water and bring it back.'

Some of the evil spirits began to exhibit their displeasure even as Kunak spoke. Chased by a north-easter, heavy clouds raced in our direction. Under our feet the loose snow, which had been hardened by the alternate thaw and frost, was screeching like sand rubbing against rock. 'Looks like bad weather again,' Kunak said resignedly. He was grateful for the stretch of fine weather of the last few days and he knew it could not last indefinitely.

We could barely make out the three teams in the distance now, and I wondered if the storm would permit them to find the spot where Akraliak went down .

Our tents were flapping furiously in the stormy evening when the searchers returned. Some of the men and women gathered around them to see if they had been successful. Save for the drivers themselves, the sleds were empty. The hunter who had spoken with Kunak on departure reported: 'We found the lane and the place where Akraliak plunged to his

death. But we saw nothing of him, not even a sign that he had
been there.'

In Akraliak's tent the widow was brewing tea for the company. There was nothing in her expression or manner to indicate her inner feelings. Everyone milled around repeating
the hollow expression of sympathy: 'Mamianar illa. It's really
too bad.' To this she kept replying: 'Mamianar ayornartok.
It's too bad but it cannot be helped.'

There were no tears, no lamentations. Everyone had
howled according to custom for a couple of minutes on first
hearing the news of the tragedy from Mittek. Now all eyes
were dry; but all ears were eager for more details. Mittek
obliged: 'Akraliak and I reached the crack in the ice and
stopped to eat the liver of one of the seals we had killed in
the middle of the day. We made tea and rested for a while.
Then my father told me he would walk along the edge and
watch for seals. I took over the dogs and drove in the opposite
direction. I was going to shoot a seal swimming ahead of me
when I heard the report of a rifle. I looked back and saw
Akraliak unwinding his niksik. He threw it and brought
Natsek to the edge of the ice. He bent over Natsek to pull
him out of the water by the back flippers, but the animal
escaped his grasp and plunged down. Akraliak lost his
balance and fell headlong into the water. I swung the sled
around, whipped the dogs, and raced to help him. But when
I got there it was too late. The seal left a circle of blood
where he dived, but there wasn't any sign of my father except
the rifle he had dropped on the snow.'

Mittek spoke slowly, easily, as if he had rehearsed his
speech. His listeners were attentive, but their faces betrayed
scepticism. Plainly they did not believe what he said. More
likely their thoughts were the same as mine: the boy had
accomplished his duty imposed upon him by tradition.

An eiderdown of fleecy wool covered the sky for days as

an aftermath of the storm. A subdued white light was diffused everywhere without a shadow to be seen. There was no way to tell the lay of the land even before one's very feet. Elevations and depressions, snow-drifts and rough ice, all lost their normal contours. We stumbled about, unable to gauge the snow underfoot or the distances ahead.

Everything wore a deceptive disproportion. The most familiar sights, like dogs curled up in the snow a few yards away, looked like remote hills. At closer range the same dogs seemed to be sinking in holes.

On some days, mostly in the afternoon, great distances were opened to us. We could see around us for miles. Yet it was practically impossible to tell what lay close at hand. At first I was inclined to think that my eyes were going back on me or that my glasses were letting me down. But Kunak reassured me. 'There are no shadows, Fala. It is like a moonless winter night. Man and dog stumble because they cannot see properly. It will pass.'

'When the good weather returns, Kunak, I think we should go back to Cambridge. We have been away long enough and I have to get ready to return to Bathurst.'

He shrugged his shoulders. It was immaterial to him.

As the weather continued to improve, some of the hunters made short sorties to the sea floor, returning with varying numbers of seals. But the excitement of the first day's hunt had clearly subsided. Only one aspect of it remained unchanged: Kunak was still the favourite target for the women's taunts. 'What were you going to do with that dog you shot? Make a parka from its skin and give it to some girl, eh?'

'*Immana*. No. I know good skins when I see them!' he retorted, winking significantly. It delighted him to be picked on, especially by women. Like a spoiled child, he craved attention of any sort.

The women scraped and sewed skins, rolled and smoked

cigarettes, continuing such badinage and gossip until the nightly dance. The men talked about their dogs, their hunting, and what they would bargain for at the trading post when they reached it.

My own thoughts wandered through a labyrinth of blurry images surrounding these people whom I might never see again and my friends at Cambridge Bay and the Mission at Bathurst Inlet. For some reason my most recurrent thoughts were of the family of Nokadlak and, in particular, of his daughter Naoyak, my little godchild.

15

GOODBYE TO CAMBRIDGE BAY

I had never built a boat of any kind before, but now I had no alternative. Scotty Moore needed his jolly-boat often to visit the RCMP Station across Cambridge Bay and also to empty his nets. I had my own nets to look after, and seals to hunt for my dogs. So I decided to build a skiff.

The only lumber I could find was some old planking that served as shelves in my fish-house. I stacked the dozen bundles of dried salmon and lake trout on the floor (there were about a hundred fish in each bundle) and took out the boards. They were ten inches wide and fifteen feet long running the length of the storage room. With a handsaw I ripped some of them into three equal strips and used these for framing a fourteen-foot flat-bottomed craft.

All went well until I came to shaping the bow. Then I realized there was no way of steaming the planks so as to bend them without breaking. Mixing imagination with a little common sense, I sawed halfway through the bow end of the three-quarter-inch planks at intervals of an inch. The job was slow and laborious but it did the trick. I was able to shape the planks at will, and as I did so the cracks contracted, seized, and held as if the boards were whole.

I had bought six dollars' worth of nails, caulking, and paint from Scotty's post. And that—apart from my sweat and toil—was the total cost of the good skiff *Santa Maria*. I gave her this name because she needed divine intervention to keep her from capsizing. I found this out the very first time I floated her with Kunak's help while Constable Ray Stewart, Scotty, and his helper watched the proceedings with frank amusement. Only the well-balanced oars I had painstakingly whittled from two-by-fours saved the launching ceremony as I rowed uncertainly into the bay while my friends yelled encouragement from the shore.

Speckled with ice floes, the water was so calm and inviting that I kept rowing towards the opening of the bay. Suddenly the bow of a low, slender craft appeared around the rocky point and Constable Tom Garland waved to me from his canoe. An Eskimo was reclining behind Tom. He held no paddle and seemed to be resting.

'Allo, mon vieux!' Tom hailed me as we drew closer.

I hardly recognized Tom's helper, Uttak. Deathly pale, he sat propped up by sleeping bags, his face thin and immobile, his eyes dull and apparently unseeing.

'It's good to see you, Tom. But what's wrong with Uttak? He looks like a ghost.'

'Uttak cut his hand opening a seal, and blood-poisoning set in. Just look at it!'

Uttak's arm was an awful sight. We hurried him to shore, took him to his shack, and left him with wife and children while I heated water and prepared to incise the wound. Tom shed his parka and karlik in favour of his uniform, and I got another shock. He had lost so much weight that his sunburned skin hung on his tall, bony frame like a wet raincoat on a hanger.

'Tom', I said, managing a smile, 'how did you pick up the clerical look?'

'To tell you the truth, Father, I've been in frozen hell.'

'Where's that?'

'Well, I went to Perry River. There I met some natives from MacAlpine Lake who told me about a murder in their camp. I decided to go there with them to investigate. As luck would have it, we hit soft snow all the way plus terrific weather. Snow, wind, bitter cold, more snow—you know, the whole works. It was so bad that I had to walk ahead of the dogs, wallowing in the mush for about eighty miles.'

Tom paused to sip hot tea and take a bite of buttered bread that Ray Stewart had prepared for him before resuming his narrative. 'The fellow I was after had supposedly shot his father because he found him whipping his mother. By the time we reached the lake camp he was gone and nobody could tell me where. I had no time to waste. The snow was melting. I hurried back to the coast to survey the camps of Sherman Inlet. It wasn't long before I regretted this move. I hadn't brought all my winter clothes along and now I paid for my optimism. Snow fell and drifted day after day. Even with my primus stove going it was freezing in the tent.

'When the weather cleared for a few days I surveyed the entire inlet. There were thousands of caribou. Seals were few, but Uttak managed to shoot a couple. That was when he cut his hand. The infection spread to his elbow, then to his shoulder. I had to take care of everything for both of us. A southeaster came along and melted the snow on the land and on the ice, too. We were in water up to our knees. Two of the dogs died from the continuous soaking. That was the kind of luck that followed me all the way.'

'I remember that when you started out you were going as far as Back River and then inland to Bathurst. And you wanted me to go with you. No-one would have found our bones.'

'I know it sounds crazy now, Father, but at the time I was so tired of this place that I really didn't care.'

'Well, if you're ready, the scalpel is, and so am I. I hope Uttak can stand the pain.'

'After what he's been through already, this will be a relief to him. Let's go, Doctor Kildare!'

Surrounded by his wife and three children, Uttak was moaning dreadfully. We asked the frightened woman to send the youngsters out to play. Tom stood by with the basin of hot water and soap.

'What are you going to do with me, Fala?' Uttak muttered defensively.

'I'd like to help you, Uttak. Let me wash your hand and take care of the wound. You'll soon feel better if you do.'

'Father will empty the bad stuff you have in your arm,' said Tom.

'I want to die!' the poor fellow cried out. 'I want to drown in the river! I want to sink to the bottom and lie dead! Can't you see I am ready to die?'

'You are *not* going to die!' Tom said with emphasis. 'Father will relieve your pain and you will be well again.'

'Tom,' I said in English, 'will you please put the basin on the floor and hold the patient down by his shoulders.'

Ignoring his protests, I washed the week-old grime off Uttak's hand and arm. He did not jerk them away, although he kept mumbling: 'Let me slip into the water and drown. I want to die!'

With mercurochrome I swabbed the dirty grey wound in the palm of his hand. I was all set now. 'The scalpel, please, Tom.'

The sharp instrument sank like a stick in deep mud. The pus rushed out, repulsively thick and smelly. Uttak didn't even wince. He groaned only when I applied pressure along the arm to help drain the matter.

'Pass the gauze, please. I'll pack a drainage in the cut.' Over the gauze I placed a pad of cotton wool and bandaged the hand. Uttak was quiet now. I was hoping he would doze off.

'Better let him sleep and rest all he wants to,' Tom whispered to Uttak's wife as we left, her thanks ringing in our ears.

A week passed and Uttak began to show a little improvement. His wife fussed over him and didn't rush him and he no longer asked to be allowed to die. I visited him daily to check and change his dressings and give him encouragement.

One fine day, as I was getting ready to row over to his shack, I was startled to hear the unmistakable drone of an aeroplane engine. I dashed outside and beheld a seaplane land gracefully in the bay and taxi towards the Mission. I ran down to the water and was soon able to see my Bishop waving to me from the plane's open door.

The pilot did not want to take a chance on damaging the pontoons and stopped the plane a little offshore. I rowed out to it in my skiff. The Bishop—a big, stout, dignified man—climbed out of the plane onto the pontoon, then stepped jauntily into the skiff. No respecter of high personages, the temperamental craft dipped crazily, the Bishop tottered momentarily, and I had a lightning vision of us floundering in the cold water of the bay. But I somehow managed to hold on to the pontoon with one hand and pull my guest down with the other. The *Santa Maria* steadied.

'You were wise to choose such a good name for your fickle boat, Father!' His Excellency said, quickly regaining his composure.

Ruffled and embarrassed, I tried to cover up my discomfiture with an excuse: 'My apologies, Monseigneur. I should have warned you to be careful. I made the skiff hurriedly and without skill.'

He grinned back to put me at ease: 'I can see you made it for a light-footed tightrope walker, not for an elephant like me! I hope you will have less trouble with the pilot when you go back to pick him up later.'

We gained the shore without further incident and I invited the Bishop to see my shack. As we walked up to it, he said: 'You know, I can stay only a few hours here. I just dropped in to look over this place and see how you were doing. I'm afraid I'll have to move you back to Bathurst. Father Adam is in poor shape and I'd like you to take over the Mission.'

'What is wrong with Father Adam, Monseigneur?'

'I believe he froze his lungs last winter during an inland trip. He is under doctor's orders to enter a hospital at the earliest opportunity.'

'What should I do with all my equipment and the remaining supplies?'

'Sell everything, or whatever you can dispose of. I have other plans for the opening of a new mission in this territory."

I warmed at the prospect of returning to Bathurst. I was tired of the endless cold and wind, the unvarying landscape, and the daily struggle for food at Cambridge Bay. I was looking forward to the comforts of the Mission I had helped build and to seeing some of my old friends like Nokadlak and his family.

Before he boarded the plane the Bishop gave me his final instructions for the following year: 'I don't know very much about the Barren Land, Father, but the merest look at it is enough to convince me of its hopelessness. Try to learn all you can about the natives at Bathurst and the other groups not yet contacted inland. But be careful not to undertake any long trip unless you find it absolutey necessary. This land is big and cruel, and priests like you are few and far between.'

By the time the Hudson's Bay Company boat arrived two weeks later I had sold several bags of dried beans, rice, corn-meal, and two tons of coal to Scotty, had packed my personal belongings, and was all set to leave Cambridge Bay.

'What about your skiff, Father?' asked Scotty when I came to say goodbye.

'Well, if you'd like to handle it for me, Scotty, I'd be grate-ful.'

'I know my helper wouldn't mind buying it, but you'll have to wait till next winter for his payment.'

'I'll be satisfied with five foxes.'

'That's a fair price, Father. Your skiff's certainly worth it.'

The *Margaret A.* was a flat-bottomed vessel of one hundred tons, originally built for the shallow waters of the Mackenzie River. When the *Fort James* was crushed by ice in August 1937 she was pressed into the thousand-mile run between the Mackenzie Delta and Perry River moving supplies and per-sonnel between the HBC posts on the way. Somehow or other she always managed to escape the iron grip of the Arctic ice and was known far and wide as a lucky ship.

All this knowledge comforted me, but my main concern at the moment was to persuade her skipper to take aboard my team of nine dogs. I asked Scotty to introduce me to Captain James McCormick. We found him in his cabin drinking coffee and checking the bills of lading. He was a small man, shorter even than I, redheaded and with a ruddy complexion. I was soon to learn that his temper was as fiery as his hair.

'Have a nice trip, Captain?' I asked politely in all in-nocence.

'A nice trip? Huh! It was a hell of a trip! I take a chance every time I come to this blasted country of yours. A nice trip? We got stuck in the ice, got lashed by hailstorms and snow squalls. In the open sea it was even worse. Wind day and night. Tremendous waves over the starboard bow. And, to top it all, this crazy pilot of mine gets drunk and falls in the forehold, damaging his precious ribs. Now the bastard's not fit to take me down to Bathurst; and if he was, I'm not so sure I'd trust him in those treacherous waters anyway.' The skipper swore a lurid oath, his reddish face turning purple.

Scotty saw the opening while I was still recoiling from the captain's language. 'Captain, Father here came to ask you for passage to his Mission at Bathurst. I wouldn't be surprised if he could take over for your pilot.'

McCormick looked me over carefully, interestedly. His colour was back to normal, his voice level. 'What do you know about Bathurst Inlet, Father?'

'I've been up and down that stretch a dozen times, Skipper. Both in my whale-boat visiting the camps and, of course, by dog-team in the winter. I think I know my way around the inlet as well as any white man.'

'You sound pretty sure of yourself. I like that. Tell you what: I'll take you in free of charge. How's that—agreed?'

'Certainly, Skipper. Only I might as well tell you that I'm not alone. I have nine dogs with me.'

I fully expected an avalanche of profanity to descend about my ears. But I was a potential pilot, the only one in sight. And James McCormick was no fool. 'That's another story, Father. There's not much room on deck, and anyway there are no spare hands to look after the cleaning.'

'Oh, I can take care of the cleaning myself. I'm quite used to that sort of thing. And the dogs could be tied anywhere along the railing. They won't damage a thing. I'll vouch for that.'

'I just hope you're right. We should be finished unloading tomorrow. Bring your dogs aboard in the afternoon.'

While I muttered my thanks, the Captain turned on Scotty. 'Get the hell outa here, you old rascal, before I lose my temper!'

'O.K., Skipper,' Scotty laughed back, 'but don't forget our party tonight. We've got a few bottles of rum to assault and the best company in the world!'

'God help you if you don't make it wonderful for me. I'll tear the hide off you!'

Scotty was still chuckling as we went ashore to help with the unloading. Kunak and Scotty's helper were working like beavers carrying sacks of coal, lumber, and crates of merchandise. Their indefatigable industry amazed the crew.

We had a cheerful farewell party that night, but I could not escape the melancholy parting at sailing time next day. I can still see Tom, Ray, and Scotty standing on the improvised jetty, superimposed on empty oil barrels, trying to look cheerful as we pulled away.

How different it was with Kunak, Uttak, Scotty's helper, and their families. The Kablunak had somewhere to go and that was that. No regrets, not even a goodbye. The People Beyond are too tough for such sentimentality.

16

NAOYAK AGAIN

Dease Strait was free of ice, but its current and the prevailing northwester were dead against us. The *Margaret A.* ploughed grimly on, driven by her diesels and the twin screws.

When the regular pilot, a tall, gaunt Scandinavian, appeared on deck for the first time, Captain McCormick introduced me. 'Ole Johnson, here's our new pilot, Father Raymond. He is taking us to Bathurst, so you can rest your broken bones.'

Ole regarded me with horror. 'Another preacher, eh? How do you expect us to have any luck on this tub, Skipper? You should know better. A preacher always brings a curse to a ship. What happened to me when we took on that minister two weeks ago? I twisted my ribs, nearly killed myself falling on the railings. And what kind of weather did we get? Snow, wind, and ice all the way.'

'You don't even remember what hit you,' McCormick retorted scornfully. 'You were so full of whisky you don't know where or when you fell. You can bet your rubber boots I'll not take a chance on you any more!'

Ole's towering shoulders seemed to slump as he slunk away below. 'He knows where he stands with me now,' the Captain said. 'And don't worry, he won't bother you none. He may be an alcoholic, but he's not a bad guy at heart.'

The *Margaret A.* took the heavy seas in her stride, threading her way between numberless islets and past dangerous reefs. I was in familiar waters now and gave my directions to the helmsman without hesitation. The Skipper seemed content, and even Ole forgot his fears and misgivings. 'You're different from those dung peddlers in your trade I've met in my travels,' he confided in the pilot house when we were within sight of Bathurst Inlet.

'Wait and see, Ole. We aren't through yet.'

As we neared Burnside Harbour at noon on the second day, violent westerly gales whipped up mountainous waves that cascaded over the deck, fore and aft, drenching my dogs and tossing them about. I was sorry for them, but I could not leave the pilot house. At the height of the storm we finally made the entrance to Burnside. A mere three miles separated us from the trading post and Mission buildings, but the Skipper wisely decided not to attempt a landing. Instead he ordered the anchor dropped in the lee of Koagiuk Island.

During the next three days we rode at anchor there while I listened to an indignant monologue from McCormick. Condensed and expurgated, it went something like this: 'It's depressing here beyond human endurance. Here we are, still in August, but look at that dark sky, the snow, the freezing temperature, and that unearthly wind. How can you stand it, Father? Everything seems empty, ugly, disgusting to me. Do you think the wind will ever stop? I certainly don't want to be stranded in this godforsaken place the whole winter. I'd go crazy!'

I could not blame the Skipper. Ahead of him lay a thousand miles through Coronation Gulf and Amundsen Gulf, and it was getting late in the season for the Arctic. Lakes and rivers were already freezing, and ice floes would be drifting towards him, blown by stiff, icy westerly winds.

Towards noon of the third day the gale abated and McCormick brightened considerably. 'The wind is still strong, but I'm itching to take a chance. Do you think we can reach the post without drifting on the rocks?'

'That'll depend on your speed, Skipper. You'll have the shoreline and shallow water to port, and the wind and waves to drive you ashore to starboard. If you can maintain your speed you should make it. The only other thing to remember is the narrow channel near the post, with a sandbar on either side.'

'Can you find the channel?'

'Yes, but then you'll have to slow her down.'

McCormick considered the dilemma at length. 'Let's go!' he snapped. 'If anything goes wrong, I'll drop anchor.'

Everything went wrong from the start. The wind kept pushing the *Margaret A.* to shore. The skipper rang for more speed. She paid beautifully, but it was too fast for me. I could not locate the deep waters of the narrow channel. Standing on deck in front of the pilot house, I made a sign to slow her down. The skipper roared back: 'Don't you see? If I slow down we won't make it!'

'Well, keep going, Skipper. I'll try my best.'

I did, but it was no use. We struck the sandy bottom portside and stuck fast. McCormick left the wheel and rushed out as if possessed by all the evil spirits of the Barren Land. 'By heaven, Father, where do you think you're taking us? To hell? What if it takes me the whole winter to dig her out of this blasted sandbar?'

Ole Johnson immediately revived his favourite superstition. 'I told you, Old Man, these spell-binders with reverse collars bring nothing but bad luck to a ship. The devil haunts them wherever they go. I say toss him overboard to the devil and be done with him!'

McCormick, who had been briefly speechless with rage, ordered fore and aft anchors dropped and then resumed his blasphemous tirade. Most of it was wasted on me, for I was watching a whale-boat heading in our direction from the post. She rose and dipped, disappearing from sight altogether in the troughs of the rolling waves, rising to the crests, and falling again. I could not recognize her two oarsmen, but the helmsman was unmistakably Father Adam.

'There's your rescue, Skipper!' I said hopefully, pointing to the approaching craft.

'Not another preacher by any chance?' said Ole.

Once aboard the *Margaret A.*, Father Adam took control of the situation. 'Skipper, send two men in my whale-boat to drop a spare anchor fifty yards aft of your ship and attach a cable to the winch. The tide is still in and that's the time to get her off.'

Unable to find fault with the reasoning, McCormick complied. He had both anchors hauled up and the winch put into action. With surprising ease the *Margaret A.* slid off the sand and was afloat again. Nonchalantly, as if he was accustomed to rescuing distressed vessels every day in the week, Father Adam guided her through the channel. We dropped anchor by the Hudson's Bay pontoon wharf and I was home.

I gathered up my dogs and thanked McCormick for the free passage. 'I'm sorry, Skipper, that I let you down in the home stretch.'

The Skipper had recovered himself. 'It was partly my fault,

Father. One must learn to take adversity in one's stride in the Arctic. And it is I who should thank you anyway.'

Father Adam and I hardly had a minute together aboard the *Margaret A.* But in the bright, warm kitchen of the Mission we made up for the lost time of the past two years over a cup of coffee. I learned that, besides chilling his lungs, he was almost sure that he had contracted tuberculosis from an Eskimo girl he had nursed in her father's iglu the winter before.

He also told me that Nokadlak and Kakagun were in the neighbourhood and that little Naoyak was now living with her prospective father-in-law.

In the evening Father Adam embarked on the *Margaret A.* over Ole's shocked protests. As he headed out towards the islands of Bathurst Inlet I turned to go back to the Mission. I had taken only a few steps when I heard the voice of Ed Kennett, the HBC trader, who emerged from the pile of freight he had been examining.

'Let's go over to my place, Father,' he said affably. 'We need a good drink after all this excitement.'

Ed had originally come to the Eastern Arctic as a lad of eighteen, apprenticed to a Hudson's Bay trader. For the next twenty years he moved from post to post until he found himself a wife among the Krangmalek tribe and settled down at Burnside. Ed always seemed happy with Ivarlo and liked to say that he didn't know of any white girl who could stand the loneliness of the Barren Land as she could.

My first move was to prepare my quarters for the rigorous months ahead. I put up the storm windows and caulked every joint as best I could. From the shore I brought up all the supplies left there by *Our Lady of Lourdes* a few days before and stacked them in the little store-house. The ground was barely covered with snow and my dogs had a hard time dragging the sled up the slope. Their harnesses and tow-lines were so torn that I had to spend hours in mending them.

Then there was the problem of fresh water. The choice lay between the Burnside River and the several tiny lakes across the channel. It was a good two miles by boat to the mouth of the river and about a quarter of a mile to the nearest lake. The choice was obvious, but the little lakes were now frozen and it meant cutting blocks of ice with a saw. I was filing the long cross-cut saw in preparation when Kakagun and Nokadlak rowed up in one of the Mission's skiffs.

'Fala,' said Kakagun, 'fish are starting up the lakes. We have brought you many fish for your dogs.'

This was payment for the use of the Mission nets. I thanked him and followed my friends to the boat to unload it. I was not surprised that the 'many' fish turned out to be about fifty salmon, lake trout, and whitefish—a mere handful from the week's catch. It would be enough to feed my dogs for three or four days, but no more. Yet the entire winter—all nine months of it—was staring me in the face, and I did not want to experiment with the day-to-day existence of the improvident People Beyond.

As we sipped tea in the Mission I said to my friends: 'I need ice for the winter. Will one of you help me cut it if I pay you for the work?'

'I'll help,' Nokadlak replied unhesitatingly.

'I'll have to return to the camp and take care of the nets,' Kakagun excused himself. 'But when I come to visit you again I'll bring you a load of ice on my krammotik.'

Kakagun rowed off to Kubiartovik Bay five miles away. With Nokadlak I crossed the channel in my jolly-boat and walked the remaining fifty yards to a small frozen lake, carrying the necessary tools. It was only mid-September, but pure glare ice covered the lake to a depth of six or seven inches. So transparent was it that we could clearly see the sandy bottom a dozen feet below. Nokadlak took the axe, walked a few yards offshore, and chipped a hole in the ice. '*Talva, inertok*. Here, it's ready!' I stuck the end of the long saw into the hole and cut two lines at right angles, like the baselines of a baseball diamond, each twenty feet long. Two feet away from the home plate, along the fourth baseline, Nokadlak made another hole, and I sawed a line parallel to the first baseline. Nokadlak followed behind, chipping two-foot-square blocks between the two parallel lines and picking them up with ice tongs. This manoeuvre cleared a lane two feet wide, enabling me to saw a grid of lines parallel to the fourth baseline at two-foot intervals. With a knock of the axe Nokadlak freed the squares, took them out, and piled them up on shore.

Six hours of steady, unhurried work later, there were enough ice blocks on shore to last me through the winter. We carried a few of them to the boat and rowed back. The rest of the blocks would wait until I was ready to come and fetch them by dog-team.

'You should stay with me tonight, Nokadlak. Tomorrow I'll go with you to Kubiartovik and set up some more nets.'

'*Illa*, Fala. I'll eat and sleep here. I am too tired to return to camp now.'

After we had eaten I asked Nokadlak about his family. Full of food and unaccustomed to the warmth of my kitchen, he became languid and was not very interested in my questions. His answers were automatic. '*Namaktun*. They are fine. All in good health. Even Manerathiak still eats and sleeps like a young woman.'

He was muttering something about his son Kudnanak having grown into a good hunter when his head dropped on his chest and he dozed off.

I left him to his dreams and his snores and went over to the trading post. In the dim light of a coal-oil lamp Ed Kennett

was restocking the shelves with newly-arrived merchandise.
I told him what I had in mind.

'Sure, I'll be glad to look after your dogs while you're
gone, Father. You just fish as long as you need to and don't
give them a thought.'

'Thanks, Ed. I knew I could count on you to help me out.
And now I'm going to bed for a rest before I fall asleep on
my feet.'

Early next morning in a flurry of snow Nokadlak helped
me pack my tent, sleeping bags, food, ammunition, rifles, and
fishing nets. The sky was almost dark and the damp cold
made me wish I had stayed in bed.

Two hours later forbidding bluffs rose steeply before us to
a tableland several hundred feet high, creating the illusion
that the channel ended right there. A sharp turn of the wheel,
however, brought us around the point into a large bay. There,
sandwiched between huge boulders that screened them from
the wind, stood my friends' tents.

A howl arose from the resting dogs. Three women, a youth,
and a little girl walked to the water to greet us. Nokadlak's
wife Angivrana and old grandmother Manerathiak smiled
their welcome as we shook hands. 'You must be Nalvana,' I
said to the other young woman, extending my hand to her.

'*Nalvanaoyunga illa.* Indeed I'm Nalvana.' Smilingly she
bent to the little girl beside her. 'And this is Naoyak, my
adopted daughter.'

'Naoyak! Last time I saw her she was a tiny baby just born!'
I patted her head, reflecting on that memorable event of two
years ago. She looked up at me, her small mouth pursed as
if to say: 'I don't remember you.'

'Naoyak has been sick lately,' Nalvana said, 'but I gave her
milk from my breast and now she is better. She follows me
around as a fawn does the caribou doe.' Her fondness for the

child was apparent from the way her eyes watched Naoyak's every move.

I had met this striking woman the first year I came to the Central Arctic at a camp on the shores of Lake Kiluitok, south of Burnside. I remembered her as a thin, strongly built young woman with an extremely delicate face of light complexion. She had then had two husbands.

One of them, of course, was my friend Kakagun, the big, dark, restless man of about thirty years, commonly acknowledged as the best hunter among the Krangmalit. The other was Niviksana, an effervescent young man with a baby-face whose protruding cheek bones were covered with a skin so red that I wondered if he used rouge. The two men appeared to be good friends. There was no strife between them, not even a harsh word. They had apparently reached a perfect understanding and were quite content to share Nalvana on an equal basis.

Several weeks elapsed before I saw Kakagun and Nalvana for the second time. 'Where is Niviksana?' I asked conversationally.

'Something happened to him inland and he died,' said Kakagun in his usual deep, dull voice. The news caught me by surprise. '*Mamianak*. That's too bad,' I murmured. 'Niviksana was well the last time I saw him here. Some kind of illness must have killed him in short time.'

Kakagun's eyes narrowed. '*Nauna, naunartok*. I don't know. Who knows what it might have been?' It was the polite Eskimo way of telling me to mind my own business.

I had not seen Nalvana since that day. Outwardly, at any rate, she had not changed. She was still stately, still unusually attractive for a Krangmalek woman. As we walked up to the tents I asked her about Kakagun. 'He is visiting the nets with my son, Kivgalo. They will be back soon. Come in and have tea.' Little Naoyak followed Nalvana into Kakagun's tent. Accompanied by Angivrana, Manerathiak, and young Kudnanak, Nokadlak disappeared into his own tent.

Caribou skins served as walls and even the floor in the tent, giving it an intimate and cosy atmosphere. The air was fragrant with burning dwarf-willow branches glowing in a ten-gallon oil drum through whose top Kakagun had attached a rusty old stovepipe he picked up at the trading post.

I squatted on the furs while Nalvana put some ice in the kettle and placed it on the improvised stove. Before long, perhaps sensing the boiling kettle, in walked Kakagun with his son Kivgalo.

'How's the fishing?' I inquired.

'The water is cold, but the fish are coming in great numbers,' Kakagun said. Kivgalo studied me for a moment, then said to his father: '*Kablunak tamna, eh!* That's a white man!' '*Illa, Kablunaoyok,*' Kakagun smiled.

There was no mistaking the six-year-old's origin. With his long black hair still in bangs and his finely etched features, he looked strikingly like his mother. But the red cheeks were Niviksana's. He came over and sat down beside me like an old friend. Nalvana poured us tea and when she sat down Naoyak asked for her breast. Kivgalo pointed to the little girl sucking contentedly. 'That's Naoyak.'

'Yes, I know, Kivgalo. Do you play with her?'

'*Immana.* Certainly not. She is too small. She is like a new-born pup.' Naoyak gave no hint that she overheard or resented the insult. She was too busy enjoying her drink.

'I could catch more fish, Fala, if the nets were not so full of driftmoss,' said Kakagun thoughtfully. 'They should be taken ashore and cleaned out.'

'I've brought along some new ones. I'll ask Nokadlak to help me set them, and then you can pull up the old nets.'

Nokadlak and Kudnanak had taken apart a 30-30 rifle and were cleaning it assiduously. Angivrana was stirring a boiling cauldron of fish heads while Manerathiak was scraping a caribou skin. So intent were they on their jobs that none of them noticed my entry.

'*Kranorikpise?* How are you?' I announced myself.

Slightly startled but smiling broadly, Angivrana spoke for the family: '*Namaktugut,* Fala. We are all fine.'

'When you finish cleaning your *pitiksi,* Nokadlak, would you set up my nets?'

'Kudnanak can help you, Fala. While you are gone I will pitch your tent.'

'Have some fish heads. It will be cold on the water,' said Angivrana. 'Eat and warm your blood before you go.' She dished up a pan of salmon heads and placed it on the floor in the centre where everyone could help himself. Kudnanak got off the iglek, went to the door, and called out to Kakagun's family: '*Niarkrotoritse! Niarkrotoritse!* Come and eat heads!'

From a youngster of twelve he had changed rapidly into a tall youth since I saw him two and a half years ago. His face was burned brown by outdoor living, yet wore a constant smile, as if he enjoyed everything he did. Proud of the man-sized assignment his father had given him, Kudnanak quickly changed into his sealskin garments and followed me to the boat. We left my tent and grub-boxes on shore and pushed off. Kudnanak leaned over the bow while my oars propelled the heavy craft towards the head of the bay. '*Ikalulik.* There are fish here,' he said, his eyes searching the dark blue waters. Then excitedly: '*Amiunertun!* All kinds of them!'

I feathered the oars and looked over the gunwale. Myriads of fish were heading the same direction as we—towards the creek. It was difficult to reconcile this superabundance of life in the sea with the surrounding Barren Land, largely void of living creatures. I recalled that when I got my first taste of the Arctic winter I expected to find most creatures in the sea, the rivers, and the lakes destroyed. That winter, as

I browsed through the meagre library of the trading post, I learned that explorers like Nansen and Sverdrup discovered living animal or plant organisms at various depths in the polar basin. By dragging nets along the ocean floor as deep as two thousand fathoms, or sinking them under the ice, they often brought up hauls of small crustaceans, planktons, and worms in great variety. Moved at random by the strong polar currents, these provided an inexhaustible supply of food for the seals and fish of the sea—a supply far greater than in the inland lakes and streams.

Some of these riches of the north now swarmed below our boat. As I watched them with irresistible fascination I could not help wondering why the People Beyond should starve part of the year in the midst of such plenty.

'Kudnanak, which do you prefer—fish or caribou meat?'

He took his eyes off the water and stared at me in astonishment. *'Tuktuk kranok!* Caribou of course!'

'Why?'

'Horlikia? Why? Why? Because fish is a woman's game.'

It was as direct and as true an answer to the Krangmalek paradox as I was ever to receive. Fishing was a recreation, not to be taken seriously by a manly hunter. Inuk fished only to supplement his meat reserves—just in case the caribou hunting did not come up to his expectations. Even at the height of summer, when fish left the lakes on their way to the sea, he did not bother much with them. He greatly preferred to go after the caribou. His woman, however, sometimes took advantage of the two-week break-up on the frozen rivers and creeks when fish rushed down to the sea. Such fish as she caught she dried out in the sun and wind or left for winter travelling.

Now that the summer was over and the fish were mustering their legions around the sandbars, fjords, and channels to launch their all-out migratory attack, the natives paid little heed to the incredible amount of food swimming under their very noses. Like young Kudnanak, they watched and laughed at the finny hordes driven by timeless instinct to the peaceful spawning grounds of the inland lakes before the freeze-up.

I asked Kudnanak what kind of fish he liked best. 'Salmon and lake trout. But I soon get tired of them,' he said candidly.

We beached the boat near the mouth of the creek and I tied the end of a bundle of net to a boulder a few feet away from the lapping waves. There was no need to worry about the tide submerging it, for the highest tides in this part of the Arctic rarely reach four feet. As I rowed away slowly from the shore, Kudnanak unwound the net and let it drop overboard. Weighted with rocks every five feet, it sank until the floats I had made from salvaged freight crates and attached to the main twine held it buoyant. When the net ran out thirty yards, Kudnanak tied the free end to a large rock he had picked up on the beach and dumped it in as an anchor.

At intervals of about a hundred yards we set up three more nets in the same fashion, grading the mesh from six to three-and-a-half inches in that order. Following the shore-line in search of creeks, some of the fish were bound to get caught by their gills in a mesh of their size. Small fry less than three inches in circumference at the gills did not interest us.

We rowed back to camp to warm ourselves, eat, and rest. Three hours later we went out to the nets again. Starting at the shore end of each net, Kudnanak and I took turns at the bow, lifting the net out of the water and picking the fish out of it.

The air was cold, the water icy. My back ached from continual bending, my fingers were numb from repeated immersions. Handling the dripping nets and slippery, cold fish offered little relief. I was ready to cry. Then it would be the end of the net and Kudnanak's turn at the next net. He took the ordeal stoically, without a word, without a whimper. He was a hunter now, and hunters are not moved to tears by such ordinary inconveniences—not even when the fish weighed fifty pounds and he had to haul it up, hold it between his seal-clad legs, unhook its bulk from the mesh to free it, and toss it behind with the others.

Not all the fish were as big as that, of course, nor were they all of the same variety. There were fat *pikuktok* or hunchbacks, for instance. Covered with silvery scales, some of them were so roly-poly that their twenty pounds took the shape of oversized rugby balls. Common were the *aogak* or tomcods, possibly relatives of the cod but not nearly so nutritious. They are not the best of marine food, but they can be caught through the ice all winter and constitute, in fact, the last resort of starving natives in the Barren Land. But most plentiful of all were *kapielik* or whitefish, which literally went to the dogs because they were infested with a worm-like parasite that even the People Beyond shun like a taboo. There were also several varieties of salmon I could not identify.

'What's this fish called, Kudnanak?'

'That's the *anakhe,* Fala. It is full of oil.'

'What kind of oil?'

'The kind that is good for a hunter or a dog when they have been starving.'

'And what's this red one here with the white belly?'

'That's one of those I like, Fala. It is the *ivitaruk.* Sometimes in the big lakes they get so big that there is enough meat in one fish for twenty hunters. This is not a big one.'

'Why do you like to eat the ivitaruk?'

'Why? Because its red meat is rich and tasty. You will like it, too, when my mother cooks it.'

'Right now I could really do justice to a nice sirloin steak, young fellow,' I thought silently. Aloud I said: 'Let's finish this net, then, and go back to camp so that your mother can give us a treat.'

17

THE SPEAKING OF THE FISH

Perched on a big flat boulder, her old eyes half closed, Manerathiak watched us bring in the fish. Her mitted hands half-
way up a walking stick and her chin resting on her right arm,
she kept up a barely audible stream of unintelligible mutterings. At the risk of frightening the spirits with whom
she was conversing, I shouted: 'Manerathiak, look at all the
fish we caught!'

'I can see,' she said in that worn, flat, lifeless voice of hers,
without looking up. 'Kablunak knows how to catch fish. He
is not so stupid at sea as I thought he would be.'

'It is easy with nets.'

'Yes, I know, Fala. When I was a young woman I used to
make the *kubiak* with the sinew of caribou and musk-ox. It
took many days. Now Nokadlak can get a white man's kubiak
at the trading post all ready for fishing.'

'Without nets I could not feed my dogs. I cannot fish or
hunt very much in the winter, like Inuk. I have to travel, see
the People Beyond, talk to them, and help them.'

'Do you fish like a Kablunak or an Inuk?'

'What do you mean?'

'Do you kill the fish with a stick when you take them out of the water?'

'No, I just throw them into the boat.'

'What do you do to fish when you catch them, Kudnanak?' she asked her grandson.

'I hit them over the head with *anaotak*.'

'That's what I mean, Fala. Kudnanak fishes like Inuk. He knows that the spirits of the land speak through the mouths of the fish. They speak evil, and they wish evil on those who hear them.'

'I'd like to agree with you, Manerathiak, but I cannot. We white people do not believe that the spirits of the land bring evil to human beings.'

'A man may be born white and still be stupid!' The old woman slid off the rock slowly, stood up creakily, painfully, and shuffled off.

When all the fish were spread out on the frozen ground and Kudnanak went back to his tent, I answered Nalvana's tea call. Little Naoyak was whimpering in Kakagun's husky arms.

'What's the matter, little one?' I asked her.

She continued to sob softly.

'She has a stomach-ache, Fala,' Nalvana said.

'Did she eat too much today?'

'No, she has not eaten since morning. She won't eat even when I offer her my breast.'

'She seemed all right this morning. When did her stomach-ache start?'

'Last night she did not sleep well and she had foam in her mouth. When you came this morning she was fine. After you went to the nets she had pains.'

I touched the little girl's head. It felt hot. 'I'll be back soon,' I said and went over to my tent which Nokadlak had pitched close to a large boulder, perhaps twenty paces away. I returned with my compact medicine kit and placed the thermometer in Naoyak's mouth while I looked her over. Her tummy was swollen a little, but there was no tenderness nor any other signs or symptoms. The mercury thermometer confirmed my guess that the temperature was abnormal. I took a small can of condensed milk out of my pocket and asked Nalvana to give me a cup of hot water. I poured some of the milk into it and set it down on the iglek. Out of the medicine bag I extracted a bottle of castor oil and a teaspoon.

'Give this to Naoyak to drink, Kakagun,' I said, handing him a spoonful. 'Good. Now another one. Fine. Naoyak is a good little girl. Now she can have some of this warm, sweet milk.'

There were tears in Naoyak's eyes, but when she looked at me she was smiling bravely. 'You will feel better soon,' I said, 'and tomorrow I will take you with me in my boat and show you the prettiest fish in the sea.'

Kakagun did not seem to be impressed with my internal medicine or outward confidence. He remained silent, a worried look on his face. As I went out I said to Nalvana: 'Let me know if Naoyak has a bowel movement during the night. Right now she should sleep.'

The evening air was cold and damp. It began to snow. Rather than sit in my unheated tent I decided to spend the rest of the evening with Nokadlak and his family. The dark waves lapped softly on the pebbly shore. Apart from that, all was quiet. The silence hung unbroken in Nokadlak's dimly lit tents as if everyone was stultified by the oppressive thoughts of winter's approach. Only the slow, dull-sounding scraping of a caribou skin by grandmother Manerathiak gave life to the gloomy scene. In her allotted corner the old woman squatted on a thoroughly worn parka, puffing over her bone scraper. 'A little controversy might enliven them,' I thought to myself.

To Nokadlak I said casually: 'I was telling Manerathiak I do not believe that fish can talk to man.'

'Our forefathers believe it to be true and so do we,' said my friend.

'White people know only one Spirit and He does not talk to men through animals. He is always good and never wishes evil to anyone.'

'May be, may be. But our land is full of evil spirits. Summer and winter they are always around us, on land and at sea. At night they whisper in the sky. Sometimes they show their displeasure. They mislead us when we travel, they chase away our game, they starve and freeze our bodies. Whatever you may say, Fala, we have many, many evil spirits with us.'

'The Land Beyond is different from the land where I come from, Nokadlak. It is always warm there, dark days are unknown, and so is hunger.'

'If your land is so beautiful, why did you come here?'

'To tell you, your family, and your friends about the Good Spirit.'

Manerathiak could hold back her mutterings no longer. 'What does Kablunak say? What is his talk all about? I should indeed be ashamed to lie here, old and useless, weak as a child. I will laugh no more, for my mother and father and my old friends are gone to the land of the dead. A strange fear has come upon me. Don't you know my grandchild is sick? The evil spirits are after Naoyak because Kablunak has listened to the fish.'

Her sinister words roused Angivrana, and there was maternal anxiety in her voice: 'Kakagun should call the *tunrak* at Kiluitok. He has the power to cure. When Kudnanak was a little boy he became very sick. He was shaking, his eyes were rolling, he could not part his teeth. We had to pry his mouth open with a flat piece of wood. Nokadlak called the tunrak. He came and lay close to my child. The next day Kudnanak was able to eat again.'

'There you are, Kablunak. What did I tell you?' Manera-thiak mumbled triumphantly.

Having stirred my friends into consciousness, I let them carry the conversation while I relaxed and listened. It all added up to one thing: our spiritual beliefs were worlds apart, and indications were that they would so remain indefinitely.

Early the following morning I called on my little patient. Naoyak was about the same. I gave her another teaspoon of castor oil and told Nalvana to make her drink some broth. I noticed that Kakagun and Kivgalo were not there and asked Nalvana where they were.

'They've gone to Kiluitok. They left at daybreak on foot.'

She did not have to tell me that they would be back with the sorcerer.

The sun rose over the bluffs in the east when Kudnanak and I rowed out to the nets. It brought cheer to my young fishing partner and gave voice to the song in his heart:

> 'Ikraluk, ikraluk . . . Fish, fish! Am I such a fool
> To let you talk to me? Aya-ya-ya-a—
> You come from the darkness beneath
> To tell evil things to young and old—
> Children, men, and women. Aya-ya-ya-a.
> I'll not let you speak to me,
> For I am but a young man still
> Who does not have a woman. Aya-ya-ya-a.'

The plaintive melody re-echoed through the rocky cliffs as we tackled the nets, heavy with a big overnight catch.

Nokadlak was readying his dog-team when we returned to

camp. 'It is such a nice day I am going to hunt bear in the mountains near Ayapapartovik. Would you like to come, Fala?'

'Naoyak is not very well. I am going to wait till she gets better.'

'Then Kudnanak will come with me. Can you visit the nets alone, Fala?'

'I think I can. There is no wind. I'll take my time.'

The women were glad to see their men disappear among the boulders that dotted the valley of the Burnside River. Their absence meant more time for themselves. Angivrana and Manerathiak wasted none of it. They trooped over to Nalvana's tent, taking their sewing with them. Nalvana looked out and saw me gazing up the valley. 'Fala, you should have gone with Nokadlak.'

'There will be another bear hunt, Nalvana. I'd like to help Naoyak if I can. Besides, I have to look after my nets.'

'Come in, then. I'll make tea and you can eat with us,' she smiled.

I could see part of Naoyak's head in Nalvana's hood. There wasn't a sound out of her.

'How is she?' I asked.

'She is asleep. But her body is very hot.'

'Naoyak is sick because the Kablunak listened to the fish,' Manerathiak murmured persistently into her wrinkled chin. I sat down by the stove and pretended not to hear.

With her ulon Angivrana was cutting caribou fur trimmings on a small box shook. She fashioned squares, triangles, and circles out of the white belly fur, contrasting them with similar geometric designs of black summer fur. I was curious.

'Are you making trimmings for Nokadlak's parka?'

She laughed. '*Immana.* No. Such pieces are cut for a woman's parka. I am working for myself.'

Manerathiak cackled gleefully: 'Kablunak is like a child.

He has to learn our ways by asking silly questions.' The wide grin exposed her yellow teeth, worn down to the gums. They were perfect for the job at hand—chewing the soft, thin, delicate skins of caribou fawns to make them more supple still for the little girl's clothing.

'Fala belongs to another land where they have different parkas,' Nalvana said in my defence. With rare skill, characteristic of the Kiluitomeun group, she was making herself a pair of caribou slippers. No wonder the group got its name from *kiluitok* (meaning 'sewing in small stitches'), I thought to myself. Like Angivrana, she had cut up small pieces of black and white fur and was sewing them in a predetermined pattern that occasionally called for the insertion of red strips of scraped caribou skin.

'How did you tint the skin red?' I wasn't going to let Manerathiak's taunts prevent me from satisfying my curiosity.

'With soft pebbles I found on the beach. I crushed them and mixed them in seal oil,' Nalvana explained simply. Then, noting the boiling kettle, she stood up and went to the stove. '*Teetorluta*. Let's have tea!' she said.

As she filled the cups and passed them around, little Naoyak woke up crying. '*Teetorlanga*. I want tea,' she whimpered.

'Give her some, Nalvana. It'll do her good,' I suggested.

Obediently she lifted the naked child from her hood, cradled her fondly in her arms, and brought the cup up to her mouth. Naoyak barely touched it. '*Mamaitok*. It's bad,' she cried.

Unperturbed and with consummate patience, Nalvana held the little girl with her right arm as she lowered the front of her parka with her left hand and eased out her bulging breast. '*Takke*. Come, drink from it,' she coaxed, gently pushing the teat between Naoyak's lips. But the sick child was not to be pacified so easily. She closed her eyes and started to cry again.

'Give her to me. I'll put her to sleep,' said the old grandmother. Tenderly she drew Naoyak close to her, rocking her and muttering the while: 'I am busy, you know. What a nuisance you are. Don't you see I'm a very old woman, weak and stiff like a worn boot sole? You ought to have been a boy; but I care for you just the same.' Having secured the child's attention, Manerathiak began to chant in her toneless voice:

'*Nunaptigne* . . . In our land—*ahe, ahe, ee, ee, iee*—
The wind has wings, winter and summer.
It comes by night and it comes by day,
And children must fear it—*ahe, ahe, ee, ee, iee.*
In our land the nights are long,
And the spirits like to roam in the dark.
I've seen their faces, I've seen their eyes.
They are like ravens, hovering over the dead,
Their dark wings forming long shadows,
And children must fear them—*ahe, ahe, ee, ee, iee.*

Naoyak had stopped crying and seemed to have fallen asleep again. There was nothing I could do to help her, and the old woman's laments depressed me. I finished my tea and went to my tent. It was cold and uninviting. I lit the primus stove and sat on my sleeping bag with a book. But I could not concentrate on reading for long. I put on my fishing clothes and spent the rest of the afternoon around the nets. They were full of fish, among them many blue herrings of the species found in both the Atlantic and the Pacific Oceans. So lonely did I feel at the moment that to me they loomed more important than all the rest of the catch. They, at least, were a link with the civilized world.

18

KRILALUGAK THE SORCERER

Nokadlak's dogs were howling and Kudnanak was impatiently signalling for me to hurry as I approached the camp. I
sensed that something had gone wrong.

'What is it?' I yelled to the youngster as I hit the beach.

'A bear has wounded my father. His head and face are
covered with blood!'

I ran towards his tent. Nokadlak's team was still harnessed,
and the carcass of a good-sized brown bear lay roped to the
sled. Most of the dogs were yelping and some were licking
their battle wounds. The bear must have given them a real
fight.

Nokadlak was sitting on the edge of the iglek, his bleeding
head bent over a basin of hot water held by Nalvana. With a
dirty old calico rag, Angivrana was trying to keep the blood
from running down her husband's face and neck. In her
usual corner Manerathiak was sedulously scraping a fawn's
skin. Naoyak was asleep in Nalvana's hood.

Apart from snorting through nostrils caked with blood,
Nokadlak sat quietly, holding his head stoically over the

reddened water. His scalp had been badly scratched, and several red furrows revealed the skull bones beneath.

'How did you let the bear get so close to you, Nokadlak?'

Keeping his eyes closed against the dripping blood and sniffing deeply, he replied: 'I am like a clumsy old woman. I forgot to load my rifle. Akhak the Grizzly was feeding on berries when we saw him. Kudnanak took care of the dogs. Using big rocks for cover, I got close to Akhak. I shot, but my aim was off. The bullet grazed his neck. I pressed the trigger, but my chamber was empty. Akhak heard me, saw me, and rushed at me. There was no chance to reload. I used the butt of the rifle to ward him off. But Akhak was too angry. I went down. He tore my parka. The only reason I didn't get killed was that I played dead, burying my face in the snow. He began to claw my head.'

'And that's when I shot him with my .22,' Kudnanak finished the account for his father. 'I fired at Akhak many times before he reared, then toppled, and the dogs piled up on him.'

'Kudnanak is a good hunter,' Nokadlak conceded, and the young fellow beamed proudly.

I clipped the surrounding hair with my scissors, bathed and dressed the wound as well as I knew how. Finding no needles or catgut in my medicine bag, I put the torn pieces of skin where they originally belonged, and was about to bandage his head with gauze when Angivrana interrupted me. 'Fala, put this hare skin on first. The wounds will heal faster.' I did not take the silky fur from her but suggested that she could do that herself. This she did skilfully, and I applied the bandage.

'Are you hurt anywhere else, Nokadlak?'

'No, Fala. *Goanna*, thank you.'

'Lie down and rest now,' I said. 'Kudnanak and I will take care of Akhak and your dogs.'

The bear was no lightweight. He weighed at least a couple of hundred pounds. When the lad and I got him off the sled, Angivrana and Nalvana came out to skin the brute. His hide was thick with silver-tipped hair that turned to gold in certain light.

'*Orsholik*. He's fat,' commented Angivrana, throwing chunks of the rich meat into a cauldron. She went about her job casually, betraying no emotion or hatred towards the animal that had nearly killed her husband a few hours ago.

Also squatting by Akhak's remains, Nalvana cut open the stomach. It was full of berries and the white roots of parsnip-shaped maso. Dexterously she stuffed these into the bladder whose contents she had earlier squeezed out. 'This will be good when it's boiled, Fala,' she said, noting my puzzled look.

The stooped old Manerathiak emerged doubled-up through the small frame door carrying a pan and her ulon. She hobbled over to the carcass and began scraping bits of fat into the pan. Her baked-apple face softened. She sounded extremely pleased: 'Now we'll have brighter light in the tent!'

Nokadlak appeared tired and depressed, but for a casualty he consumed an enormous amount of boiled bear meat that evening without ill effect. I found the meat to my taste, too, but balked as diplomatically as I could at the vegetables à la bladder. Having seen their preparation, I was quite happy to take Nalvana's word for their goodness.

Grandmother Manerathiak more than made up for my small appetite. As a result she was in difficulty. So much had her stomach expanded that she was unable to loosen her belt of braided caribou sinew. 'Woe is me,' she groaned. 'Like a wolf, I have gulped too much. Now this is choking me.' The old woman cringed while Angivrana tugged at the knot before finally untying it. '*Goanna*,' she said with a deep sigh of relief. 'I feel like an old seal cow ready to give birth to a pup.'

Then Naoyak began to cry and complain of her aching tummy. '*Anakruiunga!* I want to go out!' Hurriedly Nalvana carried the child outside the tent.

I felt Naoyak's head when they came back. It was still hot. 'Has she eaten anything at all today?' I asked.

'*Immana*. She has refused everything.'

'Keep trying to feed her some broth.'

'I will try again, Fala.'

Before we went to our tents for the night I asked Nalvana when Kakagun was expected back. 'He did not come back today. He should be back tomorrow—unless the tunrak is so busy he cannot come right away.'

There was no sign of human life when I poked my face out of the small frame door early next morning. No smoke rose from the stovepipes above the other two tents. Even the dogs were still asleep, curled up in the snow.

The weather was raw, cold and sleeting. I made myself some tea and dressed for visiting the nets. Two seagulls were picking at the fish I had stored for the winter. Their days were numbered. If they were not caught in the trap-lines, they would freeze to death before the height of winter. I left them alone to their fate and rowed to the head of the bay.

Upon my return Kudnanak met me at the landing, but now, by contrast, the camp was very much alive.

'Did you get many fish, Fala?'

'Yes, Kudnanak. A lot of *kanayok* got caught in the nets. I scratched my hands taking them out and nearly froze them.'

He smiled. 'A big wind must be coming. That's why they're seeking shelter in the bay. They're so prickly and so ugly, we call them *tupilak*, the devil.'

Looking pleased, as if he had just been to a party, Kakagun

ambled up to take a look at my catch. I asked him when he
got back.

'During the night. Krilalugak also came.'

'Who is he?'

'He's the tunrak. During the spring he moved from Hanimok River to Kiluiktok. That's where I found him.'

I was anxious to see this sorcerer, but the fish came first.
Kakagun and Kudnanak helped me unload and then we
walked up to the tents together.

'Come with us, Fala. We'll eat presently,' said Kakagun.

An old man squatted on the iglek, swaying and humming
a doleful tune. His grey hair fell to his shoulders, yet the top
of his head was closely shaven. It was the first time I had seen
an Eskimo with almost white hair. For a man of his age his
face was unusually smooth: there wasn't a wrinkle or a hair
on it. But his most striking feature was his deep-sunken eyes.
When he glanced up at me they were alert and suspicious.
As we shook hands, he smiled and said with unconcealed
mockery: '*Akorlotualuovin?* Are you the long-robe?'

'*Illa.* I am such a man—one of those your people killed at
Coppermine.'

'Sinniksiak and Uluksak, who killed your friends, were two
young fools. But your friends would have died on the trail
anyway. They had been cursed by a tunrak.'

Kakagun and Nalvana, who sat apart with Naoyak in her
arms, recoiled at this talk. It frightened them. It was even
more impressive to them than the manifestations of powerful
natural forces on which their whole belief was based. They
knew how to gird themselves against the icy will of Hilla, the
evil spirit of nature. But the supernatural powers of the
sorcerer were beyond their comprehension and therefore far
more awesome.

At the risk of breaking off our diplomatic relations I told
Krilalugak that the two Catholic priests were murdered on

orders of the sorcerer at Coppermine because he had discovered that they possessed far greater powers over evil spirits than he did.

'*Naunartok*. I don't know about that. The Kablunak may be all-powerful in his own land, but not here. Here the tunrak is better.'

'If that is so then why did Sinniksiak and Uluksak eat the livers of the two Fathers after killing them in cold blood? I'll tell you why. By so doing they hoped to gain greater powers than the tunrak!'

'Maybe. But they were fools just the same. They did not use those powers. Soon after the Amakro released them from jail in his land, they died here.'

'They were young men, as you say—not old or sick enough to die. Yet one drowned and the other died in his tent on returning to the People Beyond. Now go ahead and tell me the jealous sorcerer did not order their deaths either!'

'Nobody hurt them, Kablunak. But the power of a tunrak is great. He can cure and he can cast a spell on those who go against his wishes.' Black and shiny, like anthracite coal, his eyes receded into the tunnels of his slanting forehead.

'If you are a great tunrak, Krilalugak, why don't you cure little Naoyak? You can probably make her feel better with your good luck charms than I with my medicine.'

'She will be cured. I put an amulet on her as soon as I came in.' Instinctively Nalvana's eyes dropped to the large bird claws dangling on a string from Naoyak's neck.

'What will those claws do for the child?' I asked.

'They will give her strength.'

I was about to question him about his next move when Manerathiak's doubled-up shape eased itself into the tent amid muttered complaints of her ancient aches. She straightened up as far as her old frame would allow her and grinned at the sorcerer as if he were a long-lost relative. With an uncontrollable shiver she announced to our cosy gathering: 'I feel like having some tea. It's so cold in Nokadlak's tent.'

The old woman helped herself to a cup of tea and, with a side glance at me, said to Krilalugak: 'The Kablunak does not understand. I told him he made Naoyak sick by listening to fish talk.'

'She is sick indeed,' agreed the sorcerer. 'Everyone—even the Kablunak—must observe the rules of the spirits. Now I may have to call on them if the amulet cannot ward off the sickness.'

'Even with my misty old eyes I can see that the tunrak has given poor little Naoyak some fine charms. What are they, Nalvana?'

'They are owl's claws.'

'*Illa, illa,* owl claws.' Manerathiak paused. Eyes closed, she delved into her memories. 'The owl flies silently, even during the still winter nights. No-one can hear it. It is all white then, and nobody can see it against the snow. Orkpik the Owl talks and listens to the good spirits of the land. Its claws bring the friendly spirits closer to us when we need them.'

'Manerathiak,' I said, 'you look old and worn-out. Why don't you use some of Krilalugak's charms? Surely they can give you youth and good health.'

'I have some of my own!' She lowered her parka to give me proof. Between two withered breasts hung a small dirty bag of caribou skin. The old woman held up the bag for all to see. 'I put a caribou ear into it because I cannot hear well what people say. And there are strips of wolverine skin to help me keep my wits together, and other charms to preserve me from danger and from sickness.'

The sorcerer punctuated her talk with rhythmical nodding. 'Manerathiak speaks wisely. Amulets intervene for us with the good spirits. Sometimes they give the wearer the cunning of the animals they represent.'

'If the amulets are so wonderful and the tunrak is so powerful, why don't you help Naoyak recover?' I repeated.

'From time to time the spell is broken, Kablunak. Perhaps
it is because you are here with us!' The beady, glowing eyes
were trying to burn right through me. 'Are you an *ilisitok*
in your Kablunak country?'

The sorcerer had flung his double-edged challenge, and
both its edges were razor-sharp. I knew that literally ilisitok
meant 'the clever one'. But I also knew that it was the word
the Eskimos used to describe the tunrak's adversary or antagonist who, by his foreign incantations and his evil eye, was
supposed to bring disaster upon his enemies. As his natural
opponent the tunrak had a clear-cut course of action: he
would summon the protective spirits to his side and, on their
advice, order the death of the ilisitok.

I stared squarely at the sorcerer's incandescent eyes and
said steadily: 'I left my country and came here to help the
Krangmalit in their sickness and trouble. But I don't use
amulets to cure sickness. I use medicines taken from plants
or made by the Kablunak for everybody's benefit. They do
not dispel the evil spirits or summon the good ones. They
simply clean the blood and mend the wounds.'

He grinned eloquently, as if to say: 'And who do you
think believes you? Words, nothing but words!' Then he
went into action. He rubbed his stubby hands on his fur
breeches and beat a tattoo on his chest with his fingers. He
stretched his arms out in supplication: 'Now the feeling is
coming back to me. I hear the spirits whispering outside—
listen!'

Their faces intent, Kakagun, Nalvana, and Manerathiak
sat straining their ears. Miraculously enough, there *were*
voices outside! For the moment it was hard to tell which one
of us was the most surprised. Then, unceremoniously—yet
with a difference I had not noted in them before—into the

tent came Angivrana, Nokadlak, Kudnanak, and Kivgalo. Nokadlak's face was ashen-grey and the white bandage around his head seemed incongruous in this setting.

The spell was nipped in the bud as my friends realized it was their voices we had nearly accepted for the supernatural. But Krilalugak was not one to give up easily. His faraway eyes unblinking, he stared ahead, paying no attention to the intruders. He must have made contact with the spirits again, for now there was a fervent, repetitive plea on his lips: 'What do you wish me to do? What do you wish me to do?'

Outside, the dogs began to howl. They were bewildered by their masters' continued silence at the height of day rather than frightened by the presence of whispering spirits. The bright sunshine hardly penetrated the tent through the stretched gut inserted in the caribou skins as a skylight. In this dim abode it did not take much imagination to create an atmosphere of eeriness, and the sorcerer was a past-master at the art.

He doffed his parka and moved closer to Nalvana, in whose arms poor little Naoyak lay shivering and sobbing. Around the child's head he tied a band of caribou sinew intertwined with musk-ox and wolf hair. Attached to the band were assorted animal teeth and claws and beaks of wild birds. Then, as all but Nalvana backed away from him, according to custom, Krilalugak began to sway in front of the child like a cobra before the charmer's flute. His eyes were fixed on her navel while he weaved his naked torso back and forth, pinching his old nipples and uttering unintelligible expletives.

The preliminaries over, he raised his hands and demanded: '*Kattukmik, kattukmik!* Give me the drum!'

Among the sorcerer's belongings stored at the far end of the tent, Kakagun found a small drum and a short, narrow bone that was once a seal's rib. Solemnly, silently he handed

them to Krilalugak. With practised hand the old man began
a light staccato beat as if to sound out his audience. Satisfied
that he held our rapt attention, he started to chant in his dull,
quavery voice. Although it grew stronger and less tremulous
as he went on, I could not make out all the words. Some of
them were long-forgotten phrases, retained by tradition but
meaningless to the modern Eskimo. Yet the opponent in his
song was easily identified: it was Hilla, the malevolent spirit.

'*Uvagutle* . . . But we . . . are mere shadows,
Lost shadows of the People Beyond;
Lost amid the frightening forces of the earth and sky,
Eye, eye, ee, ee, ee.
We are but restless shadows, lost shadows,
When the sun lies dead, and the moon is veiled with clouds,
And Hilla prowls in the night through snow and wind.
Eye, eye, ee, ee, ee.
We are lost shadows that Hilla haunts
With rain and thunder, death and hunger;
Mere shadows, fleeing the inescapable forces of the land.
Eye, eye, ee, ee, ee.
Come to my aid, Good Spirits!
To the side of a lost shadow,
To the help of a little sick shadow. . . .
Eye, eye, ee, ee, ee.'

Drenched in sweat, frothing at the mouth, the old sorcerer
stopped before the crying Naoyak just long enough to remove the band from her head. Then he collapsed on the
iglek.

His half-naked form heaving from the ritual dance, he lay
panting for several minutes while none of us moved or said
anything. Eventually he rolled on his side, opened his caver-
nous eyes and sought me out. When he did, a triumphant

sneer betrayed the thought behind it: 'Could you do any better, Kablunak?'

Kakagun rowed in silence all the way up to my nets. He was visibly moved by the sorcerer's performance, and I did not wish to intrude on his thoughts with mundane talk. Besides, I was busy with my own thoughts.

Naoyak's condition remained unchanged. Nevertheless, it was clear that Krilalugak was a vastly superior type to Napayok, the sorcerer I had once encountered at Kraomavaktok, southwest of Bathurst. He was a regular devil. Like a wily old hound, he would worm his way into the hearts of men and, especially, women. He was a clever enough healer by Krangmalit standards, but he was even more adept at disposing of those patients he did not like. In short, Napayok was at once a thief, an adulterer, and an expert murderer.

Napayok's antagonist—his ilisitok—was a wiry, determined fellow called Kaodluak. He and some of his friends had grown tired of Napayok's lawlessness and decided to get rid of the scoundrel. At least three times Napayok was given up for dead after he had been either shot, stabbed, or strangled by Kaodluak and his confederates. But in each instance he was revived by his wife whom he had taught how to stop bleeding and bring him out of unconsciousness.

When he discovered this, Kaodluak contrived to have the skilful lady murdered first so that no-one remained to prevent justice from being done to Napayok.

But Krilalugak was a far cry from Napayok. At worst, he was a more acceptable kind of social parasite. Like Napayok—and other Central Arctic sorcerers whose paths occasionally crossed mine—Krilalugak hunted little and fished less, depending on the People Beyond to feed him, clothe him, and, more often than not, lodge him in exchange for his magical services and advice. Unlike his late colleague, however, Krilalugak was

193

said to lead an exemplary life, minding his own business, and protecting his followers from their supernatural enemies.

It was evident that Kakagun had great confidence in him. This was not altogether surprising. Possibly no other place on earth makes such exacting claims on a man's body and soul as the Barren Land. And no matter how capable or inventive a great hunter like Kakagun may be, he can never consider himself complete master of his surroundings. Time and again he finds himself thwarted by mysterious powers of the land, sea, and air. Manifesting themselves in insurmountable storms, famine, or disease, they hold his destiny in bondage, leaving him helpless. When any of the evil spirits thus conspire against him, there is no-one he can call upon except the good spirits or a tunrak.

My reflections had reached this point when I decided to confirm them by questioning Kakagun directly. He was rowing evenly, without haste, and smiled when I looked straight at him. 'Kakagun, when your people are starving, what do they do? Do they call on anyone for help?'

He did not answer at once. He mulled over my question, and I detected a trace of suspicion in his tone when he finally spoke: '*Illa,* Fala. We call on Munarsie, the guardian spirit.'

'Did you call on Munarsie when Naoyak became ill?'

'*Immana.* When my people are sick, we call on the tunrak. He intervenes with the spirits for us.'

'Why don't you use medicine like the Kablunak? They make them from plants and from animals that nature has provided for that purpose.'

'We follow the ways of our ancestors. They did not know about such things. They always turned to the good spirits for every undertaking and in any difficulty.'

'Do you mean that in everything you do you aim to please or pacify some spirit?'

'*Illa.* We must choose the hunting season and the method

of hunting according to the spirits' wishes. The animal must be killed, quartered, and eaten in such a way that we do not displease the spirits.'

'What about making clothes or building an iglu?'

'Same thing, Fala.'

Kakagun was growing impatient. It was the same with every Eskimo I ever met. Whenever I tried to penetrate beyond the sphere of tangible reality, they became reticent and almost sullenly uncommunicative.

It was late in the afternoon when we got back to camp with a good load of fish. Thinly coated with freshly fallen snow, the landscape around us seemed vaster and more rugged than ever. From the jagged peaks to the deep valleys the land would soon be in the throes of bitter winds and snowstorms heralding another reign of terror under the tyrannical Arctic winter.

Carrying Naoyak in her hood, Nalvana came down to watch us land. She smiled at the large catch. 'Fish are still plentiful, Fala. But winter is close at hand. How long will you be visiting your nets?'

'Until I get enough for the whole winter, Nalvana.'

She gave me a searching, incredulous look.

'How is the little girl?' I changed the subject.

'Again she would not eat today. But Krilalugak said she will live to make a good wife for Kivgalo.'

'I'll see what I can do for her tonight.'

Late that evening Kakagun woke me up in my tent with an invitation to have tea with him. Cold and tired, I had dozed off after unloading the boat and spreading the fish on the beach.

As we walked between the tents in the stillness of the clear, cold night, Kakagun said: 'Listen to the river. The ice is making a lot of noise. Soon the bay will start freezing, too.

In a few days we must take out the nets and fish under the ice. We will all be setting nets under the ice because we did not get many caribou this fall.'

In the tent Nalvana was vainly trying to get Naoyak to take her breast, while near them on the iglek Krilalugak was mumbling under his breath. I felt the little girl's forehead. The fever was still with her.

'I gave her a little broth a while ago as you said to, Fala, and she took it.' Nalvana said hopefully.

The sorcerer smiled derisively. 'I should like to hear your wisdom, Kablunak. What do you think of her illness?'

'Naoyak will be all right—notwithstanding all the noise you made this morning.'

'Do you know *why* she will be all right, Kablunak? Because the good spirits have listened to me. They always listen to me.'

Nalvana stood up and went over to the stove to fill the cups with steaming tea. Then she opened the door, poked her head out, and called: *'Teetoritse! Teetoritse!'*

Answering the call with surprising alacrity, old Manerathiak perched creakily by my side. 'It's cold outside,' she muttered. 'I am always cold nowadays.' Politely she blew her nose into her cupped hands and licked them clean.

With the arrival of Nokadlak, Angrivana, and their son, the tent was filled again, but out of deference to the sorcerer none of the natives spoke as they drank their tea. This gave me an opportunity to quiz him a little further. 'You say the Munarsie—the good spirits—are your friends, Krilalugak. Tell me, are they more powerful than Agiortok and Tupilak, the evil spirits?'

'They certainly are! When someone disobeys the Munarsie, dreadful things befall that person or his family. Their guidance must then be sought so that misfortune can be avoided.

But the calamity itself is the work of an evil spirit, and the tunrak will destroy him by recourse to the good spirit.'

'How do you call upon the good spirits?'

'You should know, Kablunak. You've seen me do it.'

'How did you become a tunrak?' I asked just as abruptly, fully expecting to be told to mind my own business. But I had flattered him by taking a special interest in him. He responded with a surprisingly direct answer: 'When I was young I often had dreams. In them I saw strange things. I did not know how to explain them so I consulted a tunrak. He said I was destined to become a tunrak myself and took me in hand. He taught me much of what I know now. At last he appointed me to take messages from the good spirits and help my people.'

Manerathiak was absorbing the sorcerer's every word. Now her memories were on her lips again: 'I had a son who was a great tunrak. He is dead now. His wife strangled him. But when he was chosen to be a tunrak the hunters built an iglu around him, and every third day they gave him a piece of meat from different animals. Then the tunrak of the camp took him in his iglu. He tied my boy up and invoked the spirits. They made my son a great tunrak. Once I was so sick I was spitting blood. My son commanded all the old women in camp to drive their family sleds around the lake in the moonlight. Round and round they went with five teams while my son invoked the good spirits and hurled challenges at the evil ones. Three starving dogs died that night, but I did not die!'

She looked around triumphantly. Still no-one spoke. I threw another question at Krilalugak: 'Who is the most powerful of the good spirits?' Somewhat astonished at the unconventional query, he said evasively: 'They are all very powerful, Kablunak. Some are stronger than others, of course, but each of them is a mighty spirit.'

'What about the evil spirits?'

'They are powerful, too. And some, like Silla, must be feared more than others.'

'Why?'

'Because his approach is deceptive. Silla manifests himself in the stillness of the land and in the peaceful quiet of the mountains. He might whisper tenderly and softly to children to lead them astray, or he may bring dreadful tidings to the hunter or his wife on the wings of the breeze.'

'Is Silla always bad?'

'*Immana,* Kablunak. He is malevolent to those who violate taboos. But he is merciful to his followers.'

'What must a hunter do to please Silla?'

'He must observe the rules imposed by the tunrak.'

'What rules, for instance?'

'At Kiluitok the people have been told by me not to eat caribou meat until the sea freezes. That is a rule they must abide by. They cannot kill or touch either the skin or any part of the meat of a newly killed caribou. If they do, the soul of the dead animal will call Silla and bring a curse upon the camp.'

Kakagun cleared his throat before restating the rules of taboo in his own way: 'A man can eat anything in our land, Fala, if it is not forbidden by the tunrak.' I took this to mean that there are no 'sacred cows' in perpetuity in the Barren Land. With food ever scarce, the Eskimo could not afford such a luxury. But he will abstain temporarily from a certain animal at the tunrak's bidding and then go back to it when the taboo is lifted.

Nalvana's excited whisper interrupted my train of thought. 'Look, Fala, she is taking milk!' I offered a silent prayer as I felt the baby's head. The fever was on the wane! I could feel Krilalugak's fathomless eyes watching my every move. Disregarding him, I said to Nalvana: 'Naoyak will be well tomorrow. But to make her sleep better tonight, give her this before you go to bed.' I put an aspirin into her palm and she studied it curiously, no doubt wondering how such a tiny white object could possibly have any effect on anyone's sleep, let alone a sick child.

'Crush the little medicine in your ladle and add a bit of water to it. Naoyak will take it that way,' I reassured her.

Slowly the sorcerer's tenseness relaxed. His sunken eyes took on an expression I had not seen before. He gave me a friendly grin and when he spoke I could hardly believe what I heard: 'I thought I hated you. I thought you worked against my people. But now I see you are helping me take care of them. You are a good Kablunak!'

I stood speechless as old Manerathiak made my day complete.

'Fala has always helped us,' she said, smiling. 'If only he could follow the customs of the People Beyond, he would be one of us.'

It was getting chilly in the tent, but I was all aglow with this unexpected turn of events. The whole unnatural atmosphere evaporated with the sorcerer's warm words, and in its place there was a mutual respect and kindliness I had not known for some time.

Nalvana handed Naoyak over to the grandmother and went outside. In a few moments she was back with an armful of dwarf-willows for the stove. She broke the longer ones over her knee and shoved them through the little door. They crackled noisily, cheerfully, like pine boughs. She made two more trips to the willow pile, returning with loaded arms each time. No-one offered to help her. It was a woman's duty to keep her dwelling warm.

19

LAKE KILUITOK

Overnight a sheet of ice covered the bay. Realizing there wasn't much time to lose, I asked Nokadlak if he could give me a hand at taking in the nets.

'I thought you were going with us to visit our friends at Kiluitok today, Fala. But I suppose there will be time for that if we go now,' he said.

Kakagun and Kivgalo joined us on the beach and helped us break enough thin ice to float the boat. 'Would you like me to come with you, Fala?' asked Kakagun. 'I can break the ice as we go.'

'*Goanna*, Kakagun, I'm sure we will need your help. With you it won't take us so long to get the nets, and then we can all go and see the people at Kiluitok.'

With Kakagun and Nokadlak breaking the ice from the bow of the boat, I did not find the rowing too fatiguing. One after the other we emptied the nets of their substantial catch, pulled them ashore, and stretched them out in the snow. They would be all ready for use under the ice shortly, once the bay was frozen solid.

My hands were red and numb from the ice-cold water, but I dared not slacken the pace set by Kakagun and Nokadlak. I was playing with professionals and I did not want to remind them that I was but a Kablunak amateur. As a result, the job was done in record time and we set our homeward course along the narrow channel we had created earlier. The ice was a mere half-inch thick, but the way the temperature was dropping it would be only a matter of days before we could walk on it with comparative safety.

I thanked Kakagun and Nokadlak for their help, and the latter said: 'Can I take some of your salmon, Fala?'

'Certainly, Nokadlak. But what are you going to do with them? You have fish of your own.'

'Your salmon are bigger than mine, Fala. I will dig a hole in the ground and bury them in it wrapped in sealskin and covered with peat and gravel.'

'Why will you do that?'

'To give the fish a strong flavour. It will be a nice change from the fresh fish we've been eating all summer.'

'Take all the big salmon you want, Nokadlak. And if you'd like to bury some for me, I'll feed visitors to the Mission this winter.'

When, with the help of their sons, Kakagun and Nokadlak had harnessed their teams, the women appeared with caribou furs for the sleds. Nalvana's hood was bulging as she came up to me with the pigeon-toed, bouncing walk of the Eskimo woman.

'Is Naoyak asleep?' I asked, hearing no childish cries.

'*Illa*, Fala. She passed the night quietly, took milk this morning, and went back to sleep. I think she is much better.'

We sat down on Kakagun's sled and were presently joined by the tall hunter and his son. Skilfully Kakagun and Nokadlak took advantage of the ice on the many small lakes to make up for slow going over the rolling tundra in its thin mantle of snow. Repeatedly we had to lighten the load for the straining dogs by walking beside them.

The camp at Lake Kiluitok lay in a saucer-like depression sheltered on all sides by rocky hills. As we descended we could see the people watching us beside two tents and three fur-covered huts strung out on the eastern shore. The latter looked unfamiliar to me.

'Kakagun,' I said, pointing, 'what kind of iglus are those?'

'They are made of peat, Fala, and covered with caribou skins.'

'Why don't your friends live like everybody else in tents?'

'They walked here last summer from their winter camp at Taseriuak leaving their belongings behind. They will live in these peat shelters until some of their relatives come down with their teams. Then they will go back to Taseriuak together.'

Poorly dressed in old caribou parkas and breeches, the campers turned on their gladdest smiles and shook hands with us all. I had met them all previously at Burnside, so that introductions were unnecessary. There was a simple explanation for their shabby clothing. It had not been very cold until the last few days, and the women were still working on their new winter wardrobe. 'Now it is getting cold. The women will work faster,' my informant told me. He was Imerak who, despite his advancing years, was still a fine hunter. Like Manerathiak, he seemed toothless when he smiled, so worn were his teeth; and like her, he was a shrivelled-up creature, bent with age.

I had heard that Imerak was one of the principals in the murder of two American explorers, Radford and Street, several years before my arrival at Burnside. The details of the crime were not known to me; these I hoped to find out from Imerak's friend and accomplice, a small, thin, Japanese-looking hunter named Haala, whose wife Kuptana was now inviting me in to their hut for tea.

To the east the huge bluffs of Kringaun were painted a rich yellow by the setting sun. It was an oasis of beauty in the ugly frozen desert. Moulded in gold, the snow-veiled rocks were built on a scale without regard to mere man. It was the way God had first made them out of chaos—a world of ice and snow dreaming the aeons away under the Arctic sky. Somewhat regretfully I turned my back on this grandeur and faced the primitive people in their squalid surroundings Mussy dogs lay in the trampled snow, their droppings in evidence all over; caribou carcasses were stacked up in disorder round about the peat huts; disembowelled fish hung on ropes drying in the wind. . . .

'I'm coming, Kuptana!' I said to the sickly-looking woman whom I had treated on several occasions at the Burnside Mission.

There was little in Haala's hut to give comfort to a man's mind or body. Roughly oval in shape, it was a narrow abode with a ceiling of furs so low that even I had to stoop a bit not to brush against it. The usual smells of unwashed humanity were augmented by the reeking dampness of the peat walls. None of the smells could escape save through the occasional opening of the fur-hung door. Oppressed by the stench and the semi-darkness, I felt as if I were locked up in a medieval dungeon.

Haala beckoned me to squat near him, and said:

'My wife has a sore on her head. Krilalugak, the tunrak, cannot cure it, Fala.'

There was a deep suppurating hole behind Kuptana's right ear. I could see a piece of decayed flesh attached to the jaw. It was an advanced fistula matted over with hair and dirt. Worse than that, it was infested with lice.

I had brought along nothing with which to help the poor woman. The best I could do under the circumstances was to cut her hair around the ear with my pocket-knife and wash the sore with hot water. She winced from the pain, but neither cried nor shrank away. 'As soon as possible, Haala, take Kuptana to the trading post and tell the Kablunak there that I sent you. He will know what to do.'

While I spoke, Kakagun came in and squatted at the entrance. Silently he watched me mop up, and then he said: 'Fala, we are not going back to our camp today. The dogs are tired and it's too late. We'll go tomorrow.'

'You can stay with us, Fala,' said Haala.

The invitation was not very appealing, but I had no choice since the other dwellings would be filled up. As long as I could, however, I was determined to stay out of Haala's hut.

'I am going to visit the other families,' I said, rising.

'I will do some visiting, too,' Haala said, unceremoniously leaving his wife with her troubles.

There was plenty of meat, fish, and tea in the camp, and the people were enjoying Krilalugak's accounts of his and my own activities at Kubiartorvik. He was an excellent storyteller and held his listeners spellbound far into the night.

When I noticed Haala heading for his hut, I followed him. He was yawning from drowsiness and the stuffy air in the huts, but otherwise seemed in a cheerful mood. Kuptana was still up, and put another kettle over the stone lamp when she saw us. As we sat down on the iglek of willow stems and fur I wondered if I should ask my host about the murder of the Americans at Bathurst Inlet. Seeing him so mellow and satisfied with himself, I said: 'Haala, I learned from some people that two Kablunan came to Kringaun in spring a long time ago from the land of the white man far, far away. Did you see them?'

'Illa, Fala, I did,' he said, bending forward to take off his boots.

'Is it true that while they were crossing the ice at Koagiuk somebody shot and killed them?'

Contrary to my expectations, he neither denied knowledge of the incident nor evaded the question. Still tugging at one of his boots, he said firmly: 'Imerak and I killed them. We had to kill them.'

'Why do you say you *had* to kill them?'

'They were angry with us and we were afraid of them.'

'What made them angry? Did you hurt them?'

'*Immana*, Fala. They came from the south by dog-team. When they reached our camp at the head of the Inlet they made signs to us, pointing with their hands to the north. We did not understand what they meant. Then one of them grabbed me and pushed me towards his sled. We understood that they wanted one of us to take them north. But we were afraid to go with strangers who could not speak the language of the Land Beyond, so we pretended not to understand their signs. They seemed confused and frightened. They argued between themselves, not knowing what to do next.

'Finally, Imerak and I decided to go with them. Their dogs were a poor lot, tired out from many days of travelling. The Kablunan made us walk all the time. When we reached Koagiuk we were worn-out from trudging in the soft snow. We stopped to rest on the sea-ice, and Imerak said to me: "The Kablunan cannot go on like this for very long. Before they go mad and turn on us, we'd better kill them."

'I was much younger then, and I was scared. But Imerak told me it was the only way we could save ourselves. "When the Kablunan start eating, take my harpoon and spear them," he said. "I'll stay close by and help you."

'When the taller Kablunak bent over his primus stove I plunged the harpoon between his shoulder blades. He shrieked, stood up grasping his chest, and fell bleeding to the ice. The other Kablunak jumped up, but Imerak was too quick for him. Seizing an axe off the sled, he split his skull. Then he finished off the taller Kablunak in the same way. We left their bodies there and returned next day to camp on their sled.'

Haala sipped his drink with audible contentment. He had told his story and that was that. He did not ask for my approval or criticism.

On the surface the story rang true enough. In a weakened condition, Radford and Street might easily have lost their tempers among the primitive people and provoked them to the breaking point. But, knowing something of the Eskimo mentality, I had my doubts about Haala's version of the crime. Most of the murders among the People Beyond are irrational and unpremeditated. They kill for the sake of killing, for the thrill of the hunt. It is one of the few excitements afforded by their dreary land. From early childhood they learn to kill every form of animal, bird, and fish life. The habit of taking other lives is as strong in them as their everlasting struggle for their own survival against unequal odds. If so inclined, a hunter will stalk and kill another without reason or remorse. Why should he have any more respect for the life of a stranger?

There was another reason for my scepticism. In their everyday occupations of hunting and fishing the Eskimos rely on inbred cunning to achieve success. And this native chicanery permeates their dealings with one another. It is a matter of personal pride to outsmart the other fellow, be he friend or enemy. Such an environment, upbringing, and mode of life can conspire to make a natural liar out of anyone. And it was a thing to remember in the Barren Land.

Unconcerned about my speculations, Haala continued to undress. His wife turned his fur socks inside out and placed them on the rack above the lamp next to the two children's pairs. Still wearing his breeches, he crawled into the krepik with the sleeping youngsters and removed his final garment. Noting that I had not brought my bedding with me, he said: 'There are caribou skins in the corner, Fala. Take them and have a good rest.'

I didn't bother to undress. I lay down and took a couple of skins for blankets. Kuptana lingered by the blubber lamp, lowering the flame for the night. Then she placed a korvik within her husband's reach, undressed, and crept into the family sleeping bag.

For a while I slept like my hosts. But before long I was awakened by an agonizing itch all over my body. I began to scratch in self-defence and, to my dismay, found that I could stop scratching only at the risk of being eaten alive by lice. Haala, Kuptana, and their children scratched themselves from time to time without awakening. With them it had become a conditioned reflex.

Only when the howling of the dogs announced the break of day did the nightmare end. Haala stretched, yawned, and greeted me with the customary: 'Did you have a good sleep?'

'*Immana*. I scratched all night.'

'Since we built this hut we have been troubled with lice. But we can sleep now; they are well fed.'

'I think mine were starved!' I managed a smile.

Kuptana's day started before the rest of us got up. She took our parkas outside and beat them with a stick, knowing that in the cold of the morning the lice would shrink just enough to lose their grip on the fur and drop off. Replacing the parkas on the iglek, she went out with a kettle to get water from a hole in the lake. When she returned we were all up. She increased the flame in the stone lamp and put the kettle on. Then she sat down on the iglek, took her daughter in her lap, and began to hunt for the little parasites on the youngster's body.

Helpfully, her son searched in Kuptana's thick black hair,

while Haala went methodically through his parka. They looked like monkeys in a zoo. When they found a louse they held it between the tips of their fingers and bit it with obvious delight. At one point Kuptana protested at her son's overzealousness with her hair: 'After all, they belong to me. I fed them.'

Their morning exercises over, everyone downed some frozen meat and tea and the children ran off to play.

'Would you like me to clean your sore again?' I asked Kuptana.

'Yes, Fala. It hurts a little when I move my jaw.'

We did not tarry long in the camp that day. The sky was clear, the air cold and bracing. Sitting next to Nalvana on the sled, I inquired after Naoyak.

'She slept all night. And she ate like a weasel.'

Running alongside, Kakagun turned towards us and said: 'It is much colder today. We can set the nets under the ice tomorrow.'

Abruptly the weather worsened that evening. A snorting northwester roared through the silence of the Barren Land carrying a cloud of snow in its path. It hit the bay with such force that the thin ice began to break and pile up on the seething shore.

In the tents it was almost impossible to keep warm. Manerathiak was suffering more than the rest of us. Bundled up in her long parka on the iglek, her hands in the long sleeves, she kept repeating: *'Alapa, alapa. Kaiornartok.* It is cold, cold. It is freezing.'

Next day the wind and cold increased their onslaught on our little corner of the Arctic. Combining their forces, they penetrated everything, including the water in the bay, lowering its temperature and serrating its surface like gelatine.

The men and the boys got outside long enough to pile up

snow around the tents for a measure of insulation against the bitter wind. The women with their young ones remained inside, except to bring in willows for the stoves.

Towards nightfall the wind dropped and by morning the bay was covered with smooth, glossy ice. A mile off-shore the sea remained open. The stage was now set for the gigantic struggle between the two. Although the outcome was a foregone conclusion, the sea could be counted upon to carry the fight into November, when it would succumb to the temporarily superior forces of the Arctic freeze.

On the third day after our return to camp, Kakagun and Nokadlak walked out on the frozen bay, punching holes in the ice to test its thickness. As soon as they had ascertained that the ice was uniformly thick, they began preparations for setting their nets below it. Their two boys, Kivgalo and Kudnanak, helped me with mine. Every three paces I chopped holes through the ice, large enough for the lads to pass twine through them by means of a pole provided with a hook for the purpose. With all the twine but its ends under the ice, I fastened the net at one end and drew it down into the watery hole while Kivgalo pulled at the other end. Kudnanak, meantime, watched to see that the sinkers and floats remained in place to keep the net upright in water. To prevent it from being seized in the ice floor, which would thicken by the day, I used willow stems to maintain both ends of the net three feet below.

By noon we had set eight nets between us and were ready for a rest and food. While we filled ourselves with boiled caribou meat and tea, Angivrana proposed that we all spend the afternoon at the creek. 'The water is still open in some places and we should catch plenty of fish at the old dam,' she said.

Kakagun did not need further coaxing. 'Salmon, lake

trout, and kapieliks are still running. We should try now while there is no wind.'

'I'll come, too,' volunteered Manerathiak. 'When I was young we used to spear many fish in that creek.'

'How about you, Fala?' asked Kakagun.

'I'll gladly come. I have never seen anyone fish that way before.'

We walked nearly an hour along the shore to the creek. Angivrana was right: the fast-running stream was ice-free at the mouth. And two hundred yards upstream the remains of a rock dam, built generations ago, were still plainly visible.

When we reached the dam I was surprised to see lesser rocks piled up in a series of twisting channels converging on the main pool at the head of the dam. Slowed by these artificial barricades, the water there was partly frozen and the hunters broke the ice with their long chisels as they stood on the surrounding rocks.

Nalvana handed Naoyak over to her grandmother and, like Angivrana, peeled off her parka amid much joking and laughing. Retaining their seal breeches and boots, they followed the men down the rocky shore back to the sea. There they waded into the creek and began walking upstream, beating the water with the trident-shaped kakivok and their free hands and shouting at the same time to stampede the fish. The women screamed with laughter every time the icy water splashed over their naked torsos. As they reached the dam, Kakagun yelled: 'The fish are in the basin. Let's lock the entrance!'

I helped them pile up rocks across the only remaining opening, sealing off the fish. Now the rest of us doffed our parka tops and jumped into the shallow basin, kakivoks poised for the unwary fish. Nalvana and Angivrana had climbed up on the rocks and were spearing the fish right and left. We stood in midstream, thrusting our harpoon-like

spears into the clear water each time a fish swam by. Loud cheers went up on all sides whenever anyone's kakivok found its mark. Even old Manerathiak and little Naoyak joined in, yelling excitedly.

I had neither skill nor luck at the sport. Worse, I thought my feet would freeze. The water was so cold that it seemed to penetrate right through my sealskin boots. I scrambled out on shore, shivering all over.

'Fala, come back and help us!' the men laughed.

'I'm too cold. Let me run around and get warm. I'll help you bring the fish ashore,' I said through chattering teeth.

Jogging up and down, flinging my arms across to speed up my circulation, I marvelled how my friends could stand the cramping cold for so long. They were wet and it was freezing. Yet to judge from their shouting and laughing they were wholly unconcerned about their numbed limbs.

It took most of my courage to re-enter the water, even though the running had warmed me considerably. Kakagun passed me his catch which he had hung on his belt, and I took the struggling fish to shore. I made several return trips, stacking the fish in separate piles for the two families.

When they were satisfied that most of the big fish were taken out of the pool, Kakagun and Nokadlak suggested a halt to the fishing. Parkas were gladly replaced on the cold, damp bodies. Then each of us filled a caribou or seal bag with a dozen fish of various sizes, the men taking about fifty pounds in theirs, the youths and women proportionately less. I picked up my bag and slung it over my shoulder. Not so the others. They had a tump-line sewn to the top of their carrying bags that fitted around their heads so that the bags hung down their backs, allowing them free use of their hands. Only Manerathiak was spared the packing chore. She was given Naoyak to carry in her hood.

By the time we returned to camp we were too tired and

cold to check the nets in the bay. We changed into dry caribou clothes and the men stretched out on the iglek in Kakagun's tent. The youths followed their father's example, but
there was no rest for Angivrana and Nalvana. Their husbands told them to take care of the damp fishing garments
and to prepare warm food for everyone.

Rather expecting the brawny Kakagun and Nokadlak to
assist their wives at least with drying the heavy wet parkas
and breeches, I said gallantly to the hunters: 'I am going to
help Nalvana and Angivrana.'

Kakagun's scornful answer stopped me short.'You must be
a fool, Fala. They are only women. And *arnak* is meant to
take care of *inuk*.' By using the word 'arnak' he made his
meaning doubly uncomplimentary, for the Krangmalit apply
the same word to a she-wolf or a bitch—creatures deserving
no special consideration. Trained to do all manner of mean
tasks, the Eskimo woman is used to enduring the weaknesses
and appetites of men. But I still could not get used to what
appeared to be a master-and-slave relationship between the
hunter and his wife.

My feelings must have shown through, because Kakagun
turned to Nokadlak and said for my benefit: 'If Fala had a
wife he would be too good to her. He does not know that
women should be given little attention or they become
spoiled. They are made to bear children and work for the
men. Who could hold them in check otherwise?'

Little Naoyak, quite well again, came and perched on my
knee. The wolverine trimmings on my chest and sleeves were
the nearest things to toys in that plain shelter, and she tugged
at these playfully.

I told her about some white men making a big boat that
could go under the water like fish in the sea. I don't know
if she understood what I meant when I said that the fish
did not take the boat for a huge whale, although it looked

like one, but swam right up to the windows and peered at the strange beings inside. She laughed and asked for another story. By the time I had finished embroidering a tale about three polar bears and a little dark-haired girl who got lost in the tundra and stumbled into their iglu, she was fast asleep in my lap. I handed the child to Nalvana and went to my tent.

Next morning, with grandmother Manerathiak and Naoyak for an audience, the camp's male population went to work on the nets. Emulating Kakagun and Nokadlak, I chiselled the ice at both ends of the submerged net. Kneeling on the ice, Kivgalo attached a long twine to one end of the net, which would later enable us to pull the net back in place under water. With Kudnanak's help I dragged out the net. Many a kapielik—the last of the fish to run for the lakes—floundered in the gillnet. There were salmon, too, and trout and the odd tom-cod—in all, a pleasing catch. Getting the nearly frozen fish off the net with bare hands, however, was anything but that. Painfully we freed them from their entanglement and tossed them on the ice, where they froze almost instantly.

Manerathiak, the unconvertible soul, made absolutely sure the fish held their peace by clouting them over their heads with a stick to the tune of an old fisherman's song:

'*Ikraluk, ikraluk*. . . . Oh, fish, where have you been?
I know where you have roamed:
In the darkness of the sea,
In the depths of the inland lakes, *Aya, ya, ya, ya*.
Ikraluk, ikraluk, where have you been hiding?
I know one place you have visited:
The distant abode of Nulialuk,
The mighty Spirit of the Sea. *Aya, ya, ya, ya*.
Ikraluk, ikraluk, to Nulialuk you have gone,

213

To the lost Spirit of the Sea.
But do not tell me what you heard,
For I shall die and be eaten by worms. *Aya, ya, ya, ya.*'

Each day that the weather permitted we returned to the nets. Gradually the catches got smaller and smaller until Nokadlak said: 'The fish are getting scarcer; the ice is getting thicker. We are going to take out our nets and move to Taseriuak for the rest of the winter. But first we want to do some trading at the Burnside post. What do you want to do, Fala?'

'I have been thinking of returning to the Mission myself. I have enough fish stored for my dogs now. Will you give me a ride?'

'*Illa,* Fala. I want to get some traps and ammunition. We shall all go tomorrow.'

Over the reasonably smooth ice of the channel it took us only an hour to reach Burnside, despite Nokadlak's heavy load.

20

FOUR YEARS AFTER

During the next four years I heard of Kakagun and Nokadlak only occasionally as I travelled far beyond the normal orbit of their Kiluitomeun and Umikmaktomeun groups. So closely knit together that they could be taken really as one, these People of the Musk-Ox traditionally inhabited the Bathurst region.

For various purposes—census taking, Mission building, and replacement duties—my travels took me to Minto Inlet, Cape Krusenstern, Coppermine River, Tree River, Cape Barrow, and Melville Sound, occupied by diverse groups of the Krangmalit tribe.

Expressive names described the different groups. At Minto and Prince Albert Sound, on the west coast of Victoria Land, dwelt the Tunuarmeun or the People on the Back of the Earth. At Dolphin and Union Strait I encountered the Aogarungarmeun or the Tom-Cod Eaters, and near them the Nuvungmeun, the People of the Cape. During my stay at Coppermine I mixed with the Krolutomeun, the People of the Falls, and with some of them visited their friends at

Richardson Island, favoured by the Nagiuktormeun, the People of the Caribou Antlers. Finally, on my return trip to Bathurst I came across several families of the Far-Away People, the Kidlinermeun group.

Apart from the fact that these groups stuck to their respective camping and hunting grounds, I found little to distinguish between them. Of necessity they had much in common. In small clusters of families they were scattered over a vast frozen land that had seen their ancestors struggle for mere existence in much the same way for thousands of years. Except for modern firearms and such utensils and provisions as they were able to acquire from the white man's trading posts, their mode of life had not changed since the glacial period. Severed from the outside world from time immemorial and almost entirely free from outside influence, they remained primitive in all essential respects.

Theirs was a world of flat marshlands in the summer, of frozen tundra for the rest of the year; of stony hills and eroded mountains; of snow and ice over frozen seas; of awe-inspiring gales and blizzards. It was a world of dead monotony; of hardships and suffering inconceivable to the white man. Only an unconquerable sense of self-preservation could have driven them ceaselessly on through the ages—only that and an accompanying determination, bordering on obstinacy, to preserve their customs and language to themselves. Geography and climate, which accounted for most of their physical hazards, miseries, and discomforts, also aided them in perpetuating their isolation from the rest of the world. Detached from their original hordes, they nevertheless responded to the same instinctive gregariousness that characterizes the musk-ox and the caribou by banding themselves in small nomadic groups and wandering together in a never-ending search for food.

It was this perpetual pursuit of game that brought me face

to face with an old friend at the delta of the Hood River. I had spent weeks on Kent Peninsula in Melville Sound and was returning to Burnside by way of the Arctic Sound when I thought I would see if anyone was at the usual campsite near the Hood River Falls. From the steep rock bank of a frozen, winding stream I could see a kneeling native covering up a trap with his snow knife and smoothing it over with the back of his mitt. A pebble slipped from under my boot and rolled down. The hunter quickly glanced in my direction, and seemed as relieved to see me as I was to see him.

'Fala, *hey!*' he cried with unconcealed surprise. 'Where did you come from? Did you drop from the sky?'

'No, Nokadlak. This morning by moonlight I left Kidlinek [Kent Peninsula]. I am going back to Burnside.'

'You look cold, Fala. My iglu is up by the falls. Let's go there. I can look at my traps tomorrow.'

'I won't say no to that. I'm cold, and tired too.'

At the foot of the falls two snow-houses nestled in a cove. Behind them lay grizzled hills topped with sedimentary rock, black cliffs, and bare granite mountain-sides. The forbiddingly desolate scene reminded me of imaginary landscapes of the moon. But the resemblance vanished as the tiny camp sprang into exuberant life. Hearing my team, the dormant dogs jumped up and started a dissonant chorus of warning and welcome. The youngsters and their parents ran out of the iglus' *torhos,* waving and shouting at us, while we climbed the intervening distances.

Mittens off, Kakagun, Nalvana, Angivrana, Kudnanak, Kivgalo, and a young lady of seven, all smiling and laughing, fervently shook hands with me. '*Falanuar utirtok!* The little Father has come back!' they kept repeating happily to one another. No conquering hero ever got a more affectionate reception. Their friendliness was so overwhelming I almost forgot my tired, half-frozen limbs.

'And who is the pretty girl? Can she be the baby that had a bad tummy ache a long time ago and slept on my lap like a newborn pup?' I asked.

'My name is Naoyak,' she said with native dignity. 'I know who you are, Kablunak. Everybody has told me about you.'

'I hope they told you good things. And where's your grandmother Manerathiak? Is she in the iglu?'

'*Tokroyok*. She is dead.'

'*Mammianar*. That's too bad. She was a good woman.'

Nalvana broke the uncomfortable silence. 'Come in and have some tea, Fala. The boys will look after your dogs.'

It was heartwarming to see the flame of the blubber lamp reflected on the snowy dome. '*Goanna, goanna*. Thanks, thanks,' I said. 'It's wonderful to be inside. It's so cold outdoors.' Still smiling, Nalvana took my parka and shook off the last clinging snow. She studied me momentarily, then said: 'Your whiskers are full of ice, and under them you look thin, Fala.'

'I have been travelling a lot, Nalvana. When I get back to the Mission I shall shave off my whiskers. They are always collecting icicles.'

'The Kablunak like to learn through hardship. Why don't you pull your whiskers out the way the Inuit do? Then your face won't hurt.'

I nodded silently.

Naoyak came closer to where I sat on the iglek and, without prompting, but with a sweet shyness, said: 'Fala, give me your boots. I'll put them on the rack.' With serious mien she beat each boot with a stick and placed them above the blubber lamp. Then she said solicitously to Nalvana: 'Fala is hungry. I'll fill the pan with meat and fish and call the people to eat.'

'*Namaktok!* That's fine! Tea is ready.'

The response to Naoyak's musical '*Teetoritse!*' was immediate. Kakagun, Nokadlak, Kudnanak, and Kivgalo hurried in. Behind them, bent forward to counteract the weight on her back, shuffled in Angivrana. She had aged visibly, and tiredness was apparent in her every step.

'Is it a boy you have in your hood?' I asked her.

'*Illa,* Fala,' she said proudly. 'He was born last spring during the caribou hunt.'

'That is a good omen. Perhaps he will be as great a hunter as his father!'

Nokadlak beamed.

Kakagun, the host, quickly diverted attention to me, his guest. 'Fala, drink some tea and rest yourself.'

Naoyak made the rounds with meat and fish, and all around my friends began to stuff themselves to full capacity. Tea and a large pot of caribou broth, brought on by Nalvana, completed the filling meal. I had been sampling the victuals in silence with the rest, studying the people after our protracted separation. I felt the gap left by the grandmother's death.

'When did Manerathiak die?' I asked Kakagun.

'Long ago during the summer. She was getting too old and useless.'

'What happened to her, Kakagun?'

'I don't know. We had pitched our tents at the mouth of the Siorkretak River. It was a rainy, windy morning. She walked along the shore towards the cliffs overlooking the bay. She did not come back.'

'And you don't know where she went?'

They all stared at me in astonishment. Nokadlak chuckled: 'She went to the top of the highest cliff facing the sea. The weather was stormy, the waves angry and high. She simply disappeared, Fala.'

'*Mammianar!* Manerathiak knew the ways of your ancestors,' I said. 'She was a true Krangmalek woman.' After that epitaph no-one mentioned her name any more. Instead, they asked me where I had been, whom I had seen, and what I had done since our last meeting.

'When I was wintering with the Tunuarmeun, Naneroak killed his brother Kapulak—'

'I know Naneroak,' cut in Kakagun. 'But I don't remember his brother Kapulak. He must have been much younger than Naneroak.'

'Naneroak was married, wasn't he, Fala?' said Angivrana.

'Yes, but his wife died a long time ago. She had adopted a young girl and Naneroak brought her up.'

'Where did Naneroak kill Kapulak?' asked Kakagun.

'They were visiting their trap-line when a storm came. They built an iglu and stayed in it for three days. On the third night Kapulak had a bad dream. Still half asleep, he tried to kill Naneroak with an axe. They fought for the axe. Naneroak finally got hold of it and stunned his brother with a blow on the head. Kapulak did not recover. He died before morning.'

'Did you see Kapulak's body, Fala?' said Nokadlak.

'Yes. One day when I came out of the iglu I saw a body lying in the snow on the river bank not far away. I went over to it. It was Kapulak, dead and frozen, with his knees bent.'

'Naneroak told you how he died?'

'Yes, Nokadlak. He said his brother's forehead turned soft where he hit him with the axe, and he died during the night.'

'Fala, did you say Naneroak is still living with his adopted daughter?' Kakagun asked pointedly.

'I did. They are always together, but they stay away from other people.'

'No wonder Kapulak is dead!'

Everyone laughed understandingly.

We exchanged several minor experiences, and then I related how I had been lost for four days in the thick fog of Melville Sound. If someone had thrown a cream pie in my face I don't think they would have laughed more heartily. When their merriment subsided, Angivrana said comfortingly: 'Everybody gets lost once in a while in our land, Fala.'

'That's right', agreed her husband. 'A man should never travel alone for long distances. Anything can happen on a long trip. The dogs might run away. You might break a leg. Or the spirits of the land will try to mislead you.'

'But I was not alone, Nokadlak. I had a young fellow from Coppermine with me.'

'Couldn't he help you find the way?'

'Help me? When I told him we were lost, he almost stopped eating for a couple of days! All he did was keep saying: "What will happen to us? We cannot see anything around us. The spirits are against us. They have put the land to sleep in this white night of fog and silence. What will happen to us?" '

'What did happen to you, Fala?' said Angivrana curiously.

'One evening, as I tried to fall asleep, the boy went out of the iglu. Soon I heard several rifle shots. I ran outside to see what was going on. Rifle in hand, he was standing on the sled, looking around and listening. I asked him what he was shooting at. He said: "At the spirits, Fala. I heard them whispering. At first I thought of killing you because you are a Kablunak and the spirits do not like you. Then I heard them talking to each other and laughing. So I fired the rifle to make a big noise to scare them off. Now they are gone." '

My listeners nodded approval. Nokadlak expressed the consensus: 'He could not do anything else.'

'How did you find your way again, Fala?' asked Kakagun.

'The following day the fog slowly lifted. I climbed a hill and in the distance recognized Krikitakapfaluk.'

'You see, the boy was wise,' concluded Kakagun. 'Sometimes, when we stand up against them, the spirits fear us and depart. If I hear a murmur or a hum of conversation coming from the land, I throw rocks around or shoot the air with my rifle. Other times I sing the song of the tunrak:

'O, Spirit, Spirit, take a good, long look at me;
I am not afraid of a worm, a creeping worm,
Hungry for my blood, gnawing at my flesh.
You are like a fox—afraid of man.
O Spirit, Spirit, bad Spirit of the Land.
You are like a weasel—afraid of a child.'

During the three days I spent at the falls the men did not bother with their trap-lines. Instead they busied themselves skinning the foxes they had caught earlier and drying the pelts on the rack above the blubber lamp. Between their other household chores Angivrana and Nalvana worked on their clothes and fancy trimmings for their parkas and boots. The feverish activity set me wondering. 'Where are you getting ready to go?' I finally asked Nalvana.

'Didn't Kakagun tell you? We've decided to go to the trading post with you.'

So that was it! I had casually mentioned that I wanted to be back at Burnside before Christmas, and now I was going to have plenty of company all the way.

'Your new clothes look very pretty, Nalvana, and I hope you will have a good time at the post,' I said.

All this time Naoyak had been following me round the camp like a friendly kitten. 'Why don't you play with Kivgalo?' I asked her.

'I like to play with him, but he is always hunting ptarmigans in the hills with Kudnanak.'

'Won't they take you hunting with them?'

'No, Fala. Kivgalo says I am too young. He says it is dark most of the time now and the spirits might take me away into the mountains.'

'Never mind, Naoyak. The boys will be back soon and maybe Kivgalo will play with you then. In the meantime, let's visit Angivrana. You can take care of her baby while she is sewing.'

'*Immana!*' she said, puckering up her nose. 'I'll play with Kivgalo when he comes back.' Before I could say another word, she turned and scampered like a caribou fawn towards Kakagun's iglu.

Something made me follow Naoyak. Perhaps it was curiosity—I don't know. The scene I saw in the iglu, however, I remember vividly.

Naoyak was crowding Nalvana, trying to get at her breasts. '*Immilanga!* I want to drink!' she kept repeating.

'I'll be making tea soon.' Nalvana was putting her off.

'I don't want tea. I want to suck your breast.'

'You're a big girl now, Naoyak. You don't need milk any more, like a new-born child,' the woman said patiently.

Sitting cross-legged on the iglek, Kakagun stopped skinning a white fox long enough to tease the youngster: 'Naoyak may be a girl, but she is more like the calf of a musk-ox. All she wants is milk, milk!'

Ignoring him, Naoyak resumed: '*Immilanga, ama.* Let me drink, mother!'

Nalvana gave in at last. '*Talva!* There it is!' she said. Her breast was surprisingly round and firm for a woman who apparently had not had children for several years. 'Or were they girls?' I asked myself.

Refreshed, Naoyak played with her adopted mother's breast as if it were a toy, drawing the mildest protest from Nalvana. 'What have I done to you that you should bother me when I am so busy getting ready to leave tomorrow?' she said with a smile. Naoyak chose not to answer, but presently stopped her play, put on her mitts, and announced: 'I'm going out to see if Kivgalo is coming.'

Nalvana and Kakagun took her whims in their stride. Their composure never wavered. They remained cheerful and gentle with her. Marvelling at their patience, I said: 'Naoyak has changed a lot since I saw you people last, but in some ways she is still a child.'

'She does not cry so much now, Fala,' Nalvana said charitably. 'She is learning to be a woman.'

'Sometimes she still wakes us up at night, but she is better now,' conceded Kakagun.

'Did she keep you awake much before?'

'*Illa*. After her sickness at Kubiartorvik, she used to wake up often, whimpering and even screaming. At first we wondered if she had pains. Then we found she wanted hot broth. So Nalvana would get up, light the lamp, and put the pot with broth over it.'

'Then I'd crawl back into the krepik and wait for the frozen broth to melt and warm up. It was cold going back and forth,' Nalvana added.

'Do the Kablunan try to please their children as we do?' asked Kakagun.

'No, they spank them when they keep asking for impossible things or do not obey their elders.'

'We leave them alone,' Nalvana said. 'That is the way of our forefathers.'

Just then Naoyak bounced in excitedly. 'Kivgalo and Kudnanak are coming! They're crossing the river. Come and see!'

Neither Kakagun nor Nalvana stirred from their work, so I went out to humour the girl. Moonlight glittered off the ice on the river, off every snow-covered slope and ridge. Sharp gusts of an icy wind from the east tore across the unearthly stillness, whipping up a gossamer curtain of snow. Nothing moved around the camp except an occasional puppy that wandered, its tail signalling friendship, between the motionless dogs strapped to the line.

'There they are, Fala!' Naoyak pointed towards two moving shadows on the glare ice about halfway across the mile-wide river. Between snow curtains I could see them sliding expertly over the treacherous surface, despite swollen hunting bags on their bent shoulders.

We walked toward them slowly along the sloping bank. When only a hundred yards remained between us, Naoyak ran out to greet them. 'You have killed many ptarmigans!' she exclaimed with radiant admiration.

The boys acknowledged the compliment with smiles. 'We went up to the large willow patch behind the falls. We found many birds there and we killed all we could,' said Kudnanak. 'It was cold, but it was fun!' Kivgalo added cheerfully.

'Let me see what you got,' Naoyak demanded, prancing around Kivgalo.

'Wait till we get inside,' he said firmly, and the girl did not repeat her request.

Kudnanak walked off to his father's iglu as I followed Kivgalo and Naoyak into theirs.

'*Alapa*. It's cold up the river,' said Kivgalo, depositing the heavy bag near the blubber lamp and flicking the hoarfrost off his light eyebrows. Naoyak dipped curiously into the bag and brought out a white bird, chubby, but smaller than a grouse. She held it up for all to see.

'I'll make my good hunter some tea,' Nalvana said. 'Give me your *attige*. I'll put it on the rack.'

'You have shot many ptarmigans, eh?' Kakagun asked.

'We should have bagged more, but we ran short of ammunition. There were many hare tracks. We will go after them tomorrow.'

'Tomorrow, if the weather is fine, we're all going with Fala to the trading post.'

'*Namaktok!* Fine! I have a few foxes I can trade for ammunition. And maybe we'll see some friends.'

'You can get me some candy, Kivgalo!' Naoyak suggested hopefully.

21

CHRISTMAS AT BURNSIDE

'We'll take the portage to Kognekoguyak,' Kakagun said as we prepared to leave camp by the light of the morning stars.

The wind had dropped during the night, but it was still raw and cold on the sled. Kakagun took the lead, followed by Nokadlak's and my team. Kivgalo sat next to me. He seemed pleased at being on the move again.

Almost at once we began to climb. When we reached the first plateau overlooking the Hood River, Kivgalo took off his outer parka, retaining the inner one. 'It is warmer up here,' he observed. 'It is always colder down the river.'

'I have noticed that, too. I think it's because cold air is heavier than warm air and flows down the mountain slopes to settle in the valleys.' Whether or not he understood me, Kivgalo readily agreed. 'Sometimes when I visit my trap-line I feel colder in the coves and narrow inlets than on the hills around them. It's like going outside from a warm iglu.'

Towards noon we gained the summit of the portage. We rested our dogs and made tea behind blocks of snow which we had piled up as a temporary shelter against the cold and drifting snow. Around us was a scene of winter desolation on a grand scale. Far below to the southwest the frozen Hood River, to all appearances like a sleeping white serpent, hid its head in a rocky canyon of the coast mountains. Beyond them to the northwest the silvery ice of the Arctic Sound stretched to the bleakness that was Cheere Island. To the east the Umikmatok Range formed the backdrop across the Bathurst Inlet. And to the southeast rose the bluffs of Kringaun or Burnside, shielding the ice-bound Kiluitok behind them.

Except for us and our dogs, the drifting snow, and the moaning wind, nothing moved or uttered a sound.

Kakagun finished his tea and dry meat, surveyed the elements, and said: 'The spirits of the air are disturbed. Let us move. Kringaun is still far away.'

The descent was dangerous. We rode the crests of eroded hills with gaping canyons on either side. Once Kakagun missed the trail. To avoid backtracking we would have to go down a steep slope to a rocky creek below. After a brief consultation with Nokadlak, Kakagun told Nalvana to hold the dogs while he pulled the sled to the edge of the incline. It balanced there for a moment and then started to slide downhill, gathering momentum and dragging the scrambling dogs after it. Kakagun sat down and slid. He came safely to rest at the frozen creek soon after the sled had ploughed into a snowbank. Helped by Kudnanak, Nokadlak sent his sled down backwards in like fashion, and I did the same while Kivgalo held my dogs. Both teams and sleds landed without damage.

'*Atkraren!* Come down!' Kakagun shouted to Nalvana, who stood hesitantly with Naoyak at her side. The girl moved first. She was doing well until the half-way mark when she lost her balance, turned over, and rolled the rest of the way like a sack of flour. Kudnanak and Kivgalo in particular thought it a grand joke and infected everyone with their laughter. Apparently none the worse for the experience, Naoyak extricated herself from the snow-drift that ended her progress, stood up, and laughed with the rest.

Gallantly Kakagun offered to climb up and help the women navigate the downhill run, but Nokadlak put him off with a smile: 'Let them try; they can't get hurt.'

With the baby asleep in her hood, Angivrana squatted down, pulled the back of her long parka forward between her legs, held the hem tightly, and was off. She negotiated the slide so well that Nalvana seemed to gain courage. But it still took a little urging on her husband's part before she lay on her back and descended, with her outstretched arms acting as brakes.

It was late evening when we finally reached the Burnside post. Tiny lights from the domes of a dozen iglus outlined the campsite, but the Hudson's Bay buildings were in total darkness. Ed Kennett and his wife Ivarlo had already retired.

As the wind was now developing into a storm, I left my friends with the other natives and hurried to the Mission. Exhausted by the long trip, the dogs lay down thankfully to rest as I relieved them of their harnesses and attached them to the line. I fed them with dried fish and went into the house. It was like an ice cavern. Some time passed before the warmth of both stoves made itself felt throughout the building. I warmed myself up with several cups of steaming coffee and went to bed.

I was getting things straightened around in the forenoon when Ed, whom I had not seen for years, dropped in. We shook hands warmly and settled down to a long talk. Before he left I invited him to attend my Midnight Mass on Christmas eve.

A sliding door separated the chapel from my large living-room, and some of the natives had asked me if they could use the latter for a dance on Christmas eve. I had replied that they could use it whenever they wanted to and that I would conduct the service at midnight. About eight o'clock the influx began. All the natives were dressed in their best. Their parkas were lined with trimmings of various designs; wolverine and weasel strips adorned their sleeves; their boots were of silvery white caribou hide embellished with beads and cuttings of wolverine fur. Some of the hunters proudly showed parkas made entirely of rare dappled caribou fur, while others looked like masquerading dominoes in white and black checks.

The women's fashions were even more colourful than the men's. They had contrived to trim the hoods of their long parkas with grey, white, or blue wolf fur; they hung two or three white weasel furs from the bodice and the shoulders; and they wore slippers of bleached sealskin decorated with caribou fur.

Ed Kennett arrived with a gramophone and records, determined to teach the guests to square-dance. He arranged the men and women in couples all over the room and took the centre for himself and Ivarlo. 'Now, everybody try to do exactly what we do!' he said to the expectant gathering.

It was a dance to remember. While the other children sat goggle-eyed on benches around the room and babies slept or cried in their mothers' hoods, Ed and Ivarlo led their pupils through promenades, allemande right and left, do-si-dos, and swing your partners. They caught the spirit of the square dance with surprising rapidity. Soon Ed was able to stop demonstrating, climb on a chair, and act as caller.

Towards midnight, as I began preparations for the Mass, Ed stopped the music and announced that the dance was over. We closed the partition between the two rooms. With much laughter the dancers trooped outside to cool off before the service.

Only a handful of the natives in camp were Catholics, but nearly every family crowded into the Mission as I tolled the steeple bells. It was one white man's show they did not want to miss.

I could hear the wind howling outside, but as I surveyed the quiet gathering before me in the light of the swaying kerosene lamp suspended from the ceiling, a feeling of comfort and security filled my heart. I offered a silent prayer for my family and friends at home. Then I spoke aloud in Krangmalek on the meaning of Christmas and the celebration of its Mass. Ed managed to play the little organ and received loud though unconcerted support from the unrehearsed choir. The audience showed its appreciation by giving the entire service quiet and undivided attention.

With Ed's assistance I treated them to a hot meal of meat and rice and frozen fermented fish. Then he took me back to his place for the richest Christmas spread I had seen since I left my Corsican home. While I shook the snow off my parka on the porch, Ed lighted the two tall red tapers on the dining-room table to reveal a Christmas pudding surrounded by plates with cheese, crackers, salami, olives, and cookies. Above all, there was a bottle of Chartreuse. I could not imagine how Ed knew that this was the drink my family invariably served on festive occasions. But the mere sight of the familiar bottle made me at once so homesick that nothing else mattered.

22

KAKAGUN'S TRAPS

There were nine reasons why I decided to spend the toughest part of the winter with my friends at their Hood River camp: my dogs. Until the caribou poured down to the sea from the tree-line in April, there would be no food for them around Burnside. Not having made any food caches there the previous summer, I now had but one choice: to move in with someone who had enough to go round. Few Krangmalit hunters were as well provided as Kakagun, and when I told him of my intention, he said: 'You can stay with us as long as you like, Fala. We will get food for your dogs. If we don't find any caribou inland, we'll go seal hunting on the sea ice between visits to the trap-line.'

'I shall set traps too, Kakagun, and I'll pay you with ammunition, tea, and tobacco for any dog food you supply.'

'What you want to give, I'll take, Fala.'

His family and Nokadlak's had enjoyed their visit to the post, but they all seemed eager to get back to their camp and its routine. The two hunters had only partially replenished their stores at the trading post. Now they looked forward to the big trading session in the spring when they would have many more foxes with which to bargain for Ed Kennett's merchandise and at the same time impress the other hunters.

Apart from numerous new tracks of foxes and wolverines, all over the camp, we found the place unchanged. But although Kakagun and Nalvana burned the blubber lamp all evening, they could not get their iglu warm. 'It's worn out. The snow has turned to ice. Tomorrow I shall build a new one,' Kakagun said resignedly.

'I'll help you,' I said. 'We can make a larger iglu so I won't crowd you during my stay with you.'

'I am glad you are going to spend the winter with us,' Naoyak said sleepily. She was lying in the krepik next to Nalvana, fondling a doll I had not seen before.

'Who gave you that beautiful doll, Naoyak?' I asked.

'I bought it for her,' Kivgalo said proudly. 'It was the only one in the Kablunak's store.' Propped up on his elbows in his sleeping bag next to mine, he lay watching the flickering flame of the lamp. Kakagun could not sleep either. A dry, hollow cough bothered him. I asked him if he had caught a chill. '*Immana*, Fala. My throat is sore. It has been sore for a long time.'

Our breath steamed up in the cold air, condensed, and fell back in snowy powder over our krepiks. Restless, and doubtless thinking of the trapping days ahead, Kakagun began a sad, slow tune:

> 'Roamers of the sea,
> Where are you? *Ya-ya-a-a-ye-e-e.*
> Roamers of the land,
> Where are you? *Ya-ya-a-a-ye-e-e.*
> Flee not the hunter,
> Beast of the sea,
> Beast of the earth.

Come, bring your skins
And your fat flesh
To my poor abode . . . .'

The song went endlessly on, unvarying, monotonous. Despite the cold, I fell asleep.

It took us—Kakagun, Kivgalo, and me—the better part of the morning to build a larger iglu next to the old one and to transfer our belongings into it. Inside the new snow-house I prepared my traps while Kakagun, Nokadlak, and the boys went out to their meat caches. For each ring at the end of the chain attached to the trap I fashioned a small peg of willow. For bait I filled an old coal-oil can with rotten caribou meat and rancid blubber. I was ready except for my parka and breeches. I asked Nalvana to look them over.

'Your *attige* has a few small holes, Fala. I'll patch them.'

'Thanks, Nalvana. That should stop the wind and the snow from coming through as it did at the end of last winter. I wore poorly sewn *aktatak* then. When the storm caught me on the trail, part of my right hip was frozen pretty badly.'

'You won't be cold on the trail this time, Fala. I'm going to make you new mittens and socks.'

Returning with two sledfuls of caribou they had killed in the fall, the hunters took care of the immediate food problem for the dogs—and partly for themselves.

The early morning sky was overcast and an Arctic greyness enveloped everything around us when we left camp. Kivgalo rode with me on top of some thirty steel fox-traps that I had bundled under a canvas along with my food supplies and bedding. When we reached the frozen Arctic Sound, Nokadlak and Kudnanak nosed their sled to the right.

'Where are they going?' I asked Kivgalo.

'They will follow the coast to Tikerak in the north. Then

they will turn south to Kagnekoguyak and go back to camp by the portage.'

'Has Nokadlak got traps all the way?'

'*Illa*, Fala, he has many.'

We left Nokadlak to his conquest of the Banks Peninsula and continued along the west coast of the Sound.

'Where does your father's trap-line end, Kivgalo?'

'At Aninek.'

A good fifty air miles away and probably more than twice that along the irregular coastline, Aninek—or Cape Barrow —held at least one advantage: Father Adam had built a shack there and stored emergency rations and fuel in it. I was gladdened by the thought of spending a night in the little wooden structure, which was comfortably heated by a coal stove.

On a small promontory Kakagun pulled up his team. He climbed to its rocky top and stooped down. I joined him while Kivgalo kept an eye on our dogs.

'*Tiriginiak tamartok*. The fox is gone,' he said, pointing to the white forepaw in the closed trap and bloodstains in the snow.

'You have been away too long, Kakagun. The fox has had time to chew his frozen paw.'

'*Illa*. And I expect to find more like this. Besides, wolverines and wolves have had time to go around and eat some of the caught foxes. This always happens when I don't visit my traps often.'

Kakagun opened the trap, tossed away the paw, and reset it. He pulled on the chain to see if it was still firmly anchored in the frozen ground. Satisfied, he cut a hole in the hard snow just deep enough to contain the snare, and laid it in. Then he covered it over with a blanket of hard snow that he scraped almost to paper thinness with his snow knife. The camouflage was perfect, yet brittle enough to break at once under the weight of an unsuspecting fox. As bait, Kakagun sprinkled bits of rotten fish to encourage the fox to walk about until it stepped upon the centre lid that would spring the trap. As he did so he said:

'Fala, cut me a block of snow. I'll place it right by the trap. It will be easier to find it when I come back again.'

'It will also attract the curious fox.'

'That's right. Especially when I spread a little blubber over it. The fox will play around it, piss on it like a dog, and eventually jump on the trap.'

For extra insurance Kakagun scooped out several handfuls of snow from the base of the foot-high pyramid on the side nearest the trap and put a piece of fish into the niche. No fox could get at it now without treading on the trap.

The canny hunter had placed his traps every half-mile or so and we visited as many of them as we could during the daylight hours. Here and there, along silenced creeks, on hilltops, and in other likely-looking spots, I set some of my own traps.

By late afternoon, while a ground wind moaned among the snow-drifts, we drove past Kater Point and entered Daniel Moore Bay. We built an iglu, fed the dogs with dry meat, and crept into our tiny shelter. Kakagun sealed the doorway with a large block of snow, Kivgalo got the blubber lamp going, and I lit my primus stove for extra warmth and a quick pot of tea. We dined on chunks of frozen meat and relaxed on the iglek.

'Kakagun, when you were smoothing the snow around your traps I heard you say something I did not understand. You did not speak to me but to the land. Do you remember?' I asked.

'*Illa*. It was an incantation, Fala.'

'What kind?'

'For the foxes, of course. Foxes listen to the voice of man. I
was taught it when I was a young boy.'

'What did you say to them?'

'I said: "Wanderer of the land, come, come and place your
paw on this fresh snow!" '

'How many foxes did you and Kivgalo catch today?'

Thoughtfully counting on his fingers, Kakagun said: 'I got
ten foxes: three *kereaotilik* [cross foxes]; one *kayortok* [red
fox]; and six *tiriginiak* [white foxes]. That reminds me, we
should skin those that are not frozen, Kivgalo.'

The youngster got off the iglek and put his parka back on.

'I forgot to bring them in,' he said. 'I'll get them.'

He let himself out by cutting around the entrance block
and kicking it forward.

'There are not many white foxes this winter,' commented
Kakagun, as Kivgalo crawled in with three white and one
red fox. The animals' feet were stiffly frozen, but otherwise
they seemed soft enough for fleecing.

'Why is this a poor winter for foxes?' I asked.

'Last spring I saw females with their young. They had only
two or three pups. During the summer, when I was hunting
caribou, I saw fewer foxes than before.'

'How many pups does a female usually have?'

'Four, five, or six.'

'How do you account for the small litters?'

'Maybe it is because the lemmings are scarce.'

The very first fox Kakagun skinned showed no fat on its
bright red carcass. 'See, Fala, this one did not have much to
eat! The lemmings are disappearing.'

'But foxes do not feed only on lemmings.'

'That's right. Sometimes they'll catch a ptarmigan or find
the remains of caribou killed by wolves. And far out on the
ice pack they'll eat carcasses of seals abandoned by Nanuk,
the bear. But lemmings are their main food, Fala.'

'You mentioned seeing foxes in the summer. Where do they live then?'

'After the ice break-up, all white foxes hide in their holes on river banks and dry, sandy mounds near places where there are plenty of fowl and eggs.'

'I have heard that white foxes are easier to trap than the others. People on Banksland often don't bother to put any bait around the traps at all.'

'Tiriginiak is not so sly and suspicious as the red fox, Fala. Many times I have seen him following my team, staying around my camp, watching moving people.'

'I know what you mean. There were a couple of white foxes under my shack at Cambridge Bay. They emerged periodically to see what I was doing. They weren't shy. They were just curious.'

Having skinned another fox, Kivgalo said critically: 'This one is lean, too. If it had been fat, we could have boiled and eaten it. I'll give it to the dogs.'

'I don't like fox meat,' I said. 'It has such a strong flavour, and I ate too much of it when I visited the People on the Back of the Earth at Minto Inlet.'

'We don't usually eat it. Only for a change,' said Kakagun. 'We like to try everything, except Tulugak the Raven.'

'Why not the raven?'

'He is taboo.'

Before piling into our krepiks for the night we stepped outside for a last look at the dogs and a breath of fresh air. Seldom had I seen the Northern Lights in a finer display. Like a glittering *corps de ballet*, they glided over nature's immense stage, now rising, now falling, ever colourful, never still. The ground wind had died completely. It was so quiet that I imagined I could actually hear the celestial show. It sounded like the delicate rustling of silk dresses. But as I bent down to the frozen ground I knew that the gentle noises came from the snow particles expanding in the cold.

At Daniel Moore Bay next day Kivgalo and I were astonished to see two wolves caught in Kakagun's traps. The great hunter himself smiled with pride. Still alive, the platinum blue *arluk* and the plain grey *amakro* were even more surprised than we at the encounter. They cringed in fright, tails between their hind legs like the beaten cowardly bullies they were.

There were natural cowards among our dogs, too. While the wolfish scent enticed most of the huskies into a sprint for the traps, some of them showed their reluctance to approach the enemy by skidding on their rumps. But Kakagun wasted no time. Within ten yards of the traps he jumped off the sled and anchored it to discourage the more venturesome dogs. Then he seized his rifle, squatted in the snow, and fired. The handsome arluk keeled over, blood gushing from his mouth. Again Kakagun took aim and shot, sealing the amakro's fate. In a few moments he and Kivgalo considered it safe to remove them from the powerful traps.

The wolves had a good reason to be there. Near by another trap held the paw of a white fox, its fur scattered about the gravelly spit in silent eloquence. And partly buried in the gravel, only a few feet away, were the ravaged carcasses of four seals.

'How did these seals get here?' I asked Kakagun.

'I hunted here last summer. Got more than I could carry in my canoe. I cached them in the gravel. They made big bait!'

I wondered what Kakagun would do next with the wolves. Answering my thoughts, he said: 'The wolves are too heavy to haul to the next camp. I'm going to skin them right now.'

'I'll reset the traps while you do that,' said Kivgalo.

As I helped Kakagun skin them, I estimated that the wolves weighed about 130 pounds apiece. 'How old are they?' I inquired.

'Two winters. They are young and from the same litter.'

'How can you tell? Their colouring is different.'

'Look at their muzzles. Both long for the head. See how their forehead slopes the same way? Compare their eyes, their ears. Notice how long their fur is over the bellies and their legs. They are alike but for the colour of their fur.'

Each time Kivgalo glanced in our direction he smiled compliments for the arluk. 'It's beautiful! It will make wonderful hood trimmings for Nalvana and Naoyak.'

'Don't you get arluks very often, Kakagun?'

'No, Fala. Amakro is the common one. Sometimes we get white and black wolves. But, like arluk, they are scarce.'

'That's strange! When I hunted with the Tunuarmeun people all the wolves we saw were white. Even in the summer they were white. But, of course, their islands are more northerly.'

'I did not know that. What I know is that you won't see many white wolves in our land.'

'Do you find that wolves like to hunt in packs, Kakagun?'

'*Immana.* Mostly the amakro hunts alone; sometimes in pairs. Rarely—and only in wintertime—have I seen packs of five or ten or more.'

'Last spring, while I was watching a herd of caribou crossing the ice at Kidlinek, I counted fifteen wolves travelling together.'

'Probably that was a family pack, Fala. Maybe two bitches, their mates, yearlings, and two-year-old cubs.'

'What is the biggest pack you have ever seen?' Kivgalo asked his father.

'One winter, when I was at Hanimor River visiting my trap-line, I saw about twenty amakro. In all my life I never again came across such a large pack.'

'Have any of your people been attacked by wolves?'

'*Immana,* Fala. Singly or in a pack, the amakro may follow or circle a hunter and his dog-team at a distance, but not for very long.'

'Why?'

'The first rifle-shot, and sometimes the hunter's scent—if it's strong enough—will scare the amakro.'

'What about dog scent?'

'That does not frighten the amakro. In the gloom of the winter night many a dog on the dog-line has been attacked and killed by him. And if a dog, or even a whole team, runs away from camp, sooner or later it will fall prey to the amakro.'

'I thought the wolves were after caribou and musk-ox the year round.'

'Not always, Fala. In summer they will eat anything—birds, squirrels, hares.'

'Wolves look so much like a species of dog in my country that I suppose they breed like dogs, too. Do they?'

'I don't know when the Kablunak's dogs breed. Mine breed almost any time. But the amakro bear their young only in spring.'

'Where do they hide at that time?'

'They seek out natural dens among fallen rock in the hills. They like to watch all the approaches without being seen themselves.'

'How many are there in a litter usually?'

'Five to ten.'

'Who provides food for the cubs while they are still too young to fetch for themselves?'

'The amakro. While the bitch watches over the cubs, he hunts alone and drags part of his kill to his family. The fittest cubs survive, grow up, go hunting together, mate with other amakros, and part. . . . You ask a lot of questions about the amakro. Have you not hunted them yourself?'

'I went hunting a few times with Nerreok when he was at Umimaktok one summer. We ran trap-lines on high ground and across passes, and set traps around caribou carcasses. And we used to lie in ambush, sometimes waiting for hours before we could get a shot at the amakro. I remember Nerreok got so tired of waiting one day that he fell asleep. Concealed by rocks, I kept up the watch. While Nerreok slept, I saw five wolves cautiously approach the caribou we had killed earlier that day. I nudged Nerreok in the side: "Hey, wake up, the wolves are coming!" I said. He rubbed his eyes, and said, half-asleep: "Where? Where?" I pointed to the wolves. They were sniffing at the carcass, licking the dried blood and biting lazily at the soft parts. They were not hungry.

'We took up our positions, and Nerreok whispered: "Let's shoot together, Fala!" We fired at the same time. Then quickly again, and again. Three of the wolves bounced up and two of them fell dead. The third tried to run away on three legs but Nerreok broke his back with a well-aimed shot. The other two escaped. Those we killed we left to the ravens and the seagulls.'

'Didn't you skin their heads to show to the Kablunak at the trading post?' asked Kakagun.

'No. In those days, at the start of the white man's big war, the police were not paying bounty on wolves. I know they do now again.'

'*Illa,* I remember, Fala. When the bounty payments stopped, my people did not bother to hold their spring and summer hunts for the amakro.'

'That's not why your people call the policeman an amakro,' I smiled.

Kakagun and Kivgalo both laughed, and the former said: '*Immana,* Fala. You were here before the Kablunan started their war. You must have heard us calling the policeman an amakro even then. It's because he goes after men like a wolf stalking a caribou.'

'Few Kablunan have ever visited this country, Fala,' Kakagun informed me as we looked across Detention Harbour from Galena Point. 'Even the Inuit seldom come here.'

'Why is that?'

'Long ago the hunting failed them, and the few caches of caribou meat that they had were eaten by wolverines. Many of them died of hunger. My people have not forgotten.'

'If the hunting is poor, why did we come here, Kakagun?'

'It is good ground for foxes, Fala. My trap-line follows the shoreline to the foot of the harbour. Let's take a look at it.'

In the intervening ten miles we snared four foxes, one of them a handsome blue that was still very much alive. Kakagun smacked the doomed animal on the nose with the handle of his snow knife. It flopped over and lay unconscious. He finished it by crushing its ribs and heart under his foot. Then he picked it up by its hind legs and examined its fur. Finding no fault, he smiled and said: 'When I was a young boy, the tiriginiak were a mere pastime for the women. And they used their fur only for children's garments and for parka trimmings. Now I can trade one at Kablunak's post for a .22 rifle or two steel sled runners.'

'How did the women hunt foxes?'

Both hunter and son looked incredulous. 'How is it you don't know, Fala? Didn't you ever see the kind of traps my people used before the Kablunak came?'

I professed forgetfulness.

'We used to make traps with heavy flat stones. We set them up like a Kablunak's box. Then we placed a rock so that it would fall and close the trap if the bait was touched.'

'Oh, yes! I've seen these old traps here and there in my travels, but I paid little attention to them.'

By noon next day we reached Desbarats Inlet, which lies a couple of miles south of the tip of Cape Barrow. There, dwarfed between 400-foot bluffs surrounding it like a horse-shoe, nestled Father Adam's little shack—a welcome half-way shelter for missionaries travelling between Burnside and Coppermine. It consisted of a ten-foot-square room equipped with a table, stove, and three wooden bunks. In its tiny en-closed porch the provident Father had stored a dozen bags of coal, a case of coal oil, and a crate of large tins of dehydrated potatoes and onions.

Blessing my friend, I got a hot fire going with the coal and cooked the vegetables in a pot of caribou meat. Quickly the cosy little place warmed sufficiently for us to doff our parkas and relax in comfort. I poured some water from the kettle into a pan and washed my hands and face for the first time in many days. It felt so wonderfully refreshing that I asked my companions if they would like to do the same. From the bunks they looked up at me and laughed merrily. 'When you wash your face you take the fat out of it. Then your nose and cheeks will freeze more easily.'

'If you Kablunan listened more to the Inuit, you would avoid a lot of trouble.'

After a steady diet of frozen or dried fish or meat, it was a treat indeed to sit down to a pot of boiled meat and vegetables. Kakagun and Kivgalo, who downed enormous quantities of the stew, expressed their approval with loud belching and the polite '*Akreartorama, goanna*. I am full, thanks!'

Cape Barrow was the anchor point on Kakagun's trap-line. Apart from that, it held no attraction for him. We left it after a restful night in the warm hut to face a bitterly cold breeze on the sea-ice. Kakagun chose not to retrace our steps by Detention Harbour and Daniel Moore Bay, but followed instead the western shore of Chapman Islands down to Stockport Islands.

Two of his older dogs developed badly frozen flanks and had to be left behind at the mercy of the Barren Land. I was thankful that my own dogs were all in good shape.

Actually, I began making sure they would be strong and well-conditioned from the time they were six-month-old pups. Gradually working them into the team to temper their growth and steel their muscles, I had them thoroughly prepared for long-distance travelling by the end of their first year. I was careful not to overburden or overstrain them, and always tried to keep them well nourished. It wasn't surprising, therefore, that Kakagun's shorthanded team soon started to fall behind. He motioned to me to stop and came over. 'I'm too heavy for my dogs. I'll ride with you, Fala, and Kivgalo will take over.'

There was little to do at most of the traps, and Kakagun's thoughts were mainly on one of the Eskimo hunter's favourite topics—dogs. 'I'd like to get some of your pups next spring,' he told me, after making several complimentary remarks about my huskies.

'You certainly can,' I said, 'but you'll have to feed them every day if you want them to withstand the constant cold and the long trips you like to take.'

'*Illa,* Fala. I'll do that, although we Inuit raise our dogs differently. We don't want their stomachs to stretch, so we feed them little when they are young. Later we give them enough food for the work they have to do and no more. They get used to that.'

Despite his seemingly heartless talk, Kakagun—like all good hunters—loved his dogs. It was a pity, but it was inevitable that at best they last only four or five years in the Barren Land. Then would come their unrewarding doom, one of the saddest features of Arctic life. For no man in the north destroys a faithful dog without a pang of grief. Inhuman though it may sound, the native hunter, for one, would sooner lose one of his own family than a dog. For a child or a woman is an extra mouth to feed. But a dog—where would he be if he could not go hunting or trapping by dog-team?

I presumed that these might be some of his thoughts as he sat moodily and silently on my sled. I had known moods like that myself caused by similar circumstances, moods as grey as the low-hanging sky, void of all colour, drained of all life. There is no telling how long they may affect a man, nor what it will take to shake them off abruptly.

A string of small islands sheltered us from the cross-wind as far as Stockport Islands, but still Kakagun said nothing. It was when we entered the narrow passage between an island shaped like Napoleon's hat and Kater Point that he dramatically broke his silence.

'Stop, Fala, stop!' he cried anxiously. 'The ice is smoking.'

'Where, Kakagun?' I asked with fear in my voice, as I automatically threw down the anchor to halt our progress.

'Look just ahead!'

Not thirty yards away a light vapour hung over the ice. It was the danger signal Nokadlak had once warned me about: 'When you see that, Fala, it means open water in the ice floor. Be very cautious.'

Right enough, worn down by the strong currents of the narrow gap, the ice had given way, and above the free, fast-flowing water hovered a grey fog.

Kakagun jumped off the sled and waved his hand to Kivgalo behind us. 'Stop! The ice is smoking!' he yelled. They obeyed at once.

Kakagun turned to me: 'Fala, I'll lead the team to the shore. We will follow it until we reach the end of the gap.

It should be safe then.' Relieved, I nodded in full agreement.

We navigated the detour safely, but it took us a good hour to get past the danger area, so rough was the ice along the shore. We forced ourselves to build an iglu and crawled in for a much-needed rest.

Out on the open sea-ice next day we were again overtaken by the gusty wind which whirled fine powdery snow in clouds that sifted through everything in sight. The dogs, the sled, and we upon it, all turned a ghostly white. The snow glued down our eyelids; it melted on our faces only to freeze again and burn the skin. But we were determined to get back to camp, and if the dogs could do it, we could, too. The huskies did not let us down. At nightfall we were greeted by Nokadlak and Kudnanak, who had arrived earlier, and stood outside the iglu with Angivrana, Nalvana, and Naoyak.

Both families crowded into Kakagun's iglu that night to hear how Nokadlak had brought back a musk-ox from Kanuyak Island.

'I was resetting a fox trap when the dogs scented something unusual,' he said. 'Kudnanak stopped them just in time from running away. Then we saw a lone *umikmak* coming down the hillside towards us.'

'It must have been an old bull wanting a fight,' suggested Kakagun.

'*Illa*. But the spirits of the land were good to me. I shot him in his tracks.'

'Did you see any more musk-oxen on that island?' I asked.

'After we fleeced the umikmak we climbed the hill to look around. We saw a herd of about forty umikmak travelling west. They were on the alert for three amakro that followed them, trying to snatch off their calves.' Nokadlak paused to puff on his cigarette.

'The amakro made a rush for the calves once, but the big umikmak quickly formed a circle around their young ones,' his son broke in. 'Standing shoulder to shoulder, with their horned heads sticking out in all directions, they left no opening for the amakro.'

'We started to descend into the valley to shoot the amakro, but they turned and fled,' Nokadlak resumed. 'This was also a signal for all the umikmak to disappear out of sight.'

'Did you bring back the umikmak's hide?' inquired Kakagun.

'*Illa*. Angivrana will scrape it and shave off the fur.'

'I would like to trade a piece of the hide. Nalvana needs some for making boot soles.'

'You can have it and some meat, too.'

'I would like to have some umikmak meat!' piped up Naoyak. 'It is so much better than Tuktuk's.'

'*Anertak*. Of course,' said Kakagun. Then he added as an afterthought: 'There is so much meat in one umikmak that it is a great pity to see so many of them get away.'

'Perhaps it is better that way,' I reminded them, 'for is it not the law of the land to leave them alone?'

23

SIRENEK THE SUN

'Let's go up to the hills and greet Sirenek the Sun!' said Nokadlak one morning. 'He should be back today, for the sky is brightening in the southeast.' It had been intensely cold for the past two weeks—so cold that even the foxes stayed in their lairs and our traps remained empty. Now the long Arctic night was on the wane and once again the sun was about to gladden our hearts.

We picked up our .22s in case we should encounter small game, and climbed the height of land above the Hood River Falls. The moment we saw the pale golden rays of the sun slant over the frozen desert, my friends removed their gloves, tossed back their hoods, and waved their arms blissfully at the low-hanging sun. I asked Kakagun, who stood smiling and waving next to me, what their gestures meant. He seemed happy to enlighten me.

'For us it is a sign of good luck and prosperity, Fala, to greet Sirenek on his first return. Sirenek harbours many kind spirits and we must welcome them back to our land.'

It was easy for me to understand how the same sun that I

had taken for granted on the shores of the blue Mediterranean became a near-deity in the Barren Land. Its long-awaited appearance brings cheer and hope to the People Beyond. It beautifies their dreary existence. It adorns their monotonous surroundings with a crown of glittering light and dancing colour. It transforms the most desolate stretch of ice and snow into a scene of transcendent beauty.

No wonder, I thought, the casual visitor to the Arctic often carries away with him little besides memories of vivid sunrises and sunsets in a setting of dazzling whiteness. 'The Arctic is picturesque beyond description,' he will tell his eager listeners at home in all sincerity. How deceived and disillusioned he would be if he remained in the same land for years instead of days! Seldom would he have occasion for such enthusiasm. Imprinted permanently on his mind would be a shadowy world of man and beast at continual grips with sub-zero temperatures and snowstorms—a world so primitive and savage that the struggle to keep from freezing and from starving is the main, and often the only, concern.

I glanced round at my companions. Their ecstatic salute to the reborn sun was over. Their faces resumed their customary serenity. They were resigned to their lot because they knew no other land, no other climate, no other life. The Barren Land was theirs from birth till death. No other people wanted it; no-one would attempt to take it away from them. This was their sole security. Yet it gave them a peace of mind that our world has always sought but has never found.

'We didn't see anything except a few tracks of Ukadlek the Hare,' Kakagun reported later in the day when he and Kivgalo joined the rest of us in camp.

'Ukadlek, and Arheliek the Ptarmigan, are hiding in the creeks,' explained the game-wise youngster. 'It is too cold for them today.'

'*Illa*,' agreed Nokadlak. 'Until spring we won't get much game inland. We'll have to hunt Natsek the Seal.'

Kakagun looked at the women busy with their sewing, at Nokadlak and Kudnanak straightening a willow stem over the blubber lamp, then said: 'There is little food left for the dogs. I'm going after Natsek's breathing holes tomorrow.' He turned to me: 'Fala, will you help us look for Natsek's aglus?'

Kakagun hardly waited for my answer, knowing it beforehand, so anxious was he to sharpen his spear on a piece of slate and tie a long narrow strip of sealskin to its detachable head.

Not having any special preparation to make, I joined Naoyak and Kivgalo in their frequent evening pastime of throwing string patterns over their fingers. Like every Krangmalit I ever met, they were very skilful at it and I could not keep up with them.

'This is a fox running,' Kivgalo was saying to the girl. 'Pick it up and make a sled.'

Naoyak passed her agile fingers through the mesh and triumphantly held up both hands with a passable string sled.

'Fala, it's your turn. Make some dancers. I'll tell you how to weave the strings!' she said excitedly. I made an honest attempt to follow her instructions, but when I held up my clumsy effort Kakagun took his eyes off his work and snorted: 'It looks like a twisted nose! Give it to me, Fala, and I'll finish it for you.' Introducing his little fingers and thumbs under the stretched strings and picking up others, he produced another combination.

'What do you think this is, Fala?'

'I couldn't guess, Kakagun.'

'That's a man and woman embracing in a krepik!'

Swiftly he made a few passes to astonish me further.

'These are female breasts! I can make many more designs

like that!' he boasted. But I had got the general idea and excused myself on the pretext of sleepiness.

Although I was tired, I could not fall asleep. I closed my eyes and tried to relax in the furry sleeping bag, but impressions and thoughts of recent events kept my mind working.

With unsuppressed yawns, Kakagun and Nalvana began undressing for bed. I could not help overhearing their whispered words.

'Kivgalo is almost a man now,' said Kakagun. 'He should start sleeping with Naoyak.'

'She is not very old yet, but she can learn to please her man,' agreed Nalvana.

Aloud to the playing youngsters Kakagun said: 'We are going to sleep. Make room for Naoyak in your krepik, Kivgalo. She will keep you warm. And some day she will be your wife.'

Kivgalo smiled, but the girl showed no emotion. They undressed and squeezed their young bodies into the boy's bag. Somehow, in those surroundings, it did not seem lascivious or even incongruous.

'Have some meat and fat, Fala,' said Kakagun. 'You'll get cold standing on the ice if you don't fill your stomach now.'

It was raw and windy on the frozen Arctic Sound where we had driven early that morning under a cloudless sky. Only Angivrana remained in camp, ten miles to the south, to mind her baby. We had anchored our three sleds, and the hunters were dishing out the food from their grub bags.

As I munched bits of frozen musk-ox meat and caribou fat I let my gaze wander across the rigid sea to the grey horizon. There wasn't a sign of life as far as my eyes could see. The only sound was the ceaseless swishing of drifting snow along the glassy ice floor.

'Let us go now and look for the seal's aglus,' said Kakagun, unharnessing one of his dogs and attaching a leash to its collar. 'This dog is one of the best I've ever had for scenting aglus,' he explained to me.

'Mine is good at it, too' said Nokadlak. 'I had a better one last summer, but he was killed in a fight.' Like Kakagun, he slung a seal bag, with his hunting implements, across his shoulders, and picked up a short harpoon in his right hand.

Just before we walked off, Nalvana, who was staying behind with Naoyak to look after the teams, told Kakagun that they would make a windbreak for themselves out of snow blocks while we were gone. 'We won't be too cold, and we will have hot tea ready for you when you return,' she said with a dutiful smile.

The dogs strained against the leash, sniffing into the wind, stopping, and trotting again, their muzzles barely skimming the snow. The hunters' sons also let the huskies choose their own direction, and they responded like trained bloodhounds. Kivgalo's dog suddenly froze in its tracks, vigorously sniffing the snow beneath it. From several yards away Kudnanak's dog swerved to the same spot. Highly excited, both dogs began to scratch the crusty snow. Covered by a drift of hard snow and totally invisible even at close range, the tiny breathing hole of the aglu now became apparent. Kakagun raised his hand to signal for silence and whispered to me: 'Can you smell it, Fala? This aglu was made by a bull seal.'

I sniffed before replying, '*Illa, tipartok*. It smells strong.' An unmistakable odour, like the mustiness of rotten onions, escaped from the blow-hole.

Lest the dog's ardent digging should warn an approaching seal, the boys pulled them off to a safe distance while Kakagun prepared to mark the aglu.

'Nokadlak and Kudnanak are going to look for some of the other aglus,' he said as they walked off quietly to the left. He knelt down and with his knife began to scrape away the top layer of snow, smoothing the rest noiselessly with his mittens. Out of his tool bag he took out a yard-long, pencil-thin whalebone with a pronounced curve and lowered it through the breathing hole. He turned it around, probing the shape of the aglu under the surface to determine its exact centre. Then he grunted happily: 'This aglu will do, Fala. Cut me a block of hard snow.'

I chopped a large slab out of a snowdrift and brought it over to Kakagun. He placed it on edge, stood up, and urinated on it. 'You, too, Fala!' he invited me. 'It will be easier to see it from a distance.'

The marker ready, we marched off with Kivgalo and the two dogs in the opposite direction from Nokadlak and his boy. The dogs led us to four other aglus within a half-mile radius. Each of these we packed so thoroughly with snow that no seal would ever break through. By the time we had sealed off the last aglu, we had gone around in a semi-circle toward Nokadlak who, in turn, had done the same to meet us.

'We found a few more aglus and kept one of them open,' Nokadlak reported.

'If we are lucky, the seal has only those two marked holes left for breathing,' said Kakagun. 'Let's try them out!'

While the two boys continued to look for holes, Kakagun and I retraced our steps to the aglu he had marked and Nokadlak proceeded to his own.

'Keep a little away from the aglu, Fala, and don't make any noise. Natsek might hear you,' cautioned my friend. He pulled out the willow stem he had prepared the night before and knelt silently by the blow-hole. The dried willow rod was forked at one end so as to spread inside the foot-wide aglu. Its other end was topped with an eider-duck feather that fluttered gaily in the light breeze, as if it sat upon an Easter bonnet. Kakagun gently swept the crust off the hole with the back of his mittens and then pushed the forked end of the rod about a foot down into the aglu. He attached a string to the stick and pegged the loose end to the snow. This sensitive marker was now set so that the least pressure on it from below would start the feather quivering. Kakagun was all set. The rest was up to the seal.

He took one last precaution. Out of his bag he produced a piece of polar bear skin that he spread on the snow as a rug to stand on. It served to insulate him from the freezing floor and deaden any creaking sound he might make by moving his feet. He picked up his harpoon and held it waist-high, bending forward slightly over the feather to await its signal.

Having mounted guard, Kakagun did not move. His eyes were glued to the bright feather. At any moment it might be pushed up by Natsek the Seal; or the wily creature might not show for hours, using other breathing holes that we might not have detected. No matter how long his vigil, a hunter like Kakagun would remain as motionless as a statue. Almost half a mile away Nokadlak was standing in the same attitude. Beyond him the two boys maintained their search. And far behind us, against the greyish twilight of a wintry sky, Nalvana and Naoyak were two tiny pebbles on a sea of white.

It was bitterly cold, but no-one would ever suspect it merely by looking at Kakagun. He was oblivious to the elements and to the passage of time; his life and the welfare of his family depended on his patience and endurance. Only the hoar-frost on his eyebrows and chin told the real story.

I stood a few yards off, watching him, trying to keep still yet warm. It was impossible not to feel the icy wind. It penetrated to the bones. It benumbed my muscles and made me ache all over. I hoped, I prayed that the seal would come soon and end this misery.

It took barely half an hour by my watch, but it seemed like eternity before the feathered indicator at last moved upward. Kakagun's body stiffened. Slowly he raised his right arm, tightening his grip on the harpoon. Then, with a grunt, he thrust his weapon down along the willow rod dead through the centre of the hole. I heard the dull thud of the harpoon's spur against the seal's head. Quickly discarding the shaft of the harpoon, Kakagun began pulling on the rope connected to the metal spur. The seal splashed and snorted, trying to plunge down the aglu, but the rope held.

'*Ikayorlanga!* Help me!' yelled Kakagun.

Miraculously my numbness vanished and I was at his side in an instant.

'Hold it tight!' he said, as I took over the line with both hands, pulling for all I was worth against the struggling seal. Kakagun went down on his knees to cut the blow-hole wide open with his snow knife. Water and blood spurted from the aperture as he worked, but he did not seem to mind. He seemed delighted, in fact, and kept encouraging me in my efforts to outlast the twisting natsek.

Led by their sniffing, yapping dogs, Kudnanak and Kivgalo came running towards us while Kakagun was chipping away the ice around the aglu with his ice chisel to make it wide enough for hauling in the prey. Together we pulled up the bleeding seal onto the ice, and the dogs leaped for the warm blood oozing out of its neck wound. Kakagun kicked the huskies to keep them off it and said: 'Let's eat the liver! It will warm up our stomachs.'

Just then we heard faint shouts. Instinctively we all looked in Nokadlak's direction. Pulling on his harpoon rope with one arm, he was frantically waving to us with the other.

'He has a natsek!' Kudnanak exclaimed superfluously.

'Let's run!' commanded Kakagun.

We dropped our catch and sprinted. I could see Nokadlak straining like the anchor man on a tug-of-war team. He was backing up, using his weight for every possible advantage.

Then he was suddenly down prostrate on the snow, sliding towards the aglu. Next moment he was struggling to stand up and pull his unseen adversary in the opposite direction. Now he was sitting on the snow, skidding forward.

'Must be a big seal, maybe an *ugiuk!*' Kakagun panted as we raced side by side.

The moment we grabbed the rope from Nokadlak we felt a powerful pull. No wonder he couldn't handle it alone, I thought. As fast as he could, Nokadlak opened and enlarged the aglu. Then, smiling proudly, he said: 'There's an ugiuk down there. I'll use your rifle, Fala.'

Aided by the boys, we drew back the rope until the ugiuk's head appeared above the bloody water. Nokadlak fired twice, point blank. The turbulent water grew redder, then quietened. The fight was over.

But we still had a job on our hands. The bearded seal must have weighed five hundred pounds, and to bring it up was a problem in itself. Nokadlak solved it by passing the rope through an incision in the animal's lower jaw and securing its snout in a loop. It took the combined strength of the rest of us to drag the massive ugiuk onto the ice floor while Nokadlak guided it through the aglu.

The happy hunter extracted the liver and passed it round for each of us to have a bite. Then he threw a piece of it on the ice as an offering to the sea spirit.

Nalvana had tea ready for us behind her snow wall, as she had promised, when we joined her and Naoyak. She could see that we had been successful, but Kudnanak surprised her and Naoyak by announcing: 'My father got an ugiuk.'

'Good for you!' Nalvana smiled at Nokadlak.

Admiringly, Naoyak echoed her words.

'We'll try another trick on Natsek,' Kakagun told me a

257

few days later when I asked why he and Nokadlak had prepared some thirty three-pronged hooks.

'With these niksiks?'

'*Illa,* Fala.'

'Are you going to put two or more in each aglu?'

'*Immana.* Only one in each aglu.'

'But you'll have more than you can use.'

'*Immana,* Fala. The ice is thick now and natsek cows carve
out resting chambers for their young at the top of the aglus.
It is easier to set niksiks in many aglus than to spear a natsek
in one of them.'

'How can a cow build a chamber in the solid ice, Kakagun?'

'She goes above the ice into the snowdrift protecting the
aglu. There she scrapes out a small iglu. In it she takes care
of her pup or sleeps and rests herself when the weather is not
too cold. If the spirits are good to us you will see for yourself.'

It would have been an enjoyable hike had it not been for
the ubiquitous cold and wind. I followed Kakagun and Kivgalo and their leashed dogs, while Nokadlak and Kudnanak
went their own way, agreeing to meet later at the sleds, which
were guarded, as before, by Nalvana and Naoyak.

Whenever we discovered a breathing-hole, Kakagun inserted a niksik through it, immersing it about a foot below
the water line in the aglu. Then he anchored the free end of
the attached rope in the ice and the trap was ready.

Setting the niksiks in the only three chambers we found
took a little more effort and skill. Each time Kakagun had to
cut open a hole on the roof of the hidden compartment large
enough to pass his arm through so that he could lay the
niksik the way he wanted it. Because I could not see exactly
how he did it, a thought occurred to me: 'Kakagun, when the
natsek enters the chamber, she will notice the niksik and
will avoid it.'

'*Immana.* I covered it with fresh snow. Natsek will come

up head first from the aglu and will glide over the niksik without feeling it. But when she begins to back out, she will get caught by the prongs.'

'From what you say, it should be easier to catch a seal that has no rest chamber but only the aglu.'

'That's right, Fala. In the aglu the niksik hangs straight down. It does not bother Natsek as he comes up for air, but often catches him on the way down because the aglu is narrow.'

'Can't the seal free himself from the hook while you are gone?'

'He will struggle and try to dive down, but in vain. He will starve or freeze if the hunter does not return to that aglu in good time.'

There was still some daylight left when we returned to camp. Naoyak and Kivgalo took advantage of it to visit some of the traps Naoyak had placed near weasel holes along the river bank. An hour later they were back, the girl proudly exhibiting five small animals less than a foot long, but with beautiful short white fur.

'What are you to do with the *tereak* fur—put it on the sleeves of Kivgalo's parka for good luck so that he can say "Tereak, tereak, come and fight good luck to its death"?'

'*Immana*, Fala. I'm going to trade it for calico.'

'Why, Naoyak?'

'To make a nice dress for the spring when we go for the big trading.'

'Too bad,' I thought, 'these handsome ermine furs will bring you only a dollar or two at the trading post!'

I was awakened next morning by Kakagun, who was the first up. 'Fala,' he said, 'Nokadlak and I are leaving early. Do you want to take a good look at the niksiks with us?'

'How's the weather, Kakagun?'

'You can hear the wind, and it is misty, but it is passable.'

'I'll be ready soon,' I said.

From marker to marker Kakagun and I went, stopping at every aglu in the four-mile circle. We gave each line a tug to see if there was anything on it. Only two of them rewarded our efforts. As we hauled in the first seal onto the ice, Kakagun turned the struggling natsek on its back, saying: 'Here's the way to kill him, Fala.' With his left hand pulling on a flipper, he raised the animal's forepart, then sharply snapped its head against the middle with his right hand. I heard the crack of breaking bones in the seal's neck, but that was all. Without so much as a cry, it lay limp and dead at Kakagun's feet.

He insisted that I apply the same merciful *coup de grâce* to the other natsek, and I found it an easy and efficient method.

'It is a good catch for one day,' Kakagun said happily when we loaded the seals aboard the sled. His eyes went past the sealskin and saw food for us all and fuel for the blubber lamp.

With the wind lashing us from the southwest, we hurried back to camp. I could not quite manage to share in Kakagun's delight. I was too cold to be anything but wretched.

Nokadlak arrived a little later. He had managed to get one seal, and had had fair luck besides in hunting ptarmigans on the return trip. He joined the rest of us in Kakagun's iglu where Nalvana passed around meat and fish until a chorus of belches announced that we were satisfied. There were happiness and good humour in the shining white abode, and an upsurge of confidence. Only those who have gone cold and hungry could really have understood how we felt that night.

24

INTERLUDE

My friends accompanied me back to Burnside for the spring trading. The morning after our arrival, I had an unexpected visitor at the Mission. It was Naoyak. She sat down on a bench in the living-room and said: 'Travellers are coming, Fala.'

'Why don't you go and greet them, Naoyak?'

'I came to ask you to come with me.'

'First let me give you some tea and candies—then we'll go.'

She drank her tea hurriedly and took a small bag of candies.

'*Goanna,* Fala. Now let's go and meet the newcomers. They should be getting close.'

We walked within sight of the fifteen iglus and tents strung out along the shore of the channel, and sat down on a drift of hard snow. '*Taku, taku,* Fala! Look, look, many travellers!' the girl cried as six teams came into view around the bend of the channel. The entire village poured out to watch them cover the last quarter-mile across the snow floor.

'Do you know any of these people, Naoyak?'

'I have seen them all before. They are from Taseriuak and

Hanimor. They have big loads. They must have caught lots of foxes.'

All the new arrivals wore well-trimmed clothing, as if they had just left their iglus. But their tired, weather-beaten faces spoke of storms, hardships, and fatigue. Lordly handshakes, broad smiles, and loud wails intermingled on all sides, re-echoing on the sloping banks of the channel. 'Somebody died inland,' Naoyak deduced.

The moans and laments—polite expressions of sympathy for children or relatives who had died recently—were quickly supplanted by the excitement of renewing friendships after months of near-isolation.

Knowing how busy Ed Kennett would be, I purposely kept away from the trading post until he could catch his breath. I took advantage of the warm sun to browse through the camp, see who had arrived, and learn the latest happenings among them. The ground was already strewn with the litter of man and dog. It had been used as a latrine by both, and as a temporary storage for caribou skins, firearms, rusty traps, harpoons, scoops, and ice-chisels. Piles of frozen caribou carcasses and bundles of dried fish lay close to the dwellings. The sleds were partially covered with snow to prevent them from melting in the sun. Hanging on ropes strung between poles and amply exposed to the same sun were boots, fur socks, caribou and seal hides, and anything else that needed drying or bleaching.

I dropped in on several families in answer to their loud tea calls. Everywhere the story was the same. The trapping had been good, starvation was avoided, the past was forgotten, the present was theirs to enjoy. Meat and fish, dry or frozen, were generously passed round and consumed with gusto.

Outside his tent I found Nokadlak unwrapping the furs

on his sled. '*Itiren,* Fala. Go in,' he said. 'Angivrana will give you a cup of tea.'

I expressed an interest in his furs. 'I am going to trade some of them,' he explained, grabbing an armful and following me into the tent.

Angivrana sat on the iglek, putting on her boots. Her baby rested comfortably in her parka hood. Nokadlak tossed the furs to his wife. 'Have a look through these. We can trade them now.'

Instead or sorting the pelts, she replied: 'The Kablunak will look at them all. But we must remember to get something from them that we really need.' In the silence of her iglu on the Artic Sound she had long since decided what Nokadlak should purchase at the trading post. But from experience she knew that once he was confronted with the wealth of the Niuvavik, her advice would be forgotten—unless, of course, she was on the spot to remind him.

We walked up the slope to Ed's store. Like a peacock displaying his bright plumage, Nokadlak entered the warehouse with his bundle of fine furs. Fluttering like a goose about to take flight, Angivrana was close on his heels. They glanced around quickly. A dozen hunters with their women and children had preceded them. Here was the moment Nokadlak and Angivrana had looked forward to all winter. Here was their one great opportunity to show off in front of their friends.

Nokadlak's eyes kept shifting from side to side. He had come in with the intention of making a brilliant impression on everyone. Yet now he stood speechless, almost breathless, before the imposing array of the Kablunak's ingenious merchandise. Sparkling hardware shone at him from the shelves or dangled tantalizingly from the rafters. Beautiful new rifles, boxes upon boxes of ammunition; harnesses and tools of all kinds; sacks of tea, sugar, flour; earthenware, chinaware, glassware; calico. . . .

He was thrown off balance, like a child in a toy shop. Mechanically he pulled the furs out of his bag and dumped them on the counter. '*Tamma! Uva!* Give me this—that!' He began pointing indiscriminately to a variety of articles, and Ed obligingly fetched them down to lay them before him.

Angivrana, practical and self-possessed despite the strange surroundings and glittering temptations, came to the rescue of her bewildered spouse. 'Why do you choose what you don't like? I don't think you will want a dog collar. We need a kettle, some enamel cups, a pot, needles . . . . '

The entranced Nokadlak hardly noticed her. But Angivrana was not so easily discouraged. She knew precisely what she wanted, and she meant to get it. 'We have little tea and tobacco left. I thought you would want to get some.'

'It doesn't matter,' he grumbled. 'If you would only leave the thinking to me. . . . '

They stayed in the store for hours, arguing back and forth over each item, trying to get the most out of the Kablunak they were set on outwitting. Ed, wise in their ways, left them alone to wait on other customers like them who were closer to reaching a final decision.

When, some time later, they left the store devoid of furs and laden with boxes of the Kablunak's merchandise, they paused just outside and I heard Nokadlak grumble: 'We have no matches.'

They went back in and Nokadlak said to Ed as soon as he got his attention: 'It's too bad, but we want some matches. How are we going to light fires without them?' He rummaged through his purchases and brought out a roll of twine. 'Look, Kablunak, I don't need this. Will you change it for matches?'

Ed accommodated him without protest. To me he said with a wink: 'They'll be back again!'

Visitors swarmed into Nokadlak's tent almost as soon as he and Angivrana returned from the store. He spread his booty out flamboyantly, with the triumphant smile of the shrewd and successful bargainer. As his visitors picked over the articles with various complimentary exclamations and gestures, one held up a watch and asked: 'What are you going to do with this, Nokadlak?'

'I don't know. The baby might like to play with it.'

'I'll trade a newborn pup for it. How's that?'

'Good. I need more dogs.'

An hour ago Nokadlak had paid three foxes for the watch, and now he was exchanging it for a puppy worth one fox at most. But it was spring, he was happy, and at the end of the year he would have a new, trained member in his dog-team.

Before the visitors left, the watch had gone the rounds, being traded next for a snow knife, then for a parka, a wooden sled runner, and finally for a night with the successful bidder's wife.

More and more families kept arriving, until by the end of the week nearly a hundred dancers were crowding into the kalgit each night. Among them was my guide at Cambridge Bay, the hunter Kunak. He had changed little in appearance or in nature. As usual, when he took the drum and sang his song, his boasting was outrageous.

He did not boast of his prowess in hunting or in love; his song was devoted to the invincible speed of his dogs. This could not go unchallenged. Towards the end of the dance, when the women had brought in their steaming kettles of tea and meat and fish, and everyone was squatting exhausted on the snow floor, Kakagun said for all to hear: 'Hey, Kunak, you said your dogs could beat anyone's team here. How about a race tomorrow?'

'My dogs brought me here from Ikalututiak in four days. They are a little tired, but they're still good enough for a race. I'll bet a fox that I'll win!'

'I'll take that bet! It will be easier than catching a fox with a trap!' Kakagun said with a laugh.

When the news of the race reached the trading post, Ed Kennett put up five foxes for first prize, three for second, and one for third, and offered a party for everybody at the end of the race. The dogs themselves must have sensed the excitement of their masters, for their howling drowned out everything else while the hunters were icing up their sleds and harnessing their teams.

I went with Ed to the starting place at the entrance of the channel, where a noisy, laughing crowd was already on hand.

The competitors decided to use only five dogs to a sled, and to carry no extra weight on it. The teams drove up to their positions at the starting line. We counted forty-five entrants in all. 'Better tell them the rules now, Father,' Ed suggested. 'Once around Krikitakapfaluk Island and back here. No running along the dogs. No whips. You can start them off with a rifle shot.'

I called out the rules as I walked behind the sleds so that all the drivers could hear. Then I stood back, waited for them to get set, and fired into the air. Amid a roar from the partisan spectators, the startled dogs scrambled in all directions. Some even turned right round and headed back for camp, despite the 'gee' and 'ha' commands of their masters. Several teams tangled, and a huge dog fight resulted. Bystanders ran to break it up. Dogs left behind on their lines yelped furiously.

'What a start! What a shambles!' Ed roared delightedly, while a semblance of order was being restored. Finally the last of the contestants was off and the teams strung out on the sea floor among the snow-drifts.

'How long will it take them to get back, Ed?'

'The course is twenty miles. The winners should make it in about three hours. While we're waiting we ought to organize something for the kids.'

The Krangmalit boys and girls took naturally to sprinting races and to a tug-of-war between the sexes. In the latter event, while their parents screamed encouragement with *'Takke, takke*. Come on!' the boys suddenly slackened the long rope. The girls lost their balance and landed on their seats. Quickly taking advantage of their opponents' slip, the boys hauled them across the middle line to win the contest. Loud praise for the cunning little men and suggestive comments about the frailty of little women filled the air. Everybody laughed heartily, and Ed gave out his candy prizes.

'Maybe the women can do better than the men,' I suggested. That was all the incentive they needed. The men expected little resistance and almost let their cockiness defeat them. The women were tenacious, if nothing else. And for a truly dependable anchor they had picked the biggest, fattest woman in camp. She planted her three hundred pounds on the snow, dug her heels in, and refused to be budged. Disconcerted by their initial attempts, and goaded by the howling taunts of the children and old people on the sidelines, the men could gain no ground for a long time. But neither would they gave any up. Very gradually the strain proved too much for their wives, and it was over at last.

We were in the midst of foot races for the women when someone sighted the first of the returning dog-teams two or three miles off. To get a better view of the home stretch, we all climbed the sloping bank.

'Who's in the lead?' was the question on everyone's lips. 'He's well ahead of the rest!'

I noticed Nalvana and Naoyak standing close together, watching intently. Tense moments passed. Then Naoyak's excited voice rang out: 'The leading dog is white. It's Kakagun's team!'

'It's Kakagun! It's Kakagun!' the word flew round.

Nearly everyone shook hands with the great hunter as he crossed the finish line. He beamed as he became the victor. When I congratulated him, he laughed. 'The race was won before we started, Fala!'

'What do you mean, Kakagun?'

'For the last three days I fed my dogs caribou meat. Yesterday I didn't feed them at all. Today they were furious because I let them smell the meat without giving them any. To earn it they ran like wolves.'

And Kunak? He placed neither second nor third. Two other young men from Hanimor did that. The boastful Kunak was sixteenth.

When all the teams were in, everybody headed for the trading post, milling outside the helper's shack where Ed served tea, pilot bread, and jam. I contributed caribou meat and rice which some of the women volunteered to cook for the hungry multitude.

Ed meantime set up a block of snow and placed a target on it. Then he paced off three hundred yards and waited for the marksmen. Each hunter was allowed three rounds, courtesy of Ed Kennett, who also provided the prizes—several cartons of 30-30 ammunition. Kakagun won again.

Finally there was an archery shoot in which my old friend Nerreok, the lone-wolf hunter, was the outstanding performer. Never once did his trusty bow falter. His arrows not only hit the thick snow target at a range of fifty yards; they went right through it and landed well beyond. No wonder

I had not been able to draw his bow when he offered it to me at Melville Sound!

Nokadlak, waiting for his turn to shoot, said: 'When we were young men, I saw Nerreok kill two caribou that were running side by side with one arrow!'

The archery championship was never in doubt, and Nerreok triumphantly carried off the prize—two one-pound tins of tobacco.

One day Kakagun, Nokadlak, and I set out on a seal-hunt. We had reached a reef north of Koagiuk when Nokadlak spotted the seal a mile off. He motioned to Kakagun and me and we all stopped our teams.

'The snow is crackling under our feet. I'll go alone,' Nokadlak said. Out of his hunting bag he pulled a long white sealskin parka and put it on. It fell to his knees, and its hood hid not only his head but part of his face.

As he ran forward in a crouch, keeping the sun behind him, Kakagun and I watched from behind rocks. 'Natsek is shortsighted. He will think Nokadlak is a piece of rough ice and will let him come close,' said Kakagun.

When he was only about fifty yards away from the seal, Nokadlak fell prone and waited for it to raise its head. When it had gone back to sleep, he ran a few more steps, flopped on the sea-ice, and uncovered his rifle. He wormed his way closer to his prey and lay ready to shoot. The seal's head came up. There was a loud report. 'Natsek's dreams are over forever,' said Kakagun; then he added: 'I'll show you I'm as good as Nokadlak. Let's find another seal.'

We drove up to Nokadlak, his team willingly following ours, and resumed the hunt. Every few minutes Kakagun stood up on his sled to get a better view of the frozen sea. 'There!' he said, pointing. 'Natsek is quite far away, but we should stop here or he may hear or scent us.'

Kakagun quickly attached a square white canvas sail to a tiny sled whose runners were wrapped in strips of polar-bear skin to deaden noise. Three feet long and not much more than a foot wide, like a child's sleigh, it served merely as a support for the four-foot sail to conceal his movements from the vigilant seal, which he could observe meantime through a peep-hole in the middle of the sail.

'Keep the dogs from howling, Fala,' Kakagun said. He looked round, sniffing at the breeze, plucked a few hairs from his parka, and tossed them in the air. 'I'll have to walk a long way or the wind will waft my scent to Natsek.'

Stooping behind the white screen, he walked off, pushing the sled before him with the barrel of his rifle. Half-an-hour later we could just discern him stalking the little dark spot that was his quarry. He was crawling now, getting within firing range. The unsuspecting seal did not have a chance.

It was natural that both hunters should offer the third seal we sighted to me. 'Let's see if a Kablunak can be as good as an Inuk,' Kakagun said, smiling.

'*Oktorlugo*, Fala. Go ahead, try it,' said Nokadlak.

I borrowed the latter's white parka, and used his tactics to approach the seal from the rear. When I was thirty yards from it I let its eyes get used to my prostrate white form. It seemed to me that Natsek stared unduly long in my direction. I was about to shoot when another seal raised his head from the same aglu. I took a potshot at the latecomer, then fired quickly at my original quarry before he could dive.

'You are like an Inuk, Fala!' Kakagun complimented me as he and Nokadlak brought up my team. 'But we heard two shots. Why?'

'Look in the aglu. The reason may be there.'

'*Ayuitutin*, Fala! You are certainly capable!' My friends pounded my shoulder.

INTERLUDE

The news of our successful seal-hunt brought a change in the life of the camp. It seemed to remind some of the natives that their dog-food was getting low and that it was time to move off to the hunting grounds. Several hunters left the very next day for Taseriuak in the expectation of encountering caribou there. But most headed during the next few days for the entrance of Bathurst Inlet, some eighty miles to the north. There, at Wilmot Island, seals would be plentiful in spring, and hunters would congregate from as far as Cambridge Bay, Richardson Island, and Coppermine to disperse in all directions two or three weeks later before the summer break-up.

The last to leave Burnside were the families of Kakagun and Nokadlak. With their impending departure for Wilmot Island, there was no point in my remaining at the Mission. My duty was to keep in touch with the natives.

25

SNOWBOUND

Rattling particles of frozen snow drifted over Wilmot Island as we arrived, bucking a cold northeaster. It was a foretaste of the miserable weather that was to dog us almost daily for the next two weeks.

Tents were pitched all round the main cove, which faced south out of its horseshoe of surrounding cliffs. A small trading post, now closed, looked over the splendid natural harbour.

So preoccupied were the earlier arrivals with looking after their tents and equipment in the howling wind, that our coming was unnoticed. There was no dance that night. The men were too tired to build a hall, and it was too cold for open-air frolicking.

Howling dogs woke me late next morning. Another team was pulling into camp. I breakfasted on coffee and started my rounds. The wind had grown stronger overnight, hurling snow on the sea, on the beach, and on the distant bluffs whose tops were rounded by centuries of erosion. Only a few hunters were outside, checking their dogs or sleds.

Kakagun's tent was crowded. Nalvana was serving tea to the latest arrivals—a young couple with two children. I

shook hands with them and asked the young hunter: 'Did
you have fair weather on the trail?' He smiled, then wrinkled
his nose as he answered: '*Immana*. We had wind every day
after we left Napartolik. And yesterday we couldn't even see
the island and camped on the sea.'

When I got up and told my hosts I was going to visit the
other people in camp, Naoyak said brightly: 'You'll find
everybody in, Fala. The weather is too stormy for hunting.
I'll come with you.' She slipped on her outdoor parka and
put on her mittens. Without saying a word, Kivgalo followed
us.

'Which tent do you want to visit, Fala?'

'Any one will do, Naoyak.'

Proudly she guided me from tent to tent. She knew everyone in camp. Her excellent memory spared me the impolite-
ness of asking the natives their names or where they were from.
The few times that she faltered, Kivgalo helped out readily.
He, too, was proud of his intimate knowledge of the families
we visited, and his fund of stories about them was inexhaustible.

'That tiny, chubby woman we just saw, Fala, is Ukayaluk.
She has passed from man to man. Five, perhaps more. She
stays with one hunter, then another. And always some stranger comes and takes her away.'

'What's her husband's name, Kivgalo?'

'Her husband now is Krisuk. He is a great fighter with his
fists.'

'I didn't see any children near their tent. Have they any?'

'Ukayaluk never had a boy. She bears only girls. She is
childless.'

In another tent I saw a tall, lean man who stood off by
himself in a corner, acting in a peculiarly restless manner. He
kept hopping from foot to foot, shaking like a dog just out

of the water, and laughing continuously at everything and everybody in sight.

'This is Kaotak,' Naoyak said quietly to me. 'He is from Ellice River.'

Outside I asked Kivgalo what he knew about Kaotak.

'I have heard that he killed two men, Fala. He took away the wife of the first victim, but he ill-treated her and she soon died. Then he lived with the young wife of the other murdered man. She bore him a child, but eventually ran away with another hunter. He has been shaking like that ever since.'

For the next three days the weather steadily deteriorated. Powdery snow fell continuously. With the wind's help it sifted through every tiny hole in our tents and buried our sleds, the dogs, and any equipment left outside. We spent much of our time digging out and cleaning our belongings. It was an exhausting, endless task. The hunters were growing impatient. It was May and still there was no sign of summer. Supplies were dwindling and it was impossible to replenish them in this weather.

Towards the end of the week the wind dropped and everybody emerged to walk about and remove some of the drifts around the camp.

Suddenly someone shouted: 'Look, *aagnek!*' We looked up to see a flock of ducks flying north.

'They are looking for open water,' said Nokadlak, 'but they will find nothing but ice.'

'At least we know that summer is coming,' observed Kakagun.

We couldn't help laughing when an hour later the ducks were back overhead, flying lower but faster in the opposite direction.

To soothe their restlessness the hunters and their families

exchanged frequent visits, despite the dangers and extreme discomforts of venturing out in the blizzards.

'*Krayguit*, Fala! Come on, Father. Come with us. You won't get lost with us,' Nokadlak or Kakagun would say to me whenever they decided to drop in on their friends in various parts of the camp. It was like preparing a full-scale expedition. Outer parkas, breeches, and a snow knife were the minimum equipment for everybody but the babies, who took the chance in their mothers' hoods. The hunters and their wives realized that losing their way in the swirling, blinding snow meant death, unless someone had an implement for building a small iglu to wait out the storm.

The women held sewing bees, which kept them cheerfully occupied and afforded them added opportunities for small talk and gossip. With Kakagun and Nalvana I happened to be detained one evening in one of the largest tents in camp where half-a-dozen women had congregated with their sewing. They chatted and laughed as they scraped, rubbed, and chewed the caribou skins they would later fashion into handsome parkas. Kakagun shifted his large frame uncomfortably: 'Let's go and see the men,' he said to me. 'These women sound like a flock of ducks!'

Overhearing him, a fat elderly woman with a pear-shaped face said mockingly: 'Nalvana has brought lots of skins. Why can't a big, strong man like you help us scrape them?'

A young woman with a baby in her hood put in: 'Men will give their urine to dampen the skins, but they don't care to use their hands!' There was more truth than humour in the remark, but everybody laughed as if it were a great joke.

This was Kakagun's cue for a string of remarkably lewd comments on women in general. The women enjoyed them immensely and kept looking at me to see if I would join in.

I pretended not to understand, and the talk ultimately returned to sewing.

'Who made your parka, Fala?' asked the young mother with a look of admiring appraisal.

'Nalvana, when I was at Kattimanek.'

'*Pignertok!* It's beautiful!'

Nalvana laughed self-consciously as I said: 'She is a very clever seamstress.'

'Do the Kablunak women make clothes like us?' asked the fat one.

'Yes, they make clothes, but they use calico because it is never cold in my country. And their dresses are of different shapes and colours.'

'Ours are the same because we use only caribou skin for protection from the wind and cold.'

'Why don't you use other animals' skins for variety?'

'We don't use seal because it isn't warm enough in the winter and it stiffens in cold weather. The white bear and the musk-ox are too warm and too heavy. Wolf and fox fur are warm and light, but they are too weak and snow sticks to them and cakes into ice.'

It was during one of these sessions that I met my old friend Krilalugak, the sorcerer. We had not seen each other since he had tried to cure Naoyak at Kubiartorvik, but he spoke to me as if there had been no break in our conversation: 'You are too much by yourself, Kablunak. Why don't you take a wife like everybody else here?'

'Many white men live without wives, and I am one of them. If I were married, I would not be here to help your people.'

Krilalugak always had to have the last word. 'Kablunak, look at the beasts. They are like us, male and female, and they always mate. It is against nature to live alone.'

'I know many young men here without mates. And you yourself have no wife, either.'

'I had a wife, but she died. I could have one now, but I like to sleep with a different woman wherever I go. That's what young men do, too, because there are too few women among my people.'

'I know, Krilalugak. That's the reason you and the young men like to move from camp to camp.'

'But whenever a young man finds a woman, Fala, he marries her,' interposed Kakagun.

'*Illa,* they must marry,' repeated Krilalugak.

'*Illa, illa,*' cooed an old woman squatting forlornly in a corner of the iglek. 'I always trained my children how to mate when they were young. Now they are all married and have their own children to teach.'

'I have already taught Kivgalo and Naoyak,' said Kakagun. 'Now they always sleep together. Kivgalo does not have to look for a wife, unless he loses Naoyak by being a poor hunter.'

'We gave Nokadlak a rifle and three dogs for Naoyak,' put in Nalvana. Then she said thoughtfully: 'When I was a girl, my parents handed me over to the parents of my first husband for nothing, just because they were good friends and good hunters.'

'I was a good hunter when I was younger,' said the sorcerer. 'I got my wife for nothing, too. I tried her out for two winters. She was good. Then she became pregnant. I don't know whether I made her pregnant, but I knew I had to take care of her. She bore me three sons and died.'

The unbroken stormy weather was getting on everyone's nerves. Repeatedly the men set out to build a kalgik for a dance, but each time the gusty winds ate away the snow blocks as fast as they could cut them, or piled up drifts to hamper their progress.

Then there was the business of getting food for the dogs,

a problem I shared with the rest. Much as I hated to go out into the storm, I went with Kakagun and Nokadlak after tom-cods, the only fish available at the time. If nothing else, these excursions to a comparatively protected cove on the west side of the island helped shake me out of my sluggishness—a form of the well-known 'Arctic mania' brought on by worry, loneliness, and bitter cold. We walked along the shore and across a narrow strip of land to the fishing spot where, in the lee of the sloping bluffs, earlier arrivals met behind blocks of snow and jigged for the *aogaks*.

'I'll make a hole for you first, Fala. Then you can help me scoop out the chips of ice,' said Kakagun.

Half an hour later, warmed by our efforts, we sat down to dangle our hooks in the dark water beneath the ice, using bits of white calico for bait. Fortunately the tom-cods were both plentiful and gullible. Nokadlak's hole turned out to be the best producer. In the two hours we spent there he pulled out no less than thirty fish. Kakagun and I between us caught forty-five, many of them weighing from ten to fifteen pounds. There was little nourishment in the aogaks, but at least they would keep our dogs from hunger until we could offer them something better.

By the time we returned to our tents we were half frozen. Kakagun's cough was worse than usual, and for the first time I heard him complain about the weather. '*Alapa, kaiornartok*. It's cold; it's freezing. Winter lasts too long in our land.' His wheezing cold at times made him gasp. He cleared his throat after one spasm and confided: 'It is painful, Fala. My throat is hard and swollen.'

I wished there was something I could do for him, but the symptoms told me there was nothing.

That evening as I visited several tents I noticed that a quiet air had replaced the customary verve of Krangmalit gatherings. They had reverted to the tranquil resignation imposed on them by winter's rigours and dull surroundings. They were again in a state of partial hibernation, their minds and souls suspended in a vacuum.

'If the weather clears, we shall just stay a few days here to hunt Natsek and then go inland,' I heard Nokadlak say meditatively.

Out of his vast knowledge of the Barren Land, Krilalugak advised my friends solemnly: 'When Silla decides to change his course, the southern wind will bring a fast thaw. It will be wise to move to the winter camps.'

Even the children, normally as lively as the husky pups they played with, were subdued. With the rest of them, Naoyak spent most of the time standing idly in the tent, her face glum, her ears half-listening to the sparse talk of the elders present.

At times the conversation degenerated into a disjointed, stammering monologue with the bystanders hardly listening at all but nodding their heads in automatic agreement. It was so with Nokadlak now. 'I was jigging for aogak with Fala,' he began slowly, lifelessly, then paused. 'We found a good spot along the bluffs.' He paused even longer. 'My bitch had a litter of five pups.' He fell silent again, gathering his thoughts. 'Fala hooked a big aogak. . . . He pulled it up. . . . The line broke. . . . As I said, my bitch bore five pups. . . . Two are female. . . . Should I keep them?'

Used to the mental processes of the Krangmalit, I listened patiently to the simple, often disconnected observations of Nokadlak and his friends. But I could imagine what an outsider would think.

'Tell me, Father,' he would ask, 'have these people no intelligence? Are they feeble-minded?'

But I would leap to their defence. 'No! They may not have our powers of logical description, but their primitive way of thinking has its own wisdom. Though they may not grasp the antecedent and the sequence of a given topic, their minds remain alert and keen-witted whenever they are with friends. But when they are alone in their iglus, separated from other families by distance and by weather, they sometimes seem drowsy and stultified.

'On such occasions, too, their better natures might be over-shadowed by incomprehensible acts of brutality. These reveal their primitive temperament, hardened by the frozen world about them. Accustomed from childhood to natural and violent death, they are not in the least troubled by an act that puts an end to a man's life.

'Their whole conception of life is different from ours, and they cannot be understood on brief acquaintance. Live with them and among them, take part in their daily routine for years and years, and then judge them, if you like—but not before.'

When the storm finally disappeared, the men spread out on the sea-ice in search of seals, just as their ancestors had done for countless generations. Soon the various families would be separated for several months, and this fact made them lose interest in each other and think and act in terms of their own family groups. With the rest, Kakagun and Nokad-lak realized that they must go their separate ways to avoid starvation.

The seal hunt proved so disappointing that many of the hunters began to pack and leave the island the following day. My two friends were among them. 'My dogs are almost starv-ing,' I told them, 'and the caribou have probably arrived. I am going, too.'

'We'll travel by way of the Kulugayuk River, Fala,' said Kakagun, whose cough seemed worse. 'We shall winter at Taserkapfaluk. Will you be coming to see us?'

'I don't expect so, Kakagun. I may have to call on the Tunuarmeun, the People on the Back of the Earth.'

The People on the Back of the Earth are so called because their land is the ultimate limit of inhabitable tundra. Beyond them lies the perpetually frozen world of longer Arctic nights, greater storms, stronger and more dangerous currents under the ice floor.

I spent nearly three years with these people. When I lived with them there were only twenty-one families in the group. They had seldom mixed with other groups of Eskimos. I found their life still more stark and harsh than those of the groups I had known before. Inevitably they had adhered more closely to the ways of their ancestors. Animal life was scarcer and less varied in their territory. Hence they were forced to follow a more limited pattern in their hunting and fishing, and to keep continually on the move. •

I came back to Burnside feeling that I had seen Arctic life stripped to its grim essentials and that I now had a far deeper understanding of all Eskimos. At Burnside I heard from Ed Kennett that Kakagun and Nokadlak were planning to winter at Siorkretak. I decided to join them there in September.

26

TUKTUK DRIVE

No-one greeted me on the beach at Siorkretak when I arrived, although four tents stood guard on a flat sand-bar at the mouth of the river. Dwarf-willows spotted the sloping hills at either side of the winding river, providing a pleasant contrast to the bare rocks and sandy river banks. Several dogs stood up to get a better view of my jolly-boat; others sat up or remained lying. All watched me with a boredom born on the dog-line.

I walked up to the tents, listened, and peered inside. They were all empty. Then I heard faint voices and laughter upstream. I sat down on a rock and waited. The voices grew louder. Still I could see no-one, for the river turned sharply behind huge boulders, concealing the approaching company.

Then I heard someone exclaim: *'Umiak kraysimayok!* A boat has come!' and several natives appeared round the bend, running and shouting. A young man and woman outdistanced the rest and made straight for me. I stood up to salute them.

'Falaoyok! It's Fala!' she cried, and rushed to shake hands.

'Naoyak! How you have changed!' I said. 'And this must be Kivgalo. How big you've grown!'

'*Illa*, I'm Kivgalo. At first I did not know you. You have taken off your beard.'

Four years had done much for the handsome young couple. Naoyak was now taller than I. No longer the little girl I remembered, she had filled out and her pretty face carried a promise of maturity, though it still retained its red cheeks and smiling eyes. Kivgalo towered over me. He looked at Naoyak with such tenderness and possessiveness that I asked: 'Are you married?'

'*Illa,* Fala,' he replied proudly.

Kakagun, Nokadlak, Kudnanak, and the young man I had met at Wilmot Island in Kakagun's tent now surrounded me. Then came the women, who had been slowed down by the weight of their caribou bags. Greetings were accompanied by shouts of laughter.

'Fala has cut off his whiskers. His face looks like a young girl's!' exclaimed Nalvana.

'Yes,' agreed Angivrana, passing her hand over my bald pate, 'but his head feels like a woman's breast!'

When the laughter—and Kakagun's coughing—had diminished, he said: 'Women, make tea! We are all thirsty and hungry. Fala must be, too.'

Picking up armfuls of fuel from the piles of willow twigs by each tent, the women went willingly into the tents to fire the stoves. I sat down on an overturned sled with the men. Nokadlak patted his bulging carrying bag. 'We got many fish at the traps, Fala.'

'Where are your traps?'

'By the rapids.'

'Agleroitok and I didn't fish; we went to look for his dogs,' Kudnanak said, glancing at his stocky friend, the young man from Wilmot. He was massively built, thick folds of flesh almost concealing his slanted eyes.

'What happened to the dogs?'

Nokadlak laughed. 'They ran away yesterday when we were looking for caribou. Agleroitok had four dogs with him to pack the meat. He tied them to a willow when we saw two bulls grazing. We went after the bulls. But as we fired on them, three more tuktuk emerged from a creek. The dogs saw them. They are still chasing them!'

'They will not catch the tuktuk,' Agleroitok drawled. 'The wolves will get the dogs.'

Kakagun nodded silently. Then a coughing spell hit him. His thin, leathery face showed his pain. He was still tall and erect; his movements expressed his enviable energy; his eyes were still piercing. But his cropped hair was now grey and his aquiline face drawn and more deeply lined.

'I cough a lot,' he said apologetically. 'Sometimes it chokes me, setting my head on fire.'

'*Mammianak*. It is too bad,' sympathized his friend Nokadlak.

By contrast, the intervening years had hardly left a mark on him. Long-legged and broad-shouldered like his son Kudnanak, he still wore that indefinably mixed expression of mirth and sadness peculiar to young Eskimos as yet unbroken by their cruel surroundings. Only the crow's feet about his eyes were more pronounced now, especially when he laughed or spoke.

'Tea should be ready soon,' said Kakagun, observing the wisps of smoke rising from the chimneys that signalled hot fires below and listening for the clattering of enamel cups within the tents. Expert fire- and tea-makers that they were, the women did not keep us waiting long. Exuding good cheer, they brought us steaming tea, then meat and half-dried fish, and, when all the menfolk were served, squatted on the gravel to enjoy the food and drink with us.

Naoyak stood out among them. In the youthful bloom of life, she flitted back and forth with the kettle, smiling, refilling the cups, joking with everybody.

Politely I said to Agleroitok: 'I don't know your wife's name.' He was so pleased at my interest that his eyes disappeared for a moment. 'Her name is Komayak.' Then, pointing to a girl about eight sitting on the ground with a little boy, he added: 'This is my daughter. She is promised to Kudnanak.'

'Is the boy yours, too?'

'*Immana*. Mine died at Taserkapfaluk. He is Nokadlak's.'

Eying his young wife, I was trying to think where, when, or in what connection I had heard her name before. She was conscious of my scrutiny, and old scars on her thin cheeks showed up more prominently in her embarrassment. Suddenly I remembered. It was she who had shot and killed a Mountie at Coppermine several years ago—Komayak, the jealous one, who wouldn't be a mistress and a plaything to a Kablunak!

Uncannily guessing my thoughts, Nalvana said with a giggle: 'Komayak was kept prisoner at Korluktok for a whole winter. She cooked for the Amakro. Then she went away with Agleroitok to Napartolik.'

I was to learn no more. Abruptly Kakagun changed the subject with the flat assertion that the caribou were returning from the north. Nokadlak picked up the hint. 'Let's prepare the pathways for them tomorrow,' he said enthusiastically.

'We haven't tasted caribou fat for a long time,' Angivrana added encouragingly.

'Last fall we hunted tuktuk for its fat. We got a full sled

of *tunu* one day. That was the time Naoyak became a woman,' recalled Nalvana.

'I remember now,' said Angivrana. 'When I learned that, I told Kivgalo Naoyak was his and that he could live with her in his tent.'

'Nalvana and Angivrana helped me make the tent,' joined in Naoyak. 'Afterwards I sewed clothes for Kivgalo all by myself.'

Angivrana began to laugh. '*Uvagor?* What is it?' Kakagun asked curiously.

'Nokadlak's brother was hunting with us at that time. His son Kublurinak tried to sleep with Naoyak. He did not know that it is taboo between cousins,' she said, as if she were telling a very funny story.

'After my first husband died,' confided Komayak, 'I used to sleep with his brother. But he could not marry me. It is taboo to marry a dead husband's relative.'

Leaving the rugged bed of the Siorkretak River, we climbed the north bank to reach a narrow valley lying between eroded hills. Over the years, boulders of all sizes and shapes had detached themselves from the bluffs and rolled to the valley floor, making passage along it extremely difficult.

In the distance several dark grey shapes almost blended into the green-grey of the granite. They were the vanguard of the caribou herds to come.

We walked the length of the mile-long valley until it opened like the top of a funnel onto a wide rolling plain that ended in a marsh.

'Any day now the tuktuk will be passing here in small herds on their way south,' said Kakagun.

'What are you going to do? Build cairns or wait for them behind the rocks?'

'They are too cautious now to be stalked, Fala. The wolves

are after them. To get them, we'll have to drive them into the valley and down towards the river by the camp.'

Quietly Kakagun exchanged a few remarks with Nokadlak, and then announced for all to hear: 'We can start erecting the *inukut*. I will go with Fala and the women to the left.'

'We will follow you on the right,' Nokadlak spoke for the men and boys.

I helped Kakagun make a pile of rocks nearly five feet high and watched him apply the finishing touches with moss to give the cairn a vague resemblance to a human form. One by one we built these inukut or man-likenesses some fifty yards apart, Nokadlak and his helpers doing the same along a parallel line two hundred yards away. It was hard work for us all—stooping, carrying, laying rocks all day long. What made it infinitely worse were the swarms of little black sand-flies that increased in numbers and ferocity as we came nearer to the swamp. They clung to our sweaty faces, necks, and hands; bit into the flesh and sucked our blood to leave our skin in itching, burning bumps. My only consolation was that it was early September and the clouds of enormous Arctic mosquitoes had vanished two or three weeks earlier. Otherwise I doubt if I could have endured the task.

By the time we reached the marshland, fifty cairns stood strung out behind us like a file of lazy soldiers. Kakagun pointed to a well-trodden path along the edge of the bog. 'Many tuktuk will come this way,' he said confidently.

A solitary shot rang out over the plain and reverberated through the valley. We looked about, but saw nothing. Everyone was here except Kivgalo. Kudnanak smiled knowingly. 'Kivgalo saw a fawn and went after it. He must have got it.'

That was sufficient notice for the eager women. They gathered resinous moss, piled it into a heap over flat rocks, and lit it in anticipation of the feast. Kivgalo did not disappoint them. He appeared presently from behind a knoll, carrying the fawn on his shoulders. Proudly he tossed his prize on the ground, flayed it, and shoved the skin into his hunting bag. Naoyak and Nalvana sliced off long steaks and passed them to Angivrana and Komayak who drew a flat rock out of the fire and used it as a frying pan.

While I savoured the tender meat, my eyes picked out several caribou bulls grazing at a comfortably safe distance among the rocks. Quite apart from them, out on the open land, a number of cows and their fawns were also feeding. It was as peaceful a scene as one might find on a well-regulated farm. And it brought smiles of joy to my friends, whose appetite for tuktuk had only been whetted by the fried fawn.

On the slope of a hill, a couple of miles away, female caribou stood by while two bulls battered each other so furiously that we could hear the thuds of their clashing antlers. The battle was fierce but brief. What looked like the smaller of the gladiators turned and ran off, shaking his antlers like a stunned boxer trying to clear his head. The victor recovered his breath, strutted over to a cow, and topped her.

The women walked ahead of us as we retraced our steps through the valley. They chattered and laughed, pausing only for potshots with their .22s at ground squirrels that peered curiously at us from all sides.

'Soon they will have enough siksiks to feed each one of us,' said Nokadlak with a laugh.

'*Mamartok.* That's good. It will be a change,' said Kivgalo.

Past the valley's throat we built additional cairns as directed by Kakagun, who led us close to the camp where the river flowed, at once wide and deep. With the cairns all ready, Kakagun and Nokadlak brought over two kayaks and hid them behind large boulders for the closing stage of the hunt.

But our preparations were far from over. Until late that evening we toiled over our hunting equipment. Rifles were cleaned and checked. Bows were strung with new twisted caribou sinew. Arrows were feathered. Short-shafted spears were made with chunks of loose copper found inland. The women sharpened their ulons and skinning knives, mended the sealskin boots, and filled hunting bags with ammunition.

A cheerful atmosphere pervaded our gathering. Sipping his last cup of tea, Nokadlak put his feelings into words: 'Tuktuk are plentiful. We shall not go hungry.'

'*Illa*, I was thinking the same thing,' said Kakagun. 'This is a good place for wintering. Tomorrow we will kill as many tuktuk as possible.'

For a time, at least, they knew they were secure from the evil spirits of the land.

'*Tuparen*, Fala! Wake up!' Nalvana was saying as she shook me from sleep. 'We'll be going soon.' Kakagun was coughing and dressing. I was the last one up.

The sun was just rising when I stepped outside. It was cold and the ground was hardened by frost. Naoyak was walking down her dog-line, checking the huskies. When she saw me she waved and shouted: '*Alapa!* It's cold! But the sun will soon warm up the land.'

Nalvana poked her head through the little door of the tent and said invitingly: 'Come in, Fala, and have some tea before we go.'

Nokadlak and Kudnanak did not come with the rest of us. 'They are going to hide near the kayaks and wait for the tuktuk,' explained Kakagun. 'We'll join them afterwards.'

As we entered the valley, Kivgalo and Agleroitok left our party to climb the north side of the rising cliffs. We waited for them to wave to us upon sighting the caribou. We could see them scanning the land, but the signal did not come. Instead they ran down again.

'Tuktuk—many of them—coming slowly!' exclaimed Agleroitok.

'They are still far away, but they are heading for the marshes!' Kivgalo reported exuberantly, and everybody laughed for joy.

'You can go and make a lot of noise to frighten the tuktuk,' Kakagun told the women.

They left eagerly, almost running, Angivrana carrying her young son on her shoulders. As they disappeared in the folds of the rolling land, Kakagun said with a smile: 'Women are good for this work. They can scare any animal in the tundra!'

Agleroitok and Kivgalo walked slowly up the valley. Kakagun turned to me: 'Let's find a good hiding-place, Fala.'

He drew my attention to what looked like a soldier's fox-hole with a wind-shield of rocks. There were many of them along the beaten caribou paths. 'These hiding-places were made long ago by our ancestors. They lay in them and shot arrows at passing tuktuk,' he explained.

'*Illa*, Kakagun. I've seen them at Uyaraktok and Ikralutu-tiak. Hunters still use them.'

'It is easier to shoot lying down in a hole than standing behind a boulder.'

More than an hour passed before the women started their ear-splitting noise. It was immediately effective. First half-a-dozen caribou, then sixty more stampeded along the trail prepared for them. Terrified, they veered off the edge of the marshland clear of the menacing cairns, ranged like giant chessmen, and headed into the valley of no return.

Kivgalo and Agleroitok let the first wave enter the narrow valley before opening fire. From his fox-hole Kakagun shot arrow after arrow with amazing accuracy. Only when his quiver was empty did he bring his rifle into play. Caribou tumbled all round us. Those that escaped raced out of the valley towards the river where we knew Nokadlak and Kud-nanak were waiting for them.

Other waves of bewildered caribou met the same fate. It was not sport—it was butchery; not aimless or wanton slaughter, but the vital provision of food for the fast-approaching winter.

When only a few straggling caribou remained on the valley floor, Kakagun shouted to Agleroitok and Kivgalo: '*Krailu-tik!* Come on! Let's go back to the river!'

Several caribou were swimming in mid-stream, and Nokad-lak in his kayak was down on their necks, spear in hand. Confused and terrified, other caribou milled on the bank where Kudnanak, unobserved, picked them off with his rifle. We opened fire on them, and before long none remained alive. The water turned red as they floated downstream. Kudnanak hopped into the second kayak to help his father retrieve them. When the last of the caribou had been towed to shore, Nokadlak said: 'I will stay behind to empty the tuktuk while they are still warm. The rest of you had better go with Kakagun to help the women skin the others.'

Here and there amid the boulders of the valley we came across wounded caribou lying helplessly and silently. A final shudder went through them as the hunting knife ended their misery.

We found the women beyond the marshes flaying caribou they had managed to shoot down themselves. Sweating over their work, they had replaced their parkas with shapeless Mother Hubbard calico dresses. Naoyak's arms were caked with blood up to her elbows. She pointed to the caribou she had just skinned and said to Kivgalo: 'Look how thick the tunu is!'

The white fat extended over the top of the animal's back. Thin between the shoulders, it thickened gradually to a depth of nearly three inches at the rump.

'*Tuktuk orshornartok*. The caribou is fat,' agreed Kivgalo. Then he added with a boastful smile: 'We killed them all!' She jumped and danced in high glee.

It did not take us long to skin and empty the rest of the caribou the women had killed. Then, laboriously, we cut out chunks of half-frozen peat with our hunting knives to conceal the piles of caribou from foxes and crows. The peat would freeze during the night and make a protective shell for the carcasses until the hunters required them.

The women worked exceedingly hard. Sweat streamed down their necks, matting their long black hair. '*Onarpadlarame*. It's too hot,' was their only complaint.

Where Kivgalo, Agleroitok, Kakagun, and I had been lying in ambush, dead caribou were scattered over the ground. I counted more than fifty. Some of those shot down by arrows were still breathing. Kakagun finished them with his deadly knife and plucked his arrows out. A few stragglers came within range and paid for their curiosity.

At last the work was over and we lounged on the rocks, sipping hot tea the unflagging women had prepared. I watched Nokadlak slice one of the caribou stomachs. The skin round the raw pouch was a dirty yellow, but inside all was green. The hunters and their women scooped out handfuls of half-digested grass and began to lap it up like porridge. It was the only vegetable I ever saw them eat.

I would have preferred not to sample it, but Angivrana insisted. With a flat stone I took a small helping of the greenish paste. It tasted rather like spinach, but I did not take to it. I pretended it was as delicious as they themselves found it, and they let me off at that.

We spent the rest of the day cutting up the carcasses and packing the life-giving meat to camp. Between us we had killed scores of caribou, yet each hunter knew exactly how many he personally had accounted for and kept the appropriate number of skins for himself and his family. As usual, I was the only one who had not kept score. I gathered up the fifteen unclaimed skins.

It took several days to slice the meat and hang it up to dry in the wind and sun. All the skins were dried by being stretched and pegged to the ground. Even bones with any meat on them were placed on flat stones to dry. Later they would be used for making soup or given to the dogs. Thus, almost every part of the caribou, from hoof to head, was used in some way.

Although the meat, the skins, and the bones surrounded every tent, I knew that they would be consumed before the long, cold winter set in. And yet, aside from fish that would be difficult to catch under the ice, there was nothing else my friends could hope to obtain in quantity. Besides, caribou meant not only better food but warmer clothing, shelter, and stronger dogs. Caribou was, in fact, the very foundation of their precarious existence.

'It is freezing. I am going back to the Mission tomorrow,' I told Kakagun and Nokadlak. They were not surprised. The former even gave his approval. 'The seagulls and ducks have left. Snow will fall and winds will blow harder and more often. You are right to go while the weather is still good, Fala.' He had been troubled with coughing attacks more than ever, but maintained his usual friendly composure.

'Are you coming after the freeze-up?' I asked.

'Kakagun and I will come to trade some caribou skins,' answered Nokadlak, and Kakagun added: 'Then maybe you can give me something for my throat. It is more painful now. Sometimes I choke at night.'

'Come as soon as you can, Kakagun, and I'll see what I can do for you.' I tried to make my words sound full of hope.

When Naoyak heard that I was leaving, she came over with

Kivgalo to Kakagun's tent that evening. 'You are going away,' she said softly. 'Here, I made a pair of slippers for you. Take them.'

It was a beautiful pair. Their tops were expertly sewn of black and white fawn hide, their soles of bleached sealskin.

'They're pretty. *Goanna*, Naoyak!' I was deeply touched.

She beamed, flattered by my praise. Kivgalo added a little of his own with a smile of understandable pride: '*Ayuitok*. She is skilful.'

27

DISASTER

I got back to the Mission just in time to see the bad weather set in. Sleety northwest winds whipped up the seas as never before. They rose to seven feet in a land where tides are almost unknown. The squalls brought frost without dry snow, and damp, penetrating cold that chilled every living thing.

Thick snow followed closely on the heels of the departing sleet. It fell continuously for several days. It covered everything in sight except Bathurst Inlet, which was still free of ice. The scene was like the negative of a photograph: white land and black sea.

It took only three consecutive nights of comparative calm and dropping temperatures to change the heaving black waters into a still, frozen mass of white. Then the wind came back. Day after day, in undiminishing fury, it tore in from the north. Clouds of powdery snow raced across the plains, swept into the creeks and the valleys, rolled over the mountains, until it was impossible to tell the land and sea from the sky. Everything was grey twilight.

Not a single Eskimo came in to the trading post. In the relative comfort and security of post and Mission, Ed and I looked out into the wild weather and constantly wondered about our friends who were somewhere out there.

In early December the winds calmed down at last. After weeks of unrelenting turbulence, the silence of the frozen land and sea was overwhelming in its own way. Only the melancholy howling of passing wolves or the yelping of my dogs on the line broke the perfect stillness of the long Arctic night.

One day the temperature slid down to 55 degrees below zero in a matter of hours, causing Ed to predict gloomily that there were more and worse storms ahead.

Later that day Kakagun, Nokadlak, Kivgalo, Kudnanak, and Agleroitok arrived at the post. They all looked tired and gaunt, with a yellow tinge of sickness in their faces. Kakagun's eyes were bulging, and a dry, grating cough contorted his strong features as we shook hands. I knew then what I had suspected before. The big man, the great hunter, was slowly dying of strangulation from a small but malignant growth in his throat. And I was powerless to help him.

'Where are the women?' I asked him, trying not to show my deep concern for his hopeless condition.

'Still at Siorkretak. They are jigging tom-cods.' Kakagun's voice lacked its usual vibrant vitality.

'We just came to trade foxes and caribou skins, Fala,' said Nokadlak.

'We're going back tomorrow,' added his son Kudnanak.

'Did you get many foxes?' I asked, and wished I hadn't.

The question merely brought sardonic smiles from the men and the answer I deserved from Nokadlak: 'Foxes, like us, don't travel during storms. And we had storms all the time.'

'*Ayornartok, illa*. It really couldn't be helped,' Agleroitok tried to soften the situation.

'We were hungry,' said Kivgalo. 'We lost some dogs.'

'Can you give me something for my cough, Fala?' asked Kakagun. 'My throat hurts. Sometimes I can't even talk. I am getting older and weaker every day.' He coughed again.

'Don't worry, Kakagun. I'll try to get you some relief.'

They partook of tea and food, then decided to call on Ed.

'If you'd like to sleep here, bring in your krepiks,' I told them. 'It's too cold tonight to stay outside.'

'*Goanna*, Fala, we'll sleep with you,' said Nokadlak for the rest.

When they returned an hour later I had a pot of steaming rice and meat for them. They ate their fill, then, drowsy with good food and the warmth of Kablunak's iglu, unrolled their sleeping bags on the floor and stretched out.

For a long time that night I heard Kakagun's raucous cough above their snores.

'The moon has a ring. We'll have to hurry,' Nokadlak remarked to his friends when they rose early next morning.

'The dogs have had a good rest. We may have time to reach Siorkretak before the storm,' said Kakagun hopefully.

'I'll visit you soon,' I assured him. 'Meantime, keep your throat warm day and night.'

'*Illa*, Fala. But, warm or cold, it is always painful.'

As they left, I glanced at the thermometer that hung by the entrance porch. It had climbed during the night and now read only 15 below. But in my living-room the barometer had dropped several millibars.

Towards noon it dropped still further and the wind was gathering force. By two o'clock it swept the snow off the frozen floor with such force that visibility was reduced to zero. Despite the six-foot-thick wall of hard snow around it, the Mission building shook under the powerful blasts. I was imprisoned by the elements.

For seven days the terrible wind continued—at a velocity of a hundred miles an hour, as I learned later. I worried about my friends at Siorkretok. Had they any food? Had they enough blubber or tunu for their stone lamps? I wasn't to know for several weeks. Though the storm centre moved on, the wind did not subside completely. Just before Christmas the post was exposed to a succession of westerly gales so violent that only Ed and his wife and their helper's family attended midnight Mass. No-one else came to Burnside.

In mid-January the temperature dropped to 40 below and stayed there. The wind disappeared, and I thought it safe to go and see my friends. I found them thinner than ever, subdued in manner, but as hospitable as ever. Kakagun was still worse. Only a dozen dogs were left: tails lying on the ground near the dog-lines spoke eloquently of the fate of the rest, sacrificed to keep their stronger brothers alive. In all this, the Eskimo comment was the same—'*Ayorama*'.

It had been a terrible winter. Even when the long, stormy polar night gave way to the spring sun, the weather continued to be treacherous, with sudden gales sweeping over the snow-covered tundra and driving every living being for the nearest shelter. Nevertheless, the natives converged on the trading post from all directions.

Trapping had been poor, and most of them had been starving off and on through the winter months. They were still cheerful and composed, but they were a sorry lot—gaunt, indolent, and aged before their time—much like their pitifully skinny dogs. It was still so cold that they all built spacious iglus instead of pitching their caribou tents. But none of them bothered to put up a kalgik for dancing. That would have taken energy they could ill afford to spare.

The few foxes brought in by the hunters were soon traded for tea, tobacco, and ammunition. Only necessities were bought. Ed Kennett told me it was the worst year he had experienced in his entire trading career. 'Even the pelts are of poor quality because the foxes have been starving, too.'

'Think of the hunters and their families, Ed! They've seldom had it so tough. Did you notice how little life was left in most of them?'

'Sure, Father, but they'll get back to normal as soon as the caribou come. By the way, I almost forgot to tell you. I got a radio message from Coppermine the other day that a police patrol is heading this way. Might be here any time now.'

'Who's coming, Ed?'

'A fellow named Reggie Aitken. He never saw the Arctic till last summer.'

When I left Ed, I went down the channel where the iglus were ranged like giant white beehives. Meeting some of the natives, I told them that the policeman was coming and would probably ask for the usual gathering of all the hunters. They seemed uninterested in the news. One hunter quipped: 'Is he going to count the foxes we trapped or the caribou we shot?'

'No,' I replied in the same tone, 'but he might ask how many musk-oxen you left inland.'

It was grim humour, but they squeezed every ounce of laughter they could from it before they turned back to their mending.

I went back to the Mission to find my living-room taken over by several natives, among them Kakagun, Kivgalo, and Naoyak. My old friend Krilalugak, the sorcerer, was also there, and I greeted him gladly. His ageless features remained the same, although he complained of getting older. Smilingly I assured him that everyone was, but he took no solace from my trite remark.

Having treated Kakagun's throat two days before, I was anxious to know how he felt now. His disappointing answer came in a choking whisper: 'I cannot swallow solid food any more, Fala. Soon I shall die from hunger.'

Pooh-poohing such thoughts, I asked Naoyak to make tea for us all. She rose willingly. As she brushed past me to go to the kitchen, I noticed how terribly thin she was. I hoped that Ed Kennett was right when he said that the coming of the caribou would bring my friends back to normal.

For lack of other drugs, I put a few drops of iodine in Kakagun's tea and gave him a couple of anti-grippe capsules with the admonition: 'Swallow these now, Kakagun, and stay for a while. It is warm in here and it will do you good.'

'What are you giving him, Kablunak?' Krilalugak asked suspiciously. 'Something to make him die quicker?'

With all the little vocal force at his command, Kakagun came to my defence: 'You are an old man yourself, Krilalugak, and soon flies will be laying their eggs in the sockets of your eyes. Why don't you let Fala alone? Can't your ancient eyes see he is trying his best to help me?'

Late the following day the dogs' cacophonous howling announced the arrival of the policeman. In bright moonlight I saw his team coming up the slope towards the trading post. I walked ahead to meet Constable Aitken. He was a tall, pleasant-looking young man of about twenty-five. I introduced myself and asked him if he had had a good trip in.

'Would've been perfect, Father, if Natsit here hadn't got the flu a couple of days after we left.'

I recognized his young guide and interpreter from Coppermine. He had earned the reputation of a fearless traveller, but at the moment he could hardly stand up by himself.

Ed Kennett came out to welcome the young Mountie, and the natives began to crowd around the newcomers, shaking

hands with Natsit and the Amakro. Spontaneously they
helped unharness the panting dogs and unload the sled while
Ed invited Reg Aitken to make himself at home in his
quarters.

'What about Natsit?' the latter asked with concern.

'He can stay with my helper, and I'm sure Father Raymond
won't mind taking care of his cold.'

'I'll be glad to give him a good dose of anti-grippe capsules,
but I'm afraid that's about the extent of my medical supplies
at present.'

When I got over to Ed's helper's house, it was jammed
with natives. Natsit lay fully dressed on his krepik, coughing
and talking to his friends. The air was blue with cigarette
smoke and, I suspected, thick with flu germs. I got Natsit to
take the pills, and strode back to the Mission for the night.

The young constable didn't waste time. He had Ed warm
up his commodious warehouse with a large coal heater and
held meetings with the natives for the next two days. With
the aid of all present, he brought his census figures up to
date and then painstakingly explained pertinent sections of
the Game Ordinance and such welfare items as emergency
rations for the aged.

His job done, Constable Aitken hurried off to other camps
at Gray's Bay, Tree River, and Kogaryuak, taking the ailing
Natsit with him.

At noon that day Naoyak and Nalvana called at the Mission. Both were coughing and looked miserable. 'Fala,' said
Naoyak, 'I don't feel at all well. My head aches and my body
is cold.'

'*Uvangalu*. The same with me,' echoed Nalvana. 'I cough
all the time. Many people are coughing now.'

After administering the cure-all cold capsules to them, I
said: 'Go back to your iglus. Drink lots of tea and broth and

try to keep warm. I'll look you up in the evening.'

During the afternoon other natives beat a regular path to my door. But my medicine shelves were bare except for first-aid supplies, aspirin, and anti-grippe capsules in which I was rapidly losing faith.

All my shivering patients complained of the same distress: '*Kallakpatugut*. We are coughing. And we are cold.'

Two boys came early next morning. '*Inuit aniartun*. People are sick. They are asking for you,' they said.

It had snowed during the night, and now a ground wind whipped the powdery snow in our faces. Apart from the sleeping dogs, there was no sign of life outside the thirty iglus. Nor could a stranger have guessed all the misery they contained within their round walls. More than a hundred people were in various stages of the debilitating disease, tossing about listlessly, moaning, coughing, and spitting where they lay.

I took the temperature of the first two victims. It was 104. I didn't bother reading the others', knowing that by now they would all have fever. I gave them cold tablets and aspirin and advised them to stay still and keep warm in their sleeping bags.

Some of the entrances were snowed over and I had to dig my way in. Inside, yellow mucus hung frozen on the walls and spotted the snow floor. Older natives did not waste their sputum. They spat into their cupped hands and sucked it in to regurgitate it later.

In Kakagun's iglu things were at their worst. Naoyak was coughing fitfully. '*Onarpadlarama*. I feel too hot,' she wailed, her face wet with high fever. Kivgalo lay prone beside her, spitting down on the floor beneath. He kept saying: '*Akoglu-lertunga*. I am getting weak.' Stretched in the krepik close to Kakagun, Nalvana courageously tended the blubber lamp. The great hunter himself was a shocking sight. Air hissed through his throat like steam out of a boiling kettle as he fought for breath. I could barely understand what he was trying to tell me, but it sounded like 'I am choking—I am finished.'

'You are all coming with me to stay in my house where I can take better care of you,' I said as cheerfully as I could under the circumstances.

'*Immana*, Fala,' Kakagun mustered a faint but determined protest. 'I am going to die like an Inuk in my own iglu.'

'I shall stay with Kakagun,' Nalvana said weakly.

Sick as they were, Naoyak and Kivgalo did not hesitate. They dressed and came along with me. As we walked to the Mission, a familiar figure crawled out of one of the iglus. His parka embellished with all the symbols of his trade, Krilalugak the Sorcerer paused to eye me curiously. Then his tired old face cracked at the mouth as he remarked in authoritative tones: 'People are coughing. They are sick. It is because they have displeased the spirits of the land.'

'I'll do my best to keep the spirits away,' I said helpfully.

His deep black eyes flashed angrily. 'Why don't you keep away yourself?'

I thought it best not to cross him in his ugly mood and moved silently on to the Mission with my two young patients. I made them comfortable in their sleeping bag which I laid on a pile of caribou skins. I gave them tins to spit in and shoved more coal into the heater. Then I served them hot tea with a strong dose of anti-grippe capsules and bade them keep warm while I went back to see Kakagun.

On the way I thought it advisable to speak to Ed Kennett about supplies for the natives. 'The flu is getting out of control,' I told him. 'All but a dozen are stricken with it. And what worries me is that most of them have little fuel left for their lamps, and their stock of dog food is meagre.'

'I've plenty of coal oil, Father, but that's not much good

because only a few of them have primus stoves. Those who want it, of course, are welcome to it. As for dog food, I am afraid I can't give them any more than you can. I'd like to help in every way I can, though. I know what this flu can do to an Eskimo. My own wife's in bed with a high fever.'

His eyes bulging wildly, his veins protruding on his temples, Kakagun was torn by convulsions. Making desperate efforts to get enough air into his lungs, he hissed faintly when he saw me: 'Let's get it over with. Give me something to make me die!'

I diluted a sedative in warm water and fed it to him, a few drops at a time. It didn't help at once. He begged me to shoot him or give him poison. 'Ayolerama, Fala. I have come to the end,' he kept repeating.

In one of his worst fits, when with wide-open mouth he gasped for air like a fish held out of water, Nalvana tried feebly to pull his tongue. Tears were in her eyes as she implored him not to leave her. 'Come back, come back!' she wailed like a lost child.

When the drug began to take effect, I told Kakagun I would be back after visiting the other sick families.

There was a noticeable change in their attitude towards me. Many would not speak to me and all refused to take any medicine. Knowing Nokadlak better than the rest, I thought I could expect to get an honest answer from him to my repeated question: 'Why do you refuse my help?' I did. 'Krilalugak warned us that your medicine would kill us. He said the spirits of the land told him we must avoid touching or receiving anything from you or we shall die.'

From the other iglek of the double iglu I heard Agleroitok's brave request: 'Give me some of your medicine, Fala. My wife Komayak and I will take it.'

'Where is your daughter?' I asked them. 'Is she ill, too?'

'*Immana,* she is out visiting.'

I invited them to come to the Mission, adding, as an inducement, that Kivgalo and Naoyak were already there. After a brief consultation with each other they decided to accept the invitation. Kudnanak, who was also suffering from the fever and cough, wavered for a time, and then said he would follow us. But none of my arguments could budge Nokadlak and Angivrana. Steeped in Krangmalit customs and superstitions, they were as adamant as Kakagun and Nalvana.

28

AYORAMA

Constable Aitken's guide Natsit had picked up his flu from shaking hands with white men who had flown to Coppermine. The flu he transmitted to the Eskimos at Burnside turned into pneumonia and was fast developing into acute broncho-pneumonia and gangrene of the lungs.

Almost everyone in camp was prostrate. The weather continued cold and windy. Yet in many of the iglus the stone lamps were lit only when it was necessary to melt snow for drinking water or making tea, so low were their blubber supplies. Dog food was all but gone, too, and more than three hundred huskies lay starving in the snow.

Even in the Mission, notwithstanding the relative comfort and care, the condition of some of my patients grew steadily worse. Flushed, and breathing with extreme difficulty, Kivgalo told me he could not stand the suffering much more. Hardly feeling any better than her husband, Naoyak tried vainly to smile when she complained of an aching head and pains in her chest. I did what I could for both of them.

Later in the day Kivgalo became delirious. I could not

make any sense out of his mutterings, but Naoyak stoically informed me that he was trying to say he was nearing the end and wanted to die. I talked quietly to him, but there seemed to be no understanding in his feverish eyes. When approaching death suddenly lifted him out of his unconsciousness, he said slowly to no-one in particular: '*Ayorama*. It can't be helped—but must I leave this wonderful land?'

'You will find a better place,' I said. 'I have told you about it often. Remember?'

'*Illa*, Fala. And I remember the song we used to sing about it.' His eyes closed and he began to hum the refrain of a Christmas hymn I had taught him:

> '*Kuvianartorle* . . . How wonderful
> For us all that God was born
> To make us friends of His
> In a land of happiness. . . .'

His voice grew fainter. He wetted his feverish dry lips with his tongue and said hoarsely: 'Give me tea, Fala, with lots of sugar.' I raised his sweaty head with my left arm and brought the sweet tea to his mouth. He tried to sip, but couldn't. Like a whipped puppy he looked up at me and whispered: '*Goanna*, Fala. Take care of Naoyak.' He did not speak again.

'*Anerneyertok*. He is without breath,' cried Naoyak softly.

'*Anerneyertok*,' repeated the others unemotionally.

I went out and got two hunters who were still miraculously free from the flu to help me bury the boy. We wrapped his thin body in a caribou skin and carried it out to the waiting sled. Slowly we pulled it for three hundred yards to the Mission's burying ground and laid the remains on a snow-covered knoll. We placed blocks of snow all around the corpse and I said the prayers for the dead.

As we trudged back, Agleroitok's daughter ran up to me.

'Kakagun is dying and he wants you,' she said shyly, avoiding my eyes. I dropped the sled rope and hurried over to my friend's side.

Kakagun had all but crawled out of his krepik and sat almost naked, choking for breath. I took his pulse. It was racing. I dissolved some bromide tablets in water and attempted to spoon the liquid down his throat. He spat out every drop. 'I can't swallow!' he gasped. 'Give me my attige. I'm freezing!'

Nalvana pointed to Kakagun's best parka and I helped him put it on. He stretched out in the krepik, as if to sleep, but the fever kept him twisting and shuddering.

'Kakagun,' I said levelly, 'you tell me you are going. Would you like to go to the Land of the Great Good Spirit—the one I told you about?'

'*Illa*, Fala. Baptize me. I have been thinking about it for a long time.'

'I'll be gone by tomorrow, too, Fala,' said Nalvana. 'I want to see the Land of the Great Spirit.'

I baptized them both with a little water from the kettle. Kakagun was quieter now, thinking. Finally he whispered: 'Are you going to put my body into the ground?'

'I can't while the ground is frozen.'

'But when summer comes, you will. I am afraid.'

'There is nothing to be afraid of, Kakagun. Burial in the ground is a protection against foxes and wolverines.'

'My people never put bodies under the ground.'

'I know, Kakagun. We'll wait and see.'

He fell silent again but for his laborious breathing. Suddenly it stopped, too.

Nalvana shrank into her krepik. She knew her great hunter would never rise again. And whatever will to live she might have had was now gone.

308

Three other bodies were taken out of camp by dog team that day to Tikerar, a narrow promontory a mile away from the post.

While their dogs died from starvation and exhaustion on the dog-lines, whole families crowded together in the same sleeping bags, spitting their lungs out.

Once I found a group of fever-ridden natives standing completely naked in the snow porch.

'Why don't you listen to me?' I demanded angrily. 'Why don't you try to keep warm as I've told every one of you?'

Their teeth chattering in the sub-zero temperature, they chorused: 'Krilalugak told us to go outside to lose our sweat.'

'Tomorrow you'll all lose your lives!' I said bitterly.

Some of them laughed at me through their shivers. Others coughed in my face.

'Where is the sorcerer?' I asked in desperation.

'*Nauna*. We don't know.'

It wasn't difficult to locate Krilalugak. He was crouching in his krepik, shivering, coughing, and moaning, like the rest. Regarding me blankly, he blurted: 'Leave me alone, Kablunak! The spirits will help me.'

'They are powerless to help you and your people. They are dying right and left now, and you are hastening their deaths,' I retorted.

'*Ayornorman*. There is nothing one can do,' he said, and his tone, for once, was subdued.

That night I woke up in a cold sweat. Someone was calling me from the living-room. By the dim light of a storm lantern I saw Naoyak propped up against her folded parka. 'I cannot stand it any more,' she sobbed, her wasted body torn in agony. She was choking now, and her formerly pretty face portrayed nothing but pain and hopelessness.

Komayak, who lay coughing next to the girl, said dispassionately: 'She cannot pull through.'

I slid a cushion behind Naoyak's head and tried to cheer her up. 'You'll feel better when I get you some tea.'

'*Immana,* Fala. Don't leave me!'

I sat down on the floor. 'I won't leave you, Naoyak. Don't be afraid.'

As I wiped the sweat off her thin face and neck, she asked: 'Am I going to see Kivgalo soon?'

'Yes, and Kakagun and Nalvana. Then some day I'll come, too.'

'We'll all wait for you, Fala.'

I kept talking to her quietly, recalling all I had tried to teach her about the Good Spirit over the years, and filling her heart with Christian hope. Towards dawn the smile I knew so well returned to her sunken cheeks. 'I am not afraid any more,' she said calmly. 'Go to sleep. I'll be all right.'

'No, I'll stay with you. You just close your eyes and rest.'

Courageously Naoyak tried to relax, but her breathing was too hard. Like a wounded fawn, she lay staring at me with imploring eyes, waiting for the final merciful blow. It came with the sunrise. Without a word or gesture of emotion, she passed on beyond, the true Eskimo to the end.

I wrapped her slender young body in caribou skins and laid it close to Kivgalo's.

Ed Kennett was gazing through his office window when I called on him. He had shaken off the flu, but wisely stayed indoors as much as he could. Unlike so many natives, his wife was also on the mend.

'Say, what's going on out there?' he greeted me, pointing to a commotion among the dogs at Tikerak.

'Those are the surviving dogs, Ed. They have lived so far on their weaker brothers. Now they are dining at the cemetery.'

Several huskies lumbered back to camp past the trading post. Their bloated paunches hung low, like toy balloons filled with sand. I shuddered, and walked over to the window in the living-room which looked out in the direction of the Mission burial ground. I was relieved to see no dogs there. The blocks of snow provided enough protection against them for the time being.

Curled up and stiff, Nalvana lay dead in her krepik. There was no-one else in her iglu. In accordance with Krangmalit custom, she had dressed herself in her best parka when she knew the end was near. I tried to stretch her body out to wrap it for burial like the rest, but *rigor mortis* proved stronger than I. Covering her in caribou skins, I took her away as she was.

Nokadlak died stoically, without a murmur. And so did his son, Kudnanak, and the latter's friend, Agleroitok. All three might have survived if they had not passively surrendered to an enemy they could not see or understand. With Nokadlak's little daughter, I buried them all side by side.

Left alone, Angivrana and Komayak put up a surprising fight until gangrene set in, in their mouths. Their cheeks swelled enormously, with pus exuding from the extended pores. They died helplessly in a state of partial putrefaction.

The biggest surprise of all proved to be Krilalugak, the old sorcerer. Only a few days earlier he had been plagued with a tubercular cough, but now he seemed almost completely recovered. While I marvelled at his stamina, I could not help criticizing him for turning the people against me.

'They must listen to me, the tunrak, or a greater calamity still may befall them,' he said in haughty anger. 'There isn't room here for you and me!'

A frightful coughing fit shook his Spartan frame. He doubled up, throwing his arms across his chest to allay the pain. Blood gushed from his mouth and splattered over the snow floor. He reeled like a drunken man and fell in his own blood while I watched, horror-stricken.

It was like the raising of a siege when the caribou came at last and the stronger hunters were able to kill several dozen for the camp. Slowly the surviving natives and their dogs picked up strength. By the second week in May they had dispersed to their winter camps at Taseriuak, Krimakton, and Taserkapfaluk. Their numbers sadly depleted, some families rode along with others. Several replaced the fallen dogs in their harnesses and pulled their sleds and belongings like beasts of burden. Even so, they were glad to move away from the scene of death.

In their fresh surroundings they soon forgot the recent disaster. Like their ancestors, oppressed by countless centuries of privation and failure against the evil spirits of the land, they were too concerned with their daily fight for existence to worry about the past.

When, at long last, Bathurst Inlet became free of ice, Ed Kennett, his wife Ivarlo, and I enjoyed several trips among its many inlets in my trusty whale-boat equipped with an outboard motor. We gathered flowers and ore-bearing rocks and generally idled the sunny days away to restore our undermined health and morale.

Later that summer, when it grew too windy and cold for these pleasure trips, I asked Ed if he would help me bury the dead at the Mission cemetery.

'Sure, Father,' he said. 'How many are there?'

'Fifteen grown-ups and several children. We can put two youngsters in the same grave. The ground should be sufficiently thawed now to make digging comparatively easy.'

Still packed in the caribou skins, now bleached by the sun, the corpses lay on the mossy ground. 'The foxes have been here,' Ed said, pointing to scattered bits of caribou fur.

Clouds of bluebottle flies swarmed over the dead, and even with the wind behind us, the stench of decaying flesh was overpowering.

I strode right up to the bundles for a closer look. Ed was right about the foxes. They had torn holes in the wrappings and feasted on the contents. The state of the bodies was indescribable.

Our shovels bit into the top few inches of mossy soil. After two feet of gravel we reached the level of permanent frost. We pulled the corpses into the shallow graves, covering them with what we had dug out. I prayed silently for each of the dead.

GLOSSARY

The Eskimo words defined here are italicized the first time they appear in the narrative. Eskimo dialogue is translated in the text.

aagnek, ducks
aglu, breathing hole of a seal
akraliak, northern lights
aktatak, breeches
amakro, wolf
anakhe, whitefish
anaotak, stick (with which to beat things)
anernek, breath, soul
angiptain, clods of moss (from *angun,* man, because of their resemblance to human heads)
aogak, tom-cod
arluk, blue wolf
arnak, woman
attige, parka
ayorama, it can't be helped; life is like that (*lit.* because I am helpless)

iglek, built-up platform of snow, bed
iglu, snow-house
ilisitok, the clever one (used to describe the tunrak's adversary)
iluvek, burial ground
inuk, person, Eskimo
inukut, like a man, man-likeness
ivitaruk, type of salmon living in certain lakes in the islands

kakivok, trident made of caribou antlers and a steel spike
kalgik, community iglu
kanayok, sculpin (type of fish)

kapielik, whitefish
karlik, short ornamented breeches
kattuk, drum
kayak, boat
kayortok, red fox
kereaotilik, cross foxes
kiluitok, sewing in small stitches
kisak, sled anchor
koglunek, heavy ridge of ice
komak, larvae of the botfly, louse
korvik, tin can (chamber pot)
krammotik, sled
krarkolak, hardtack bread
krepik, sleeping bag
kubiak, fish-net
kudlek, blubber lamp

nanuk, bear
nanurak, bearskin
natsek, seal
niapkrotain, heads
niksik, four-pronged hook

paunrain, the most common Arctic berry
pikuktok, hunchbacks (a type of fish)
pirtok, storm
pitiksi, arrow, rifle
puelluk, mittens

siksik, ground squirrel
sirenek, sun

taktuk, fog
taptaoyak, children's game, similar to blind man's buff
tereak, weasel
tikerk, forefinger

tiriginiak, white foxes
torho, porch-tunnel of an iglu (*lit.* throat or gullet)
tuktuk, caribou
tunrak, sorcerer
tunu, caribou fat
tupilak, devil

ugiuk, large seal
ukalek, hare
ulon, fan-shaped knife
umikmak, musk-ox
uyaluk, tornado

Generally nouns ending in *k* are singular, in *t* plural, e.g. Krangmalek (*sing.*), Krangmalit (*plural*).

V I C T O R I A

I S L A N D

C.C.
Minta Inlet

THE PEOPLE AT THE BACK OF THE EARTH

Holman I.

Prince Albert Sound

—70°

THE FISH
PEOPLE

Cambr
Bay

Read Island

Dolphin and Union Strait

Dease Strait

Melb

Richardson I.

PEOPLE OF THE ANTLERS

Kent Peninsula

CORONATION GULF

Cape Barrow

Melville Sound

PEOPLE OF THE
FALLS

Coppermine

TOM COD EATERS

Elli

Coppermine R.

(Bathurst Inlet)
Burnside Hbr.

PEOPLE
OF THE
NOSE

PEOPLE OF T

GREENLAND

ALASKA

—65°

C A N A D A

110°

H. GUZEWSKA